# REWRITING THE THIRTIES

# Studies in Twentieth-Century Literature

*Series Editor*:
Stan Smith, Professor of English, University of Dundee

*Published Titles*:
Rainer Emig, *Modernism in Poetry: Motivations, Structures and Limits*
Lee Horsley, *Fictions of Power in English Literature: 1900–1950*
Peter Brooker, *New York Fiction: Modernity, Postmodernism, The New Modern*
Richard Kirkland, *Literature and Culture in Northern Ireland Since 1965: Moments of Danger*
Keith Williams and Steven Matthews, *Rewriting the Thirties: Modernism and After*

By Cesar Abin. A caricature of James Joyce which first appeared in the magazine, *transition* (issue 21, 1932)

# Rewriting the Thirties: Modernism and After

*Edited by*
*Keith Williams and Steven Matthews*

*Longman*
London and New York

Addison Wesley Longman
Edinburgh Gate
Harlow
Essex CM20 2JE
England
*and Associated Companies throughout the world.*

*Published in the United States of America
by Addison Wesley Longman Inc., New York.*

First published 1997

ISBN 0 582 29449 5 CSD
ISBN 0 582 29448 7 PPR

**British Library Cataloguing-in-Publication Data**

A catalogue record of this book is
available from the British Library

**Library of Congress Cataloging-in-Publication Data**

A catalog entry for this title is available from the
Library of Congress

Set by 35 in 10/12pt Bembo
Produced by Longman Singapore Publishers (Pte) Ltd.
Printed in Singapore

# Contents

Acknowledgements                                                              viii

Notes on Contributors                                                          ix

1. **Introduction**   KEITH WILLIAMS AND STEVEN MATTHEWS          1

2. **The Age of Anxiety and Influence; or, Tradition
   and the Thirties Talents**   VALENTINE CUNNINGHAM          5

3. **Illusion and Reality: the Spectre of Socialist
   Realism in Thirties Literature**   PETER MARKS          23

4. **'Alien Experiences': Virginia Woolf, Winifred
   Holtby and Vera Brittain in the Thirties**
   MARION SHAW                                                                37

5. **Remembering Bryden's Bill: Modernism from Eliot
   to Auden**   STAN SMITH                                                   53

6. **Believing in the Thirties**   PETER MCDONALD          71

7. **'A Marvellous Drama out of Life': Yeats, Pound,
   Bunting and Villon at Rapallo**   STEVEN MATTHEWS          91

8. **Thirties Poetry and the Landscape of Suburbia**
   SIMON DENTITH                                                             108

9. **Politics and Beauty: the Poetry of Randall
   Swingler**   ANDY CROFT                                                  124

10. **'Irritating Tricks': Aesthetic Experimentation and
    Political Theatre**   STEVE NICHOLSON                                  147

11. **Post/Modern Documentary: Orwell, Agee and the
    New Reportage**   KEITH WILLIAMS                                        163

12. **Modernism and the People: the View from the
    Cinema Stalls**   JEFFREY RICHARDS                                      182

13. **Blood and Marmalade: Negotiations between the
    State and the Domestic in George Orwell's Early
    Novels**   LYNETTE HUNTER                                               202

Index                                                                        217

# Acknowledgements

We are grateful to the following for permission to use copyright material:

Faber & Faber limited for all T.S. Eliot quotations; The literary agents, A.P. Watt Ltd and the U.S. publisher Simon & Schuster for the poem 'Crazy Jane Talks to the Bishop' by W.B. Yeats.

We have been unable to trace a copyright holder for the Cesar Abin sketch, which appears as a frontispiece to this publication, and would be grateful for any information which would help us to do so.

# Notes on Contributors

**ANDY CROFT** has been active for many years in community writing projects on Teeside, where, until recently, he taught literature and creative writing for the University of Leeds. He has published and broadcast widely on the literary history of the Labour Movement, including a study of British novelists and the Popular Front, *Red Letter Days* (1990), and has edited (with Keith Armstrong) *The Big Meeting* (1994) and (with Graeme Rigby) the autobigraphy of the Durham miner and novelist Harold Heslop, *Out of the Old Earth* (1994). His first full-length book of poems, *Nowhere Special*, was published in 1996. He is currently writing a biography of Randall Swingler.

**VALENTINE CUNNINGHAM** is a Professor in English Literature and Fellow at Corpus Christi College, Oxford. He has written a study of dissent in Victorian fiction, *Everywhere Spoken Against* (1975), and edited two volumes of writings on the Spanish Civil War, *The Penguin Book of Spanish Civil War Verse* (1980) and *Spanish Front* (1986). He is also the author of *British Writers of the Thirties* (1988), and of a collection of critical essays, *In the Reading Gaol: Postmodernity, Texts and History* (1993).

**SIMON DENTITH** is Reader in English at Cheltenham and Gloucester College of Higher Education. He has written on George Eliot, rhetoric, and nineteenth- and twentieth-century topics; his most recent book is an introduction to Mikhail Bakhtin.

**LYNETTE HUNTER** is a Reader in the School of English at the University of Leeds. She is author of *G.K. Chesterton: Explorations in Allegory* (1979), *George Orwell, the Search for a Voice* (1984), *Rhetorical Stance in Modern Literature: Allegories of Love and Death* (1984), *Modern Allegory and Fantasy: Rhetorical Stances of Contemporary Writing* (1989) and *Towards a Definition of Topos: Approaches to Analogical Reasoning* (1991).

**PETER MARKS** is a Lecturer in the Department of English at the University of Sydney, where he specialises in twentieth-century British literature. He has published essays on George Orwell and imperialism, and on 1930s literary periodicals. He is co-editor of a forthcoming volume, *Literature and the Contemporary*. Currently, he is working on an extended study of the literary periodical, and on the essays of George Orwell.

PETER McDONALD is Senior Lecturer in English at the University of Bristol. He is the author of *Louis MacNeice: The Poet in his Contexts* (1991), and the co-editor (with Alan Heuser) of MacNeice's *Selected Plays* (1993). He has written widely on twentieth-century poetry, and in particular Irish verse: his work on contemporary poetry includes *Mistaken Identities: Poetry and Northern Ireland* (1997). He has published two volumes of poetry: *Biting the Wax* (1989) and *Adam's Dream* (1996).

STEVE NICHOLSON taught for four years in the Workshop Theatre at the University of Leeds, and is now Senior Lecturer in Theatre Studies at the University of Huddersfield. He has published a number of articles about British political theatre between 1917 and 1945, on censorship, right-wing dramas, and left-wing writers such as Montagu Slater. He is currently contributing to a major new encyclopaedia of censorship. He has also staged several rarely performed plays from the thirties, including Irwin Shaw's *Bury the Dead*.

JEFFREY RICHARDS is Professor of Culture History at Lancaster University and author of *The Age of the Dream Palace* (1984), *Happiest Days: the Public Schools in English Fiction* (1988) and *Films and British National Identity* (1997).

MARION SHAW is Professor of English in the Department of English and Drama at the University of Loughborough. She has written extensively on nineteenth-century poetry, and is editor of the *Tennyson Research Bulletin*. She has also written on women writers of the nineteenth and early twentieth centuries, including a book on Agatha Christie. She has edited an anthology of writings about work, *Man Does, Woman Is: The Faber Book of Work and Gender* (1995); she is also editor of a volume of essays, *An Introduction to Women's Literature from the Middle Ages to the Present* (1997). She is writing a biography of Winifred Holtby and editing a collection of her short stories; both books will appear in 1998.

STAN SMITH is Professor of English at the University of Dundee. Amongst his publications are *Inviolable Voice: History and Twentieth-Century Poetry* (1982), *W.H. Auden* (1985), *Edward Thomas* (1986), *W.B. Yeats: A Critical Introduction* (1990) and *The Origins of Modernism: Eliot, Pound and the Rhetoric of Renewal* (1994).

# CHAPTER ONE
# *Introduction*

KEITH WILLIAMS AND STEVEN MATTHEWS

Our reason for putting this anthology together is that we thought it long overdue to challenge the persistent aftermyth of the thirties as a homogeneous anti-modernist decade. Outdated cultural maps of the time sustain a damagingly restricted canon centred on a narrow genealogy of polarised relations between aesthetics and politics, or between difficulty and accessibility, textuality and content. According to this tradition, let us say, Auden fathers out of Socialist Realism a prodigal generation whose lasting literary value resides in subsequently recognising the disastrous inadvisability of their own attempts to mix writing and 'commitment', and in disowning their immature output. Against this distortive narrative, this book seeks to configure an alternative history – that, at least in terms of the avant-garde aspect of their culture, the thirties were more accurately a troubled but symptomatic transitional phase between modernist and postmodernist writing, art and politics, a complex mutation that defined itself within, and in some ways against, the wider background of the popular writing and mass culture of the time. Following on from this, it is vital to locate any reassessment of this kind within a suitably broad and contested cultural context.

Ezra Pound famously declared that 'We do not all inhabit the same time.' Such a sense of mutiplicity blows apart the homogeneous chronology which has dogged our sense of the period: the idea that cultural history is a mosaic is especially applicable to the culture of the thirties. There were many overlapping, competing and contradictory theoretical tendencies and practical alignments in the decade. So-called High Modernists, such as Pound himself, were still writing both 'impersonal' high art and egregious political propaganda. Joyce, in drafting *Finnegans Wake*, and Woolf, in writing *The Waves* and *The Years*, were moving into extended explorations of the possibilities of formal experiment, which for Woolf became, paradoxically, increasingly indivisible from ever-closer engagement with sexual politics, whatever the arguably more open-ended nature of the Joycean project.

As for the popular literary audience, they were still largely dieted on texts in the pre-modernist modes of Ian Hay and Edgar Wallace. A growing

1

'middle-brow' (to use the period term) sector of the population, on the other hand, were busily making best-selling authors of novelists such as J.B. Priestley and poets such as John Betjeman. But despite such mediating figures, the mass-civilisation/minority-culture split, diagnosed as the chief condition of cultural ill-health by the Leavises, was all too apparent. As demonstrated by Jeffrey Richards' chapter, this was particularly the case in relations between literature with a big 'L' and popular cinema, though it was being gradually (albeit ambivalently) modified by poets, prose-writers and dramatists increasingly fascinated and enthused by the artistic potential and popular impact of modern media forms. On the other hand, paradoxically, the attitudes of feature film audiences (rigorously policed as the industry was by the British Board of Film Censors) were, in terms of their sensibility, morality and expectations about narrative form, still largely located in the nineteenth century. Similarly, there were few signs of modernism arriving at all in mainstream British theatre.

Writers as different in themselves as Auden, Orwell and Winifred Holtby, whose careers are virtually synonymous with the thirties, were under the 'anxiety' of modernist influence – as much a case of repressing some aspects of it as admitting others. This made them often ambivalent towards the presumed cultural entailments and political responsibilities of innovative form. Conversely, the role of Joyce, Woolf and Eliot as mentors and – in Woolf and Eliot's case at Hogarth and Faber – literary midwives to the younger writers of the thirties should not be underestimated. In turn, as Stan Smith's and Steven Matthews' essays argue, the work of High Modernists was being modified by its rewriting in, and by their reading of, the texts of the next, upcoming generation. This is not only true of Eliot and Auden, but also of the serial encounters between Yeats, Pound and Bunting. All of these parameters and trends throw into question the neat paradigms of ending which have been imposed on the decade. Such periodising, as Peter McDonald shows, is essentially myth-making and drastically inadequate for the task of illuminating the actual matrix of creative relations between MacNeice, Auden, Spender and their High Modernist precursors.

For themselves, writers such as Auden, Orwell and Holtby were on the one hand anxious to adapt pragmatically the legacy and, indeed, currency of modernism, and on the other to resist its perceived obscurantism and indifference to social and economic facts. They adopted a whole variety of self-consciously *ad hoc* theoretical formulations and provisional solutions in their practice, which cannot simply be subsumed by any single aesthetic or political category because they stemmed from such a plethora of hybridised elements. Freud, Marx, Catholicism, Homer Lane, D.H. Lawrence, I.A. Richards, the Leavises, the Surrealists, Socialist Realism, Documentarism and Epic Theatre, to name but a few of these elements, all jostle in uncoordinated

chorus for the attention of thirties writers. The sometimes unstable positions that resulted from volatile mixtures undoubtedly anticipate more fully
postmodern thinking about the relations between culture and politics. For
example, Lynette Hunter's essay shows how Orwell's precocious hunches
that ideology is 'naturalised' by processes of historical dismembering and
obliteration, as well as about the torturous negotiations between private self
and public space, foreshadow post-structuralist debates in this area.

This thirties polyphony of ideas, issues and discourses was also being
played out – in underlying rhythm, if not to exactly the same score – in
the theory and practice of many proletarian writers, as Valentine Cunningham
and Peter Marks demonstrate in their case studies of Joycean novelist James
Barke and the heterogeneous editorial 'line' of *Left Review* on what would
constitute a properly proletarian kind of writing. No less symptomatic of
the leading contemporary debate about the nature of 'realism' and the real,
as Keith Williams shows, are the self-conscious aesthetics of documentary
form. Whatever the myth-making says to the contrary, thirties writers did
not necessarily proceed in a vernacular naturalistic vein, anymore than in a
prescriptive Sovietised one. Indeed Andy Croft argues that Randall Swingler,
in many ways close to the nominal centres of committed cultural activity
in the period, was representative precisely because he confronted the per-
plexing nature of modernity neither as a modernist nor a hard-line Socialist
Realist, adapting instead the home-grown, more populist poetics of Georgian accessibility and place to the contemporary scene. However, there is
little doubt that through the work of both bourgeois and working-class
writers, definitions of the political underwent significant metamorphoses
in practice. Besides the public 'macropolitics' of the decade – the clashes
between Fascism and Communism, dictatorship and social democracy – a
whole new agenda of 'micropolitical' concerns was being opened up, consciously or unconsciously, and addressed by writers. Take, for example, the
explicit and implicit social values of style, and what they reveal about the
material conditions and cultural ideology of the writer, as demonstrated by
Simon Dentith's account of the poetry of suburbia, or Steve Nicholson's
discussion of the shifts in the performance–audience relationship sought by
the innovators of radical theatre. Not least, the politics of gender, unfairly
regarded as neglected in thirties writing, were in fact continuously objectified
and scrutinised in the later work of Virginia Woolf and of her acolyte/
antagonist, Winifred Holtby and others, as Marion Shaw contests. In this
way, the writing of the thirties emerges as both *less* and *more* political than
hitherto assumed, in more complex and inflected senses.

The revised map of the period this collection plots is a topography riven
by cultural fault-lines and by intellectual cross-currents of sometimes politically edgy, even indeterminate direction, though always dragged by the

unpredictably tidal influence of large-scale historical events. Moreover, to regard the British writing of the thirties as a resurgence of cultural 'Little Englandism' also ignores the wider geography of cosmopolitan modernist influences, continuous from the American and Irish, but also the European, spheres. Eliot and Auden's trajectories, for example, are parallel but inverted in this respect. Eliot naturalised both his statehood and critical assumptions in a cultural vision which, contradictorily, laid claim to both universal tradition and essential Englishness. Auden, in turn, began the thirties by deconstructing these assumptions and then took the opposite route at the end of the decade, by assuming American citizenship. Similarly, it is an error to marginalise or demonise the influence of Joyce in the period, because unlikely Joyceans, like the proletarian Glasgow Communist James Barke, brought into focus many of the key critical and political debates in their writing. By such unprogrammatic means, the cultural and linguistic hierarchy between the heteroglot 'margins' and mandarin, unitary 'centre' (to use Bakhtin's terms) was contested. The actuality of perpetual displacement of lives in travel and exile, of political alignments, and of forms of reading and writing patently defies the kind of canonical selectivity all too often imposed upon the thirties, and resists any master-theory about its nature and aftermath. The map is of course a favourite and most highly-charged metaphor in thirties writing. Since the last major collection of essays on the period appeared well over a decade ago, it is high time that it was culturally reconfigured: *Rewriting the Thirties* will provide an indispensable pathfinding chart for subsequent undertakings in this long overdue process.

# CHAPTER TWO

# The Age of Anxiety and Influence; or, Tradition and the Thirties Talents

## VALENTINE CUNNINGHAM

Two large focuses or frames of analysis confront us in any approach now to thirties writing. The first is literary-historical, and involves a sort of traditional knee-jerk division between modernism and the thirties. This is the crude bit of historicising which defines the Thirties as an Age of Utter Reason, a period only of Political Art, of Documentary deviationism, a time of sad Realist cravings, of rampant anti-Formalism, anti-Textualism, and so a sort of unfortunate historical blip or bypass on which writing got snagged and slowed down in the good long march of the twentieth century from modernism at the beginning to postmodernism at the end. This view sees the thirties as a very unfortunate, even inexplicable, parenthesis, and one which we can now, especially since the fall of Eastern European Communism and all that, simply overlook as a species of shortsightedness, a deviant moment in a larger textualising progress, involving crude ideological preferences which history has not sustained and literary-critical category errors we can only wonder at our immediate literary and critical fathers for indulging themselves in. This is a reading of literary history greatly ministered to by seeing the thirties as thoroughly Leftist and so extremely, even absolutely, hostile to the modernism that flourished before it and continued despite it. And, of course, vice versa.

A symptom of this making of stark historical contrasts is the reissuing by Lawrence & Wishart of their 1935 volume *Problems of Soviet Literature* with the rebarbatively new title *Soviet Writers' Congress 1934: The Debate on Socialist Realism and Modernism in the Soviet Union* (1977).

The second large analytical frame which now inevitably has thirties writing in its grip has to do with value and values. There is a common reading of much thirties literature which concedes it a certain, even momentous, cultural and historical value, but denies it anything like the highest *literary* merit. On this view the greats of our time are Eliot, Pound, Woolf, even – still – in our feminist age, D.H. Lawrence; whereas the thirties boys are scarcely up to snuff. Even if W.H. Auden, say, just about makes it into the pantheon of the great and good, Spender and Day Lewis (not to mention the raggletaggle army of poets who wrote for Spain or the gang of proletarian novelists of the period, or the women authors brought back into the light by Virago Books, Rosamond Lehmann and such), certainly do not get into the Premier Division. We certainly would not choose their sort to save our First Fifteen. This kind of demarcation is based, of course, on a very usual set of judgements about literary value, prejudgements or prejudices no less, heavily reliant on the very traditional assumption that overt political propaganda, in fact instrumentality of any kind, let alone sentimental disposition of materials, and simplicity of address to readers, will axiomatically mark a poet or poem down. According to these views, temporal or worldly interests and commitments automatically make a work of less importance than more formalist, or more language-centred, or (save the mark) more 'eternal-verity'-centred writings – even if the 'eternal-verities' in question are, in the end, just as ideologically skewed as the propagandistic dispositions which are being disallowed.

What is at issue here, of course, sooner or later, is canonicity. Canon-making, questions of what constitutes canons, how canons get formed, were utterly central to the critical debates of the thirties, and they are main questions in the critical debate about the merits now of thirties writing. Not surprisingly then, certain positions in current canon debates seem to have particular force in the light they can cast on thirties materials. There is the case Michael Bérubé makes, for example, for the black American poet Melvin Tolson, involving a critique of how literary-historical modelling is done. Bérubé asks how an American version of modernism gets to be constructed so as to exclude Tolson, and along with him most Leftist US work of the thirties:

> Richard Chase's canonical 'modernism' allows him to conflate aesthetic experimentalism and social protest under one sign, that of an 'insurgent movement' which 'defended "modernism"' – which is to say that Chase's account leaves no room for avant-garde social protest that attacked (or was at best ambivalent about) modernism, no room for Joseph Freeman, Michael Gold, *New Masses*, or, for that matter, writers of the Harlem Renaissance. More generally, Chase has no record of what happened to the insurgent movement in this country which defended the strikers at Passaic, New Jersey, in 1926, or the insurgent movement that made up the Abraham Lincoln Brigades a decade later; for him, these 'insurgent movements' have dropped out of sight, their oppositionality subsumed under the rubric of the Euro-American avant-garde.[1]

Or there is Jane Tompkins questioning the circularity of the valuation processes that keep a populist classic of sentimental humane propaganda such as the anti-slavery novel *Uncle Tom's Cabin* out of the high canon of great American fiction. Harriet Beecher Stowe's reformist text usually fails to get past the question 'But is it any good?', because it fails to live up to certain criteria of literary value which, however, and in the first place, consciously exclude its kind of thing from the top table. The merits of *Uncle Tom's Cabin* are, Tompkins suggests, precisely ones normally downgraded. It is female, domestic, sentimental, pious. It is an evangelical and missionary fiction which works well precisely because it is moral, purposive, simple and thus popular. And if the traditionalists' canonical criteria deplore all that, it is they that are lacking, not the novel.[2]

The upshot of such canon scepticisms is that if the model, the current of historical-interpretative assumption, the regular literary-historical framing devices, the criteria of value don't fit, and in fact seem to miss entirely the literary phenomena in question, then one should try changing the model and the criteria rather than just turning a blind eye to those awkward phenomena. And I agree. And so, interestingly, does T.S. Eliot. That is a notable agreement not least because it helps bring sharply into focus the alleged gulf that divides our High Modernists, the likes of T.S. Eliot, from our thirties realists and propagandists. It is the position T.S. Eliot arrived at, quite openly, and I think actually in response to certain thirties Leftist discussions, in relation to Rudyard Kipling. Kipling is a stone of stumbling. He doesn't fit. 'I confess', says Eliot, 'that the critical tools which we are accustomed to use in analysing and criticizing poetry do not seem to work' on Kipling. But Kipling can't just be written off. So Eliot sets about making a case on some other grounds for this writer for whom, despite the normal judgements of the tradition, he feels certain strong admiration. And Eliot's scepticism about the literary history and the valuations and the canonicity that would keep Kipling out, at bay, is, I would argue, exemplary.[3]

I want to test my own scepticism about the ordinary rigidities of literary history and evaluation, and so of canonicity, as they relate to the thirties, by looking at what I take to be a pretty exemplary text of the period – a passage (pp. 122–5), from a novel by James Barke, *Major Operation: A Novel* (London: Collins, 1936), about a socialist celebration of May Day, a people's protest, a street demonstration in Glasgow. This section of the novel has, in common with every division of the text, a mock newspaper headline: 'RED MUSIC IN THE SECOND CITY'. The narrative voice is a very free sort of direct discourse, a dramatically outered interior monologue, the voice of many citizens and of none in particular; the people, that elusive desideratum of Leftist politics and poetics, is speaking; the text is inside, as it is with and for, the common mind.

## RED MUSIC IN THE SECOND CITY

The flutes sounded shrill and distinct. The noise of the drums, flung back from the high walls of the tenements, gathered in force and in rhythm. Shopkeepers came to their doors, windows were flung up, children ran. On the sidewalks groups gathered, heads turned in the direction from which the music came.

A slight drizzle was falling: the weather was murky and unpleasant. But the citizens of the Second City had more to worry about than a miserable day.

For one thing, Labour was in control of municipal affairs of the City. Michael Mullrooney would be the next Lord Provost. Sir Michael Mullrooney. Nice name that for a future Lord Provost of the Second City, etcetera. What was it Derry's walls were built with . . . ? Top av the mawrnin' to ye, Sir Michael—

> O, Sir Michael was a gintleman:
> He came av dacent pape'l.

What do you think Mr Timothy O'Rafferty with your white apron and your black lustre jacket? Apply for another licence, will you? Labour on the bench: Red Biddy in the Family Department! Arra me bhoy: there'll never be any Red Clyde so long as there's Red Biddy. Ah, the bhoys would rather have a night with Red Biddy than a night with Burns. With Labour on the bench, me bhoy. It's a darlin' party the Labour Party: a darlin' Party. I wonder, now, if them flutes will be Orange or Hibernian?

Now you, Mr No-mean-citizen-of-no-mean-city: you said something just now about boiling a can? Sorry and all that . . .

You're canned if you ask me.

In Xanadu did Kubla Khan—

Kubla Khan? I've got you, mister. In the 3.30? I can take you on, sir, up to twenty quid. Pay out in the lavatory of Tim O'Rafferty's bar at six o'clock. James MacMaster, sir, a God-fearing bookie's runner at your service. Kubla Khan is a good thing.

What about Red Biddy?

Don't touch it, sir. Been a Jake drinker in my day. Meth – lavender water – green paint. Pain in the guts now. Think of the money spent on drink that might bring back a fortune – a double coming up once or twice a week . . .

Politics, thy name is acrimony. Let's have – music!

Sit, Jessica! Let the sound of music creep in our ears. Your name isn't Jessica by any chance?

Getting fresh, are you? My name's Sarah. Sarah Cannan. Call a flute band music?

Sorry, can't give you Henry Hall and His band. But don't despise the flute, dear lady. Orpheus and his lute – which, as you doubtless were told at school, is just the polite name for flute. It is the little rift within the flute . . . Afraid it's the flutes that are causing the rift, however. Suppose you'd rather hear a Mae West story? Ah, Mae West! Sex! Taboo! Wonder what Mrs Bloom would have thought about Mae West?

Or Mae West about Marion Bloom? Mummmh! Bulged right out in his face! Seven miles! Guess I've nothing on you, dearie.

Labour on the bench and a smutty story round the corner: under the trees. Music down the street. Hold the mirror up to nature and you get – sex and politics (moonlight is extra, but always in request) . . .

Well, we don't mind a little sex, sir, providing it's treated in a light, aphrodisiacal manner and provided ther's a high moral tone prevailing throughout. Nothing the public likes better in fact. But – no politics! No, siree. Keep politics out of literature.

A little bit of bread and no chee-e-e-se? Well, them flutes don't seem to be coming any nearer . . .

But the Mirror and Nature, you know. I must bow to your superior knowledge of what the public wants. The syndicate that runs your library in there . . .

Hold the Mirror up to Nature by all means. But hold it up to her *face*.

Ain't nature grand! (How'ma doin' boys?) You mean: put the blind eye to the telescope?

Unless you're a Peeping Tom.

Sorry you've been troubled. Rather afraid there's a spot of trouble coming to you all the same . . .

Fifty quid. That's my price. I've got to square another two. We have the majority vote. Guarantee the contract.

Ah! no sex or politics here. No holding the mirror up to nature. Just a little bit of business between friends. Well, well, well! If it ain't me old pal, Pro bono publico.

Did you say a hair, madam? Infra dig, infra dig. Our fish suppers, madam, have positively never been known to contain a hair . . .

A hair of the dog that bit me, you know. I was at a dinner of the Incorporation of Graftsmen – and mind you, I never thought I would live to be a Bailie . . .

The writing on the wall, Bailie. Can't you hear dem flutes?

I was never near the place. That was Bailie –

Now, now. No names: no pack drill. Don't think this is the complete low-down on the whole rotten situation here at hand. I'm only trying to find my feet in the flux of time: paddle my own canoe in the stream of consciousness: make ends meet: solve the jigsaw: earn an honest livelihood . . . Oh, you want to know what it's all about? Well: have patience. When dem flutes come into view I might be able to give you an idea. Who am I? I'm the Voice that breathed o'er Eden: I'm the Fly in the Ointment: I'm the Wet Blanket: I'm Saftest o' the Family: I'm Here, There and Everywhere: I'm Gone To-day and Here To-morrow: I'm Alpha of the Plough and Omega of the Furrow: I'm the Eternal feminine and Mr. Public: I'm Quantity changing into Quality: I'm the Negation of Negations . . . Ah, here comes the Bride.

Toot-toot, toot-toot, toot-toodli-oot . . .

You always find plenty of police at a swell wedding. Love's old sweet song. The world moves. Walk up, walk up! Walk up where? Cunarder finished. Are you weary, are you sad? Jog along, little dogie: jog along. There's a hell of a lot of you swell guys heading for the last round-up.

Think things are getting better a little: turning the corner? Bottom out of the depression? Nice to listen to Sir James Jeans, now. Got the breeze up a little back! Lawn Tennyson's (good lad Joyce) red revolution and the breaking up of laws nearly had you by the-throat! Never mind, son. Blow your nose. The bogey man won't get you this time. Zez you! The moving finger writes . . .

Something phoney about all this huey! You'll say there is, will you? Well, just what do you think about it all? All what? Just life on this little old planet. Gota job? Feel secure? Enjoy excellent digestion. Never known a day's illness? Trust in God and do the right? Once a week won't do a man any harm! What's that? Don't feel it's going to last for ever. So you admit your little world got a nasty jog there? Can't encourage you to be optimistic. Balance of imports over exports. What about a nice little reassuring speech by Ramsay over the air? No? Losing confidence, are you? Bring on the Welsh Wizard! What is a wizard? Please, miss, the inside of a hen.

But seriously: things can't go on like this. Damnation – sorry, m'dear, sorry, m'dear. Confound you, sir! The country's going to the dogs. What we need is a strong hand at the helm. (Chorus: We need a strong hand at the helm!) Record a bit worn, eh? You're all a bit worn. Things are beginning to prey on your nerves.

When the hell is it going to end? I'll be shrieking in a minute. Father's got the sack from the water works, the brick works, the rivet, bolt and nut works.

Where's the entrance out? Stop crowding, can't you! Take your bloody elbow out of my face, damn you. Another blind alley. Sally in our alley. Put a sock in her. Hit her across the gub with a beer bottle. How'd you like to live on the dole? Two bob to stop a bastard's grub trap. Apples and rusks: juice of orange if slightly costive? Shut it, you! Cut out the high hattin'. We'll bloody soon let you guys see where to get off. Done our little Lord Fauntleroy too long. Problem of life, eh? Sir James Jeans on the wonders of the starry universe? Kant! Cut the dope clean out from now on. Problem of getting the next bit of grub. Sounds too simple and elementary. Rather do a spot of speculation: the World considered as Will and Understanding: or a little of Mr Beethoven and the BBC symphony orchestra. Cultural heritage of the workers. Comrade Beethoven's last quartets. Okay then! Time and place for everything. Rebel Song played by the Springburn Unemployed Workers' flute band.

> Then we'll sing a rebel song
> As we proudly march along . . .

So that's what all the noise was about? Well: see you later: also hear.

*Major Operation* is a Communist novel. It's about the need for a Communist solution to a terrible time in a very needy city – depression Glasgow, the Second City of Scotland, currently in grave economic crisis. The novel is written by a Communist, a so-called proletarian novelist, the son of a farm-worker who was himself a shipyard worker and engineer. Barke is a writer who was conspicuously active in the public thirties debates about the role of literature in socialist and Communist politics, debates centred not least around the reports coming back to Britain from the Moscow Writers' Congress of 1934. These debates were promoted particularly in Britain by the journal *Left Review* which had been set up precisely in response to the Congress's summons to writers to get behind the cause of proletarian revolution, especially in the wake of Hitler's coming to power in Germany. Barke was a contributor to *Left Review*, and his novel takes its title from an already notorious long poem by a poet closely associated with the magazine, namely Cecil Day Lewis's Communist, or at least Ur-Communist, poem *The Magnetic Mountain* (1933). Section 25 of that poem ran:

> Drug nor isolation will cure their cancer:
> It is now or never, the hour of the knife,
> The break with the past, the major operation.

The break with the past. In political terms the novel *Major Operation* is clear where the break will come. Its goal is socialist revolution. But for the writer there is a question of just what the break with the literary past might consist of. Where should that particular cut come? What exactly of the old culture is to be cut away? And what should the Communist literary surgeon's knife leave behind? What, in fact, is cancerous about the tradition, the literary past, the bourgeois and modernist past, which the Moscow Congress had tried so vociferously to root out?

What Barke's title announces in embracing Cecil Day Lewis's brisk vision of necessary surgery is that he accepts that he is working in a crisis time, an age which, for very good reasons – economic depression, threats of war, the rise and rise of Fascism – is deeply anxious, sunk in a set of anxieties writers and writing must respond to: 'it's now or never'. As Auden would formulate the matter: the writer is 'in this hour of crisis and dismay' ('August for the People'); he's 'in a late hour of apprehension and exhaustion' ('Oxford'). The writer, the epoch, the reader are all in it, and in for it. And for the writer this age of widespread anxiety inevitably includes the anxiety of influence – that is, the question of which tradition and traditions she or he will work in or against, variously promoting, revivifying, demolishing. What, in other words, in the formula Eliot issued in the immediate aftermath of the First World War, should be the nature of the individual writing talent in the thirties in relation to the many possible literary ways and means and models the tradition supplies? Is any of that bourgeois past worth saving? Should any of those dry bones be made to live again? Could any of them go on living? How much of the literary past should be blown up, blasted to smithereens, how much blessed and continued (in those muscular oppositions announced by Wyndham Lewis as the First World

War was about to break out)? How, in fact, is the thirties text to make the modern world possible for art? How, in such times as these, can art be made possible for the modern world?

These are all of them questions which in some senses all writers have asked, but they are ones which T.S. Eliot had most recently asked as the very essence of what survival and pertinence might amount to in a modern writing and for a modern writer. After Eliot's essays 'Tradition and the Individual Talent' (1919), 'The Metaphysical Poets' (1921) and '*Ulysses*, Order and Myth' (1923), nobody could be in any doubt that the very nature of being modern was a raising of the question of what to do with and about the past. In *A Hope for Poetry* (1934) Cecil Day Lewis had agreed: the younger sons of poetry must acquire the right fathers, the right elder brothers. And if any doubt lingered about this on the Left, the Moscow Congress had confirmed the diagnosis. For his part, Eliot had suggested that the success of Joyce's *Ulysses* in 'making the modern world possible for art' had lain in its adoption of the 'mythical method' – its 'manipulating a continuous parallel' between ancient Greece and modern Dublin, 'between contemporaneity and antiquity'. This is the 'method which others must pursue after' Joyce. This is the only way of 'controlling, or ordering, of giving a shape and a significance to the immense panorama of futility and anarchy which is contemporary history'.[4] But could the thirties Communist writer go Joyce's way? Joyce looked to the classical, the mythical past. What past, what traditions, what fathers, what telos should the new, politically aroused thirties writer look to?

In 'RED MUSIC IN THE SECOND CITY', the great names of the British and European tradition are there in some number, available for the imitating and the serving in, as it were, the collective mind of Barke's Glaswegians, on his streets, on his page: Burns, Coleridge, Beethoven, Tennyson. Coleridge and Tennyson are supreme figures in the High Tradition of English Letters. But, quite clearly, what Barke's rhapsody of the popular street recognises is that the Great European Tradition, as we might call it, is one which the workers are estranged from except in some wry or queered and wrenched version, some ironically mis-taking and mis-conceiving trace. Burns is less of a delight than the booze. Kubla Khan is a race-horse running in the 3.30. The Springburn Unemployed Workers' flute band is hardly the musical equivalent of Beethoven's Last Quartets ('Call a flute band music?'). The Glasgow unemployed's musical efforts are a far cry from the BBC Symphony Orchestra. 'Dem flutes' (twice): darkie-speak has invaded the popular consciousness – Dem Bones, Dem Bones – negro spiritual stuff from the world of American popular culture. And it is echoes of that kind of demotic text – the films, the talkies, jazz, blues – that really animate the popular voice on the streets of Barke's Glasgow. And at such moments as this it is as if the novel is wondering, with Auden's *Letter to Lord Byron*, 'what the Duke of Wellington / Would say about the music of Duke Ellington'. Or, more precisely, 'Wonder what Mrs Bloom would have thought about Mae West? Or Mae West about Marion Bloom?'

And, of course, what *we* are driven to wonder, in this opposing of these two modern sex symbols, Mae West and Molly Bloom, is what Karl Radek, the great Communist promoter of Socialist Realism, would have thought of the Communist James Barke thinking of Molly Bloom. And, what's more, about his trying to write not unlike Molly Bloom – apparently imitating (or paddling his own canoe in) her kind of stream of consciousness from *Ulysses*, quoting *Ulysses*, putting his novel into the tradition of *Ulysses* and the recyclers of the *Ulysses* method, of writers like the American John Dos Passos. 'Good lad Joyce': can Joyce possibly be, or become, part of the cultural heritage of the Scottish workers? The novel evidently wants its Scottish citizenry, however poor, to have some access to the real world of Beethoven and Burns and Coleridge. But Joyce?

It was simply normal on the literary Left to denigrate Joyce. Karl Radek, Prince Mirsky, Edward Upward, Ralph Fox, Alick West, Christopher Caudwell – they all lined up, eager to cast their stones at the unrepentant modernist and his keen sponsor T.S. Eliot. Joyce, according to Prince Mirsky, illustrated the extreme limits of decadent aestheticisation: 'the path of Joyce and the path of Soviet literature form an angle of 180 degrees'.[5] The best that Joyce could do, suggested Edward Upward in his notorious 'Sketch for a Marxist Interpretation of Literature', was to distort reality and provide a limited field of social and human vision.[6] Caudwell dismissed Dorothy Richardson and Proust and Joyce as the 'last blossoms of the bourgeois novel': they were depleting the important study of social relations into an account merely of the subject's experience in society, 'complete "me-ness" '.[7] At the Moscow Congress Radek ranted lengthily against Joyce's investment in the wrong kind of realism, the wrong sort of heroic, the wrong kind of form – *Ulysses* was a 'phantasmagoria of the madhouse ... delirious ravings.... A heap of dung, crawling with worms, photographed by a cinema apparatus'; 'for him the whole world lies between a cupboardful of medieval books, a brothel and a pothouse'; his language is aberrant, comma-less – 'some kind of Chinese alphabet without commas'. (Radek had evidently heard of Molly Bloom's contribution to *Ulysses*, maybe he had even looked at the novel's 'Penelope' section, but just as clearly he had not paid too much attention to other parts of the novel with their massive amplitudes of punctuation.) And were you to imagine that Joyce's use of newspaper-style headlines and story-telling in *Ulysses*'s Aeolus section was at least a nod in the direction of quotidian history-making, you would be in error. John Dos Passos, imitator of the Joycean news-headline technique, is equally feeble – he 'puts in insertions and excerpts from newspapers in order to glue together that background which his inability to generalize prevents him from portraying'.[8]

Clearly, though, James Barke was not persuaded. His novel is organised, like the Aeolus section of *Ulysses*, in sections divided up by imitation newspaper headlines. Barke's investment in 'Love's Old Sweet Song' unashamedly looks towards Joyce's comma-less Molly Bloom as example and type of modern woman; Lawn Tennyson comes straight out of the Night-Town episode that Radek so deplored – as did Alick West ('an orgy of this blending of the materially real and the mentally real is the scene in the brothel').[9] Barke's stream-of-consciousness mode is exactly the sort of difficult textual interiority that Radek and his British imitators, such as Ralph Fox, took strongly against: 'subjective struggles, sexual intrigues'; 'that false outlook on life which in Proust and Joyce has led to the sole aim of art being . . . the dissociation of human personality'.[10] This was the kind of specialised consciousness that Nikolai Bukharin attacked Boris Pasternak for at the Moscow Congress: 'egocentric . . . convolutions of unintelligible image combinations . . . so subjective and so intimately subtle . . . associations inaccessible to "socialized perception"' – which is a violation of the laws of 'complex simplicity'.[11]

But for all this barrage of anti-Joycean feeling, this wide campaign against modernist devices and assumptions that was coming from the heart of the Communist aesthetic movement, Barke's Joycean endeavour found much support, a good deal of it from circles close to the Party, and indeed from deep within the Party itself. Jack Lindsay praised Barke's 'organic vitality'. The *Daily Worker*, official newspaper of the Party, claimed that *Major Operation* was 'Certainly one of the greatest novels of working-class struggle yet written'. The Glasgow Unity Theatre would go on to stage a version of the novel a little later, during the Second World War.[12] And, adding perhaps insult to the injury being done to the Socialist Realist Party line, John Sommerfield's novel *May Day*, which also came out in 1936, used an even more closely Dos Passos-like technique of newspaper headlining.

What emerges clearly here, then, is that no hard and fast divide existed in the thirties along the lines conventional literary-historical storytelling is prone to suggest. The Barke case simply will not sustain any clean-cut opposition between Realism and modernism, socialists and modernists, Social Realism over against Joyceanism. James Barke is, plainly, offering his novel in the cause of radical, socialist, proletarian truth-telling at the same time as he is shutting his ears to the word from Moscow and staring down Karl Radek and his British supporters in the matter of Joycean modernism. Barke is at one with the Scottish Communist Lewis Grassic Gibbon, who in effect bluntly opposed the Radek-ites in the new British Section of the

Writers' International. The Moscow Congress's 'Resolution on the Report of Karl Radek on International Literature' had declared 'the decay of the literature of the ruling classes'. But for Grassic Gibbon, 'To say that the period from 1913 to 1934 is a decadent period is just, if I may say so, bolshevik blah. . . . Capitalist literature is not in decay.' Those who believe so just do not read their contemporaries (and indeed they had not: Radek's comments showed a raw ignorance of *Ulysses*). The anti-modernist, said Grassic Gibbon, is simply full of hatred and 'moronic envy'.

What is more – and this only underlines the point about the lack of strictly drawn aesthetic borderlines in the period – Grassic Gibbon's hostility to 'bolshevik blah' was not some hole-in-corner blasphemy uttered in the wings of the Leftist thirties, a bit of politico-cultural dyspepsia whispered in the pub among chums after some Party meeting had not gone quite his way. His comments appeared in *Left Review*, in the first year of its life, in issue No. 5, in 1935, in a busy to-and-fro of critical opinion about the nature of left-wing writing and the role of the left-wing writer. They were utterly characteristic of the aesthetico-theoretical disagreements the magazine aired, especially at this early stage of its career. It was, for instance, one the editors of *Left Review*, Amabel Williams-Ellis, who reported extensively in the magazine, in November 1934, the Moscow Congress speech of Ilya Ehrenburg which the more Moscow-minded Martin Lawrence omitted from the Congress book *Problems of Soviet Literature*. Ehrenburg declared that Soviet simplicity in fiction was not everything a socialist aesthetic should aim for: 'we must foster and care for those forms of literature which today seem only the privilege of Soviet intellectuals.' 'Songs for the accordion are easier than Beethoven', he went on, but that doesn't mean to say that difficulty in art – modernism, Pasternak, Joyce – is automatically bad. One can see there, as it were, where Barke's worry over the aesthetic force of the Flute Band is coming from, and so, obviously, could any reader of *Left Review* who looked at Barke's novel. In such a context Stephen Spender seems to be mongering no great revisionist hindsight, or paradox, when he claims, as he does for example in his volume *The Thirties and After*, that Yeats, Eliot, Pound and Lawrence were revered in the thirties, that 'They were indeed our heroes', and that 'In their endgames were our game-beginnings.'[13]

What Barke's text is offering is a synthesis of modes and directions – a compound of realistic proletarianising intent and of modernistic textualising interiority. His fiction is a coupling of the subjectively experienced, sexualised, Joycean city, a daytime excursion into the Night-Town mode Alick West explicitly deplored in his book *Crisis and Criticism*, with the political purposes, the ideological slant, the ideological sentiment and sentimentalism that is to be found in the novels of, say, Harold Heslop – which West particularly opposed to the Night-Town section of *Ulysses* ('social sense . . . social activity . . . class forces . . .').[14]

Synthesis is what Ilya Ehrenburg had proposed as the way forward for socialist art, a resistance to either/or-ism, an acceptance both of songs for the accordion and of Beethoven. And Barke's synthesising practice in *Major Operation* has two arresting features – both of them important for the light they shed on the nature of thirties writing, both of them having power as they relate to modernism (rather than as existing in opposition to, or isolation from, modernism), and both of them, as it happens, involving critical manoeuvres which the Russian critic Mikhail Mikhailovich Bakhtin devised, and used, precisely to subvert the iron hand of controlling Soviet Realism doctrine, namely the carnivalesque spirit and the dialogic or heteroglossic polyphonic.[15] The modern critical world which has welcomed these two topics of discourse so warmly (and loudly) to its bosom generally forgets that Bakhtin invented them as a way of making certain old and bourgeois writings acceptable to the Soviet canoneers because they could be read as really revolutionary – Rabelais as really expressing the revolutionary potential of carnival, Dostoevsky and the Classic Realist Novel as really filled with a democratic play of human voices. And Bakhtin was right – carnivalesque and dialogism are indeed revolutionary and democratic. But any Soviet Realist antagonist of Bakhtin would also be right – Rabelais and Dostoevsky are at the same time pre-revolutionary and bourgeois. These modes are duplicitous, they cut both ways. Their presence as compelling features of Barke's synthesising text is as instructive as it is unsurprising.

James Barke's unemployed citizenry in holiday processional mood is obviously carnivalesque. This novel gives us classic carnival on the Bakhtinian model; it celebrates the workers, the lower orders, uprisen for the day, powerful, *en masse*, at play. Sexy, rude, boozy, gambling, rough; a people licensed unpuritanically to express the needs and urges, the lack of niceties, of the lower parts of the body. This is a Scottish, a British, version of the world of Rabelais according to Bakhtin. It is a Foucauldian world of the satirically excrementitious, a madhouse, brothel, pothouse atmosphere and zone where institutionalised authority has been inverted. All of which Bakhtin relished, and Radek sniffed anarchy in (compare his distrust of Joyce's 'cupboardful of medieval books'). On this day, the people are Lords of Proletarian Rule – of Misrule, according to the Master Class, those usual temporal rulers – at least for this day, this moment, on this page. And all this is characteristic of the several Leftist fictional celebrations of thirties crowd-power, when the workers occupy the city and the page, quenching and quelling for the moment the usual powers-that-be, the bourgeoisie, the owners, the police: in novels such as Grassic Gibbon's *Grey Granite* (1934) and Sommerfield's *May Day* (1936), as much as in *Major Operation*.

In many respects, of course, this all represents wish-fulfilment, a written fantasy, the bringing forward in a fiction, on a page, of the wished-for day of revolution. What Barke is giving us is a proleptic, anticipating experience of what might, perhaps, maybe, come about Tomorrow, if History allows it. It is a vision now amidst all the real anxieties and crises of Today, of the Utopia promised by Communism (what Auden's poem *Spain* allows itself to envision beyond the Struggle of Today, beyond that awkward *But* of history and of realistic assessments – 'But today the struggle'). And in its sexiness, its Rabelaisianism, indeed its Joyceanism, this enactment of carnival is just what the revolution, what the USSR, were thought at first to stand for, and indeed did for a while, before Stalinism and the puritanism so manifest at the Moscow Writers' Congress took over (to the dismay of the likes of Naomi Mitchison and Edward Upward, Christopher Isherwood and Stephen Spender, who all, and representatively of thirties writers, looked to the Sovietised people's utopia as a refuge from the sexual repressions and restraints of Christian Europe).

But fantasy or no, in the Joyceanism, the modernism, of this textualised carnival there is an important recognition and welcoming of a linguistic overturning which I think we now realise is a *sine qua non* of true revolution, certainly for writing. This was, I suggest, something well known to Mayakovsky and Viktor Shklovski (that great advocate of the merits and importance of the English language's major Rabelaisian novelist before Joyce: Laurence Sterne) and the other Russian experimentalist poets and critics who were also being put down, along with Joyce, by Karl Radek's colleagues at the Moscow Congress (most notably in Bukharin's long speech on 'Poetry and Politics'). It is no accident in Joyce's Night-Town when King Edward VII and Alfred Lawn Tennyson appear, and the British Tommies beat up the Irish Bard Stephen Dedalus, that Leopold Bloom, a prime twentieth-century example of the little-man hero so vigorously derided in so much Leftist thirties polemics, should be denounced as 'Caliban'. For Jewish–Irish Bloom is a modern Caliban – an updating of the oppressed, colonised servant and slave, who is a type of the subaltern, of Joyce himself, who has learned his master's and mistress's language and so acquired a potent instrument with which to curse them and, eventually, to bring their hegemonic imperialists' house of culture tumbling down. Alfred Lawn Tennyson's particular Victorian red revolution was one thing – and there was a kind of warning note of Darwinian inevitability about the redness of its tooth and claw. But the revolution being contrived by the good lad Joyce – the Revolution of the Word which was also a sexual, bodily, political overturning, forceful with all the power of modernism's neo-Rabelaisianism: the revolutionary dynamic and potential which Radek and Alick West were simply turning their Stalinised backs on in Circe/Night-Town – was potentially even redder.

Certainly the modern Caliban's kind of rebel song brings its own kind of cultural threat, even if it will be only heard for this one elated day of allowed Misrule. Arthur Calder-Marshall seems to have detected something of it when he talked of modern fiction in 1935: 'I detect in men's voices, in their excitement, even in their shocked horror and anticipation, a joy and relief, dating from the depression. Economically it has been a depression. Emotionally it is an elation.'[16]

The excitement of 'men's voices': dialogism, polyphony, a sea of up-raised voices, the cry of the city, of the *Massenmensch*. They had, as such, as Bakhtin recognised, their own kind of demotic power, and a power that (once again) the Radek-style cultural commissars were not up to perceiving in the helter-skelter of the Joycean (and Eliotic, for that matter) linguistic kaleidoscope: the whole urban Babel of voices that modernistic texts like *The Waste Land* and *Ulysses* and the novels of Virginia Woolf rejoiced in. And it is no accident that Barke's narrative wish to have 'the sound of music creep in our ears' echoes *The Waste Land*'s echo of *The Tempest*, '"This music crept by me upon the waters."' This babble was what Ralph Fox meant, perhaps, by his hostile reference to 'iridescent cuttings pasted on the microscopic slide. Such cuttings are often exceedingly curious, interesting or beautiful, but they are not living men or women'.[17] That Barke the Communist recognises the revolutionary power of the multivocal urban voice as practised in the modernist text is a tribute to his political good sense as well as his Bakhtinian perceptiveness (after all he could have done a Radek and rejected this kind of discourse for its massive conservative associations in the pages of Joyce and Eliot and Woolf, much as those Leftist enthusiasts for 'Helter-Skelter' John Skelton – Philip Henderson, W.H. Auden, and so on – might have been tempted to turn a blind eye to the powerfully demotic polyglottism of that Renaissance poet because it happened that the grouchy Tory radical Robert Graves also loved his writing and actually gave him the Helter-Skelter nickname). It is also a notable feature of Barke's astuteness about the power of the popular voice that the city babble his text celebrates is so much a domain of song.

Barke's Glaswegians sing, and have minds filled with song. Barke's Leftist discourse of the Glaswegian street is a compound of popular song: the Irishness of 'Sir Michael was a gintleman', the popular twisting of 'Here Comes the Bride' ('Toot-toot, toot-toot, toot-toodli-oot'), the Joycean and Irish 'Love's Old Sweet Song', the Americanism of 'Little Dogie' and 'Last Round-Up', the Flute Band's version of James Connolly's Irish Republican 'Rebel Song', and so on. The world of popular music, of jingle, ballad, musical hit and hymn, is the world of a really popular art of feeling, sentiment, crowd emotion. These are the texts and the inter-texts truly of the masses; and of course they comprise an ideologically inclusive, transgressive textuality. Eliot's Londoners and Joyce's Dubliners are just as steeped in song as Barke's Glaswegians. All the crowd-pullers, and would-be crowd-pullers of the thirties, of every stripe and persuasion, exploited song with all their might. And song is master of every party and servant of none in particular. Song defies the boundaries of ideology. Music's fluidity, its adaptability, its transgressive resistance to the corrals and boundaries of any particular politics, is what makes it so useful to all and sundry. Why should the Devil have all the best tunes? And why should the Christians? 'Revolutionary Music was throbbing throughout the City. Even American crooning songs were being adapted to revolutionary ends.' So *Major Operation* (p. 474). And the kaleidoscopic capacity of this most adaptable of popular discourses to have its coat turned and to serve any and every side in the thirties – Left, Right, Socialist, Christian, Serious, Unserious – was simply enormous. The American popular repertoire was vigorously plundered on the Left: 'Red River Valley' provided Alec McDade with the most popular song of the British International Brigade, 'There's A Valley in Spain called Jarama'; 'John Brown's Body' became 'March of the Workers' (just as Auden wrote 'Miss Gee' to be sung to the tune of the 'St James Infirmary Blues' and 'Victor' to the tune of 'Frankie and Johnny'). *The Left Song Book*, edited for the Workers' Music Association and the Left Book Club by Alan Bush and Randall Swingler (1938) is a monument to the Leftist effort to capture the low ground of popular music: 'Land of Wales, so long subjected' (to the tune of 'Cwm Rhondda' – 'Bread of Heaven'); 'Prices Rise' ('Three Blind Mice'); 'Cities Burning' ('London's Burning'), and so on. 'Music has been one of the banners at the head of every great progressive movement', declared *The Left Song Book* editors. But, of course, music has also been at the head of movements Bush and Swingler would not have accounted progressive.

A crowd art, an instrumental art, an art issuing in action through inspiring sentiment, and so also a woman's art (in Jane Tompkins' terms), the song – the ballad, the hymn – is a womanly art also in the sense of sharing with woman, anciently viewed, a daunting fluidity, worrying unfixity, awesome boundarilessness. (Derrida is not the only one to have noticed the etymological network linking *hymn* and *hymen*.) And in the thirties music proved itself quite literally a polemically transgressive business in a particular woman's preacherly hands:

> We'll hold the Foursquare banner high;
> And beneath its folds we'll live and die!
> May it proudly wave, 'til Christ's power to save
> Leaps each bounding ocean wave.
> Then let our banner be unfurled;
> Forward march to all the world,

> And forth the Foursquare message pour
> 'Til He reigns from shore to shore.

So went the 1935 rewrite of *The Red Flag* which they sang in the revival meetings of the American evangelist Aimée Semple McPherson. This was music for another kind of people's carnival, the mass Christian crusade.[18] It was Mrs McPherson's shrewd practice of adapting worldly tunes for her Christian purposes (why indeed should the Devil have all the best ones?) that attracted her to Evelyn Waugh's satirical attention. He turned her into Mrs Melrose Ape in *Vile Bodies* (1930), the itinerant preacher whose choir of Angels is renowned for coarse ditties like 'There Ain't No Flies on the Lamb of God'. Her brisk way with *The Red Flag* brings rather startlingly home the instructive multivalence of the popular musical text, of musical discourse, the way the same music can be at home in quite different mouths and on quite opposite occasions. Which is a belief somewhere near the very centre of Barke's syncretist left-wing Joyceanism.

On the other side of the politico-poetical fence, it is Rudyard Kipling's populist balladeering that gives him a value to T.S. Eliot which we might not have anticipated. Certainly, as Eliot grapples with what he thinks good about Kipling in his essay on the poet referred to earlier which forms the introduction to Eliot's *A Choice of Kipling's Verse* (1941), the pioneering modernist offers Kipling as an excellent kind of surrogate popular poet of the thirties in what amounts to the best of anti-modernist terms. Kipling is declared to be good precisely because he provides simple, political, popular, instrumental and balladic verse. Kipling is a 'ballad-maker'. His 'lucidity' is 'excessive'. He writes 'jingles', 'intended to arouse emotion', but with the 'inspiration and refreshment of the living music-hall'. They are 'best when read aloud'. 'I have in mind . . . the reader who, if he believes that Kipling wrote "political jingles", stresses the word *jingles* rather than the word *political*.' 'I know of no writer of such great gifts for whom poetry seems to have been more purely an instrument.' 'For Kipling the poem is something which is intended to *act*.' 'I am not implying any inferiority of craftsmanship, but rather a different order of values from that which we expect to determine the structure of poetry.' 'If we belong to the kind of critic who is accustomed to consider poems solely by the standards of the "work of art" we may tend to dismiss Kipling's verse by standards which are not meant to apply.' 'Political imagination . . . not ephemeral.' 'Public purpose.' 'Instrumental.'[19]

Eliot may not intend it – though he is a notorious sly-boots, always covering his tracks, always dodging and waiving, and offering the pipe of peace without professing to do so – but his defence of Kipling in these terms is not simply a justification of his own personal relish for Music Hall and of that love of popular song which so informs the demoticism of *The*

*Waste Land* and of his pageant *The Rock* (1934) and which lies behind the populism of *Murder in The Cathedral* (1935), as well as being a part of what he is drawn to in *Ulysses*. It is also, in effect, a defence of what Randall Swingler and Alan Bush were about in their Workers' Music Association and Left Book Club Musicians' Group work. It is an effective defence too of many a Spanish Civil War propaganda ballad (and it is no accident, of course, that the tones of Kipling should lie behind so many Spanish War poems – Somhairle MacAlastair's 'Battle Song of "Irish Christian Front": Off to Salamanca', for instance, which is in the verse form of 'Gunga Din'). In other words, it is in effect a sturdy sticking up for a great deal of thirties left-wing poeticity of the kind that can only be accorded high value if we grant it merit in Eliot's Kiplingesque terms. They are, of course, the terms Jane Tompkins wants us to apply to *Uncle Tom's Cabin*.

And the fact that Kipling is usually regarded as the darling of the jingoistic Right, and that T.S. Eliot is one of the highest priests of modernism, is very much a main consideration here. And what is important is not just that balladeering and song are kinds of poetry which appeal to Left and Right, cut across distinctions of socialist and modernist practice and taste and emerge hereabouts as an allegory or parable or symbol of that radical transgressivity. That is all true. But, also, and in particular, what we have here is a very potent further set of reminders: that any Radek-type attempt to close the literary borders was simply not on in the thirties; that our reading of the thirties cannot shut out modernism and the modernists; that our high valuation of the modernists cannot be deployed as a simple stick to beat the red thirties with. And, of course, that literary history, and literary value, and the canoneering they sustain, are very tricky businesses indeed.

NOTES

1. Michael Bérubé, *Marginal Forces/Cultural Centers: Tolson, Pynchon, and the Politics of the Canon* (Ithaca and London: Cornell University Press, 1992), pp. 40–1.
2. Jane Tompkins, 'Sentimental Power: *Uncle Tom's Cabin* and the Politics of Literary History', *Sensational Designs: The Cultural Work of American Fiction 1790–1860* (New York and Oxford: Oxford University Press, 1985), pp. 122–46.
3. T.S. Eliot, 'Rudyard Kipling', *A Choice of Kipling's Verse* (London: Faber, 1941), pp. 5–36. I will return to Eliot and Kipling at the end of this chapter.
4. T.S. Eliot, '*Ulysses*, Order, and Myth', *Dial*, November 1923. Reprinted in *Selected Prose of T.S. Eliot*, ed. Frank Kermode (London: Faber, 1975), pp. 175–8.
5. Quoted in John Cournos, 'Russian Periodicals', *Criterion*, XV (LVIII), October 1935: 176.
6. Edward Upward, 'Sketch For a Marxist Interpretation of Literature', *The Mind*

in *Chains: Socialism and the Cultural Revolution*, ed. Cecil Day Lewis (Frederick Muller, 1937), p. 52.

7. Christopher Caudwell, 'D.H. Lawrence', *Studies in a Dying Culture* (1938): *Studies and Further Studies in a Dying Culture*, intro. Sol Yurick (New York and London: Monthly Review Press, 1971), pp. 47–8.

8. Karl Radek, 'Contemporary World Literature and the Tasks of Proletarian Art: 7. James Joyce or Socialist Realism?'; 'Speech in Answer to the Discussion: 4. Where to Direct the Eyes of Literature', *Problems of Soviet Literature*, ed. H.G. Scott (London: Martin Lawrence Ltd, 1935), pp. 150–62, 178–82.

9. Alick West, *Crisis and Criticism* (London: Lawrence & Wishart, 1937), p. 171.

10. Ralph Fox, *The Novel and the People* (London: Lawrence & Wishart, 1937); new edn (London: Cobbett Press, 1944), pp. 96, 104. We should, incidentally, be arrested by the echo of T.S. Eliot's notorious catchphrase, 'the dissociation of sensibility'.

11. Nikolai Bukharin, 'Poetry, Poetics and the Problems of Poetry in the USSR', in *Problems of Soviet Literature*, pp. 235–6.

12. All of these reactions to Barke are from Andy Croft, *Red Letter Days: British Fiction in the 1930s* (London: Lawrence & Wishart, 1990), p. 279, and note 7, p. 305.

13. Stephen Spender, *The Thirties and After: Poetry, Politics, People (1933–75)* (London: Fontana/Collins, 1978), p. 203.

14. West, *Crisis and Criticism*, pp. 192–3.

15. Mikhail Mikhailovich Bakhtin, *Rabelais and His World*, trans. H. Iswolsky (Cambridge, Mass.: MIT Press, 1968); *The Dialogic Imagination: Four Essays*, ed. M. Holquist, trans. C. Emerson and M. Holquist (Austin, Texas: Texas University Press, 1981).

16. Arthur Calder-Marshall, 'Fiction To-Day', *The Arts To-day*, ed. Geoffrey Grigson (London: John Lane: Bodley Head, 1935), p. 122.

17. Fox, *The Novel and the People*, new edn, p. 96.

18. Edith L. Blumhofer, *Aimée Semple McPherson: Everybody's Sister* (Michigan: Eerdmans, 1993), p. 232.

19. T.S. Eliot, *A Choice of Kipling's Verse*, pp. 6, 9–12, 18–19, 26, 34.

CHAPTER THREE

# Illusion and Reality: the Spectre of Socialist Realism in Thirties Literature

PETER MARKS

The literary culture of the thirties sometimes suggests an anarchic Speakers' Corner: any writer able to put pen to paper appears to have had musings, complaints and analyses speedily published. Opinions, it seems, were as regularly produced as poems. The preferred (and certainly the most accessible) soapboxes for such pronouncements were periodicals and weeklies, some already established, others worked up in response to the decade's literary and political imperatives. These journals provided swift access to sometimes small, but often well-defined audiences, enabling vigorous consideration of the interplay between literature and politics. Periodicals allowed for rapid debate on crucial matters of the moment, matters which might develop in ways unforeseen by critics and writers. Free from the revisions of hindsight, positions put forward in periodicals offer valuable contemporary records with which to consider important, though often short-lived, disputes.

The potential for Socialist Realism in British literature constitutes such a dispute. Socialist Realism might be seen as a spectre haunting European literature during the thirties and beyond, though its impact varied measurably from nation to nation (see Scriven and Tate 1988). In Britain it certainly commanded advocates, but the evidence from periodicals suggests that the impact of the approach was not as pronounced as its supporters expected, or as its opponents feared. Certainly, in the politically engaged *Left Review*, fiery debates raged over something approaching Socialist Realism. Even there, however, views were anything but homogeneous, and no clearly defined method was prescribed. Additionally, the very absence of debate in other periodicals suggests a wider indifference to, or ignorance of, Socialist Realism. Beyond the heat (if not the light) of disputes in *Left Review*, many British writers of the thirties were left largely unscorched by the flames of this ideological debate.

Some preliminary remarks on periodicals are necessary, for the periodical culture was somewhat less democratic than might first appear. To generalise sweepingly, a disproportionate number of editors were middle-class, male, university-educated and London-based; so too were many of the contributors. Periodicals necessarily reflected these biases, even as they aspired to eclecticism. Readers provided a more diverse constituency, but it seems reasonable to assume that the majority bore a family resemblance to those whose work they read. In most cases readerships were small, *Left Review* reaching a respectable but hardly prodigious 5,000 (Croft 1990: 50). Periodicals also might be remarkably short-lived: *Cambridge Left* lasted barely a year. Furthermore, while providing a site for literary and political debate, journals did not in themselves determine what writers produced. Nevertheless, they can be seen to function centrally in the literary discourse of the decade, and their sheer number testifies to an informed, attentive audience for analyses and disputes.

Socialist Realism provided one potential issue for those in Britain concerned with the relationship of literature to politics. First given international publicity at the All Union Congress of Soviet Writers held in Moscow in August 1934, Socialist Realism as a general code of practice was the outcome of debate in the Soviet Union since 1932. The approach was itself a critique of previous attempts, most notably Proletkult and RAPP (the Russian Association of Proletarian Writers) to formulate a place and strategy for literature in the post-Revolution environment (Ermolaev 1963: 9–138). The Congress was attended by international writers, including delegates from Britain, some of the key statements being published in Britain the following year as *Problems of Soviet Literature* (reprinted in 1977 as *Soviet Writers' Congress 1934*). Communist Party functionary Andrey Zhdanov provided the introduction, 'Soviet Literature – The Richest in Ideas. The Most Advanced Literature'. Understatement clearly a low priority, Zhdanov waxes lyrical on the uniqueness of Soviet writing: 'Never before has there been a literature which has organized the toilers and oppressed for the struggle to abolish once and for all every kind of exploitation and the yoke of wage slavery' (Gorky et al. 1977: 17). He denounces the 'decadence' of contemporary bourgeois literature, with its 'orgies of mysticism and superstition [and] passion for pornography' (ibid.: 19). Soviet writing, by happy contrast, 'is impregnated with enthusiasm and the spirit of heroic deeds'. The heroes of this literature, Zhdanov reveals, 'are the active builders of a new life – working men and women' (ibid.: 20). Invoking Stalin's demand that writers be 'engineers of the human soul', Zhdanov suggests that this entails 'knowing life so as to be able to depict it truthfully', not in a 'dead, scholastic way', but in its 'revolutionary development'. Crucially, realism must be allied with socialism, for 'the truthfulness and historical concreteness of the artistic portrayal can be combined with the ideological remoulding and education of the toiling people in the spirit of socialism. This . . . we call the method of socialist realism' (ibid.: 21).

Maxim Gorky, often considered the first great practitioner of Socialist Realism, echoed Zhdanov's criticisms of bourgeois literature, arguing that European writing languishes in a 'state of creative impotence' (Gorky et al. 1977: 40). Gorky places the Communist Party at the centre of the Soviet literary project, requesting that 'Party members active in literature must not only be the teachers of ideas' but that 'the Party leadership must, in all its conduct, show a morally authoritative force.' Soviet literature, he continues, 'should be organized as an integral collective body, as a potent instrument of socialist culture' (ibid.: 64). Karl Radek launched a sharp polemical attack in 'Contemporary World Literature and the Tasks of Proletarian Art', boasting fearlessly that '[w]ithout any fear of boasting we may say that Soviet literature is now the best literature in the world' (ibid.: 130). Unlike societies which had hitherto crushed budding literary talent, the Soviet Union's fecund artistic soil allows that 'one hundred times better chances [exist] that more Shakespeares, more geniuses will be found among us' (ibid.: 148). Radek attacks two recognised geniuses of bourgeois literature, condemning T.S. Eliot for 'fascist declarations' (ibid.: 115), while luridly describing the work of James Joyce as 'a heap of dung, crawling with worms, photographed by a cinema apparatus through a microscope' (ibid.: 153). Joyce's method, Radek declares, 'would prove utterly worthless if the author were to approach with his movie camera the great events of the class struggle, the titanic clashes of the modern world' (ibid.: 154), a plausible, though hardly pertinent comment. Amid the hyperbole and the denunciation, however, speakers admit that Socialist Realism in 1934 itself remains a goal. Zhdanov acknowledges that '[o]ur literature does not yet come up to the requirements of our era' (ibid.: 23), while even Radek confesses that 'Soviet literature's process of development is a lengthy one. Achievements in this domain can only be won at the cost of persistent labour' (ibid.: 131). Even within the unique circumstances of the Soviet Union, then, the promise of Socialist Realism had still to be fulfilled.

The Moscow Congress had undoubted importance for the imposition and development of Socialist Realism, though recent commentators have presented differing views on the method's rationale and effect. Herman Ermolaev has argued that, rather than developing naturally from literary debate, Socialist Realism 'originated as a set of Party-postulated demands which aimed to transform literature into an effective instrument for the practical realization of Marxist doctrine' (Ermolaev 1963: 159). Geoffrey Hosking, less critically, explains that the method required that a work be 'popular', both in being about the lives of ordinary people and being comprehensible to them; that it reflect a 'mature, correct and fully formed ideology'; and that it be 'imbued with the ideals of the party' (Hosking 1980: 3). Hosking contends that while Socialist Realism was a doctrine imposed by the Party, 'even in the most rigid Stalinist times, external controls did not wholly determine the form and content of fiction . . . [it was] a hollow frame which the writer filled with the products of his own imagination' (pp. 19–20). Hosking nevertheless accepts that Stalin oversaw the building of that frame.

Even before the congress, however, discussion of the place and aim of a more politicised literature in thirties Britain was already established. Michael Roberts, in his introduction to *New Signatures* (1932) considered it natural that for some young poets in the collection 'the recognition of the importance of others should sometimes lead to what appears to be the essence of the communist attitude', continuing that poetic 'impersonality comes not from extreme detachment but from solidarity with others' (Roberts 1935: 18–19). Hardly an incitement to the barricades, admittedly, but one small sign of a more general attitude. Much of the material in *New Signatures* and in the Roberts-edited 1933 *New Country* derived from periodicals, and one of these, *The Adelphi*, carried 'The Poet and Revolution', by C. Day Lewis, in its September 1932 number. This proves a more substantial call to arms than does the piece by Roberts, Day Lewis explicitly challenging writers to involve themselves in the struggle for Communism (Day Lewis 1932).

*The Adelphi*'s editor, John Middleton Murry, had himself argued the case for Communism in the periodical seven months earlier, in 'The Necessity of Communism', a tenet of his thesis being that Communism should be English in character (Murry 1932). He argued this at greater length in a book of the same name. Murry's 'Communism and Art: or Bolshevism and Ballyhoo' appeared in the January 1933 *The Adelphi*, Murry arguing for 'creative', 'imaginative' Communism and against the 'negative and reductive' Communism of the Bolsheviks (Murry 1933: 266–8). In 'the formation of the revolutionary nucleus', Murry foretells rather airily, 'the dynamic relation between man and man, and man and the living universe, feels towards its own creation' (p. 270). The essays of Day Lewis and Murry signify that discussions of the relationship between Communism and literature were taking place in advance of the Moscow Congress, and that versions of Communism other than the Soviet model were being argued for. Crucially, the periodical provided a ready platform for the broadcasting of these ideas.

*Cambridge Left*, a platform now little remembered, was constructed in the summer of 1933. Though it survived only five issues, *Cambridge Left* could boast J.D. Bernal, Naomi Mitchison and W.H. Auden among its contributors. The periodical's political commitment was clear, 'A Note on Poetry and Politics' in the first number stating that '[t]he motives for writing, and the motives of those writing for this paper, have changed, along with the motives for doing anything. It is not so much an intellectual choice, as the forcible intrusion of social issues' ('A Note' 1933: 10). Eager to analyse such issues was the young radical John Cornford, whose provocative essay 'Left?' appeared in the 1933 winter number. The title's question-mark presents a challenge, Cornford demanding that the writer 'must actively participate in the revolutionary struggles of society if he is not going to collapse into the super-subjectivity of the older writers' (Cornford 1933–34: 26). Among these writers Cornford names Joyce and Eliot: the same targets Radek was to attack a year later. Declaring that '[t]he traditional writer's "impartiality" is unmasked as a denial of the class struggle', Cornford tendentiously detects 'the beginnings of a politically conscious revolutionary literature for the first time in the history of English culture' (p. 25). Similarly, in his analysis of the Soviet writers' congress, J.P. Tuck applauds the 'serious collective attempt . . . to use literature as a means for the creation of a conscious, free, educated, cultured, classless society'. He goes on to claim that '[s]uch aims are the reverse of those of the middle-class critics of England and America, who seek a purely personal art and a purely personal truth' (Tuck 1934: 11–12). This review appeared in the final number of *Cambridge Left*, but clearly its contributors aspired to a politically conscious revolutionary literature in advance of the Moscow congress.

Naturally, not all periodicals were as politically orientated as *Cambridge Left*. *New Verse*, for example, confidently proclaimed its independence from politics in its first number, editor Geoffrey Grigson claiming an alignment 'to no literary or politico-literary cabal' (Grigson 1933a: 2). The second number threateningly reiterated this purported lack of stance: 'Every poet is to send in his work, and is warned again that *New Verse* has no politics' (Grigson 1933b: 1). Despite these protestations, the journal was not entirely uninterested in the political leanings of poets. The 1934 August issue proposed an 'Enquiry' into the role of the poet, stating explicitly that 'poets of all parties or no parties and of every age' had been asked to respond (Grigson 1934a: 1). Questions ranged over the usefulness of poetry, the impulse to write, and what distinguished the poet from ordinary men. To this last enquiry Laura Riding tartly observed, 'as a poet, I am distinguished from ordinary men, first, in that I am a woman' (Riding 1934: 5). Twenty-two out of the forty poets questioned replied, Grigson commenting that 'in general those poets who have passed their lives walking backwards down an ascending escalator . . . appear to have thought the enquiry DANGEROUS, a Bolshevik trap' [original emphasis] (Grigson 1934b: 2). Grigson concedes, however, that Stephen Spender, W.H. Auden and C. Day Lewis, poets more sympathetic to Bolshevism, had not responded.

The question, 'Do you take your stand with any political or politico-economic party or creed?', not surprisingly drew diverse responses. Wyndham Lewis declared that he stood 'exactly midway between the Bolshevist and the Fascist' (Day Lewis 1934: 8), while Robert Graves advised that 'everyone should fight their own battles and no one else's' (Graves 1934: 6). From those likely to incline towards the Left, no uniform position emerged. Louis MacNeice apologised that '[i]n weaker moments I wish I could [stand by a creed]' (MacNeice 1934: 7); Hugh MacDiarmid did stand by the Communist Party (MacDiarmid 1934: 19); while Edwin Muir championed the politico-economic creed of Social Credit (Muir 1934: 17). Others, though they expressed support for Leftist ideas, did so either with such timidity or bombast as to make their political resolve highly suspect. Norman Cameron, for example, dithered that, though 'I believe that Communism is necessary and good . . . I am not eager for it' (Cameron 1934: 15), while Dylan Thomas proclaimed both vaguely and ostentatiously that 'I take my stand with any revolutionary body that asserts it to be the right of all men to share, equally and impartially, every production of man from man and from the sources of production at man's disposal, for only through such an essentially revolutionary body can there be the possibility of a communal art' (Thomas 1934: 9). How such noble sentiments might translate into practical political activity remains unclear. Nevertheless, the *New Verse* enquiry suggests two things: the difficulty for thirties writers in entirely ignoring political concerns, and, equally importantly, the manifold shadings of their political opinions.

*New Verse*'s avowedly apolitical stance contrasts markedly with that of *Left Review*, the most politically engaged of the decade's literary periodicals. The first number appeared in October 1934, two months after the Moscow Writers' Congress, and in this journal occur the most extended and heated arguments regarding anything approaching Socialist Realism. As with *Cambridge Left*, *Left Review* from the outset championed the Soviet Union, the first number opening with Louis Aragon's poem 'Waltz', a panegyric to the Tcheliabinsk tractor works (Aragon 1934: 3–5). Pro-Soviet puffs by such writers as George Bernard Shaw, reviews of books favourable to the Soviet Union and occasional reports from travelling correspondents reinforced *Left Review*'s promotion of the Soviet Union. The joys of Soviet literary culture were readily proclaimed. A report on the 1934 Moscow Writers' Congress by co-editor Amabel Williams-Ellis, for example, enthused that when the congress was held 'it would hardly be too much to say that . . . the whole of Russia listened' (Williams-Ellis 1934: 17). Georgy Dimitrov's speech before the Soviet Writers' Association, published a year later, declared that '[w]riters in the Soviet Union live in the most favourable conditions for their literary production. . . . Abroad revolutionary writers are at grips with exceptional difficulties. They suffer poverty, they are thrown into prison or into concentration camps' (Dimitrov 1935: 345). If this claim seems overstated, it was not out of place in the *Left Review* of the time. Christina Stead similarly extolled the virtues of the Soviet Union in her report on the first international Congress of Writers on the defence of culture, held in Paris in June 1935. Stead writes that 'the problems of most serious liberal-minded writers outside the Soviet Union are real. If they are not persecuted nor in exile, they pant for a public' (Stead 1935: 453). The possibility seems not to have occurred that, if the liberal-minded writer panted for a public, the feeling might not be mutual.

*Left Review* had attempted to mobilise such writers in its inaugural issue. This carried a statement of aim from the Writers' International (British Section) which disclosed 'a crisis in the capitalist world today no less considerable than the crisis in economics'. The statement continues that 'the decadence of the past twenty years of English literature and theatre cannot be understood apart from all that separates 1913 and 1934. It is the collapse of a culture' (Writers' International Statement 1934: 38). Against this bleak (though, for some, promising) prospect, the statement registers the need to organise writers under three guidelines: (1) those who see Fascism as the 'terrorist dictatorship of dying capitalism' and consider that 'the best in civilization of the past' can only be preserved and developed by a new socialist society; (2) working-class writers wishing to express the struggle of their class; (3) writers willing to write 'against imperialist war and in defence of the Soviet Union, the State where the foundations of Socialism have already been laid' (p. 38).

Though correlations exist between this statement and the broad aims of Soviet Socialist Realism, clearly crucial differences abound. Preserving from Fascism the 'best in civilization of the past', and further developing it, suggests the protection and cultivation of supposedly outmoded bourgeois culture – culture that in the Soviet Union was being transformed in the smithy of Socialist Realism. Importantly, the declaration does not propose a particular literary method which writers might adopt. In more general terms, setting working-class writers in a distinct category (a sort of literary apartheid) foregrounds the gap between the majority of potential British Writers' International members (*Left Review* writers included) and the class they ostensibly champion. Additionally, while joining the organisation entailed both an antagonism to Fascism and a defence of the Soviet Union, their placing in different subsections of the statement allows for the possibility of being anti-Fascist without being particularly pro-Soviet, or vice versa.

Responses to the statement, bearing the collective title, 'Controversy', enlivened subsequent issues of *Left Review*. Several writers welcomed the setting down of these aspirations, C. Day Lewis believing 'that the substance and object of this statement are of vital importance' (Day Lewis 1935a: 129). Alec Brown provided easily the most provocative contribution, however, demanding an answer to the question 'WHOM ARE WE WRITING FOR AND HOW?' Brown declares the need for a 'permanent propaganda committee' working towards the 'proletarianization' of outlook and language. Decrying the 'jargon most of us put out' (an example close to hand being proletarianization, perhaps) Brown suggests several slogans: 'LITERARY ENGLISH FROM CAXTON TO US IS AN ARTIFICIAL JARGON OF THE RULING CLASS; WRITTEN ENGLISH BEGINS WITH US; or another slogan: WE ARE REVOLUTIONARY WORKING–CLASS WRITERS; WE HAVE GOT TO MAKE USE OF THE LIVING LANGUAGE OF OUR CLASS; also: ALLUSIVE WRITING IS CLIQUE WRITING: WE ARE NOT A CLIQUE' [original emphasis] (Brown 1934: 77). While such hectoring hardly amounts to a worked–out literary method along the lines of Socialist Realism, it does present a demand for a populist, radical, proletarian literature.

Yet even within the ranks of *Left Review* readers and contributors, such comments drew sustained criticism. Hugh MacDiarmid, having testified for Communism in *New Verse*, protested that Brown's drive towards proletarianisation represented 'a kind of "talking down to the people"'. Highly allusive writing, MacDiarmid contends, has long been understood by workers 'and appeals to a deep–seated human desire, just as the obvious, the over–simplified, the pre–digested "pap" is abhorrent' (MacDiarmid 1935: 182). In the same issue, Stephen Spender's 'Writers and Manifestos' launched a furious attack on Brown, Spender judging there to be 'a great difference between even the most stupefying and severe censorship and the attempt to regard art as the mere instrument in the hands of a party. The difference is that censorship cuts or bans books that have already been written: but the principles laid down in [Brown's] manifesto order the manner in which they should be written. . . . No censorship has ever gone so far as this' (Spender 1935: 149). No censorship in Britain, at least.

The specific denunciation of Brown by both MacDiarmid and Spender testifies to the heterogeneity of opinion in *Left Review*. Lewis Grassic Gibbon's more general critique of the original statement only underlines this diversity. Gibbon dismisses as 'bolshevik blah' claims of bourgeois literature's decadence, seeing the Writers' International statement as 'inspired by (a) misapprehension; (b) ignorance; or (c) spite'. While keen to emphasise his own radical credentials, Grassic Gibbon prefers not to sully them by association: 'Not all revolutionary writers (I am a revolutionary writer) are cretins. But the influence of such delayed adolescents, still in the thrall of wishfulfilment dreams, seems to have predominated in the drawing up of this resolution' (Gibbon 1935: 179). Whatever else, these and other contributors to *Left Review* could scarcely be criticised for a lack of rhetorical vigour. After several issues, however, the aptly titled 'Controversy' section was wound up. Ultimately, manifestos could only provide a spur to action; writers needed first to produce.

Even so, discussion of the role of writing, literature and criticism continued to prompt *Left Review* contributors. In his 1935 essay, 'Revolutionaries and Poetry', C. Day Lewis warns the periodical's readers against 'that form of literary sentimentality which would accept any piece of verse evidently written from a revolutionary standpoint and reject everything written from any other angle' (Day Lewis 1935b: 399). Despite his positive response to 'Controversy' earlier in the year, Day Lewis had warned then that the mechanical use of characters to express a political philosophy would result in 'an illuminated textbook' (Day Lewis 1935a: 129). In 'Revolutionaries and Poetry' he argues that '[t]he first qualification of a poem is that it should be a good poem – technically, I mean . . . a poem may have been written by a reactionary bourgeois and yet be a very good poem and of value to the revolutionary; *The Waste Land is* such a one' (Day Lewis 1935b: 399). Day Lewis' defence of *The Waste Land* implicitly challenges the argument of Alec Brown, for the poem epitomises the allusive, clique writing Brown had condemned. Day Lewis also calls into question the blanket denunciation of bourgeois literature in the British Writers' statement. Might Eliot, Eliot's poem and literature like it (*Ulysses*, even) be other than decadent?

*Left Review* fought on vigorously until 1938, but while the call remained for writers to depict social and political reality, no aesthetic template was adopted by contributors. Charles Madge's 1936 review of *Problems of Soviet Literature* registers Socialist Realism's lack of impact, Madge asking 'what signs are there in England of any conscious response to this "beginning of a new era in the history of literature". There has been practically no conscious response' (Madge 1936: 228). This, remember, eighteen months after the Writers' International statement, and the subsequent discussion in *Left Review*. By way of explanation, Madge complains that British writers 'lack the political and social guidance from which Soviet writers are able to benefit' (p. 228). More positively, he suggests that Socialist Realism, 'like socialist revolution, not only *is* being invented but . . . must inevitably be invented' [original emphasis], before prophesying that 'it is the beginning and only the beginning of the long drawn-out historical process, which we see in England today' (p. 230). Despite the optimism, Madge's linking of the development of Socialist Realism in Britain to socialist revolution consigns the approach to a long historical march.

The figurative length of that march can be measured by stepping outside *Left Review*. Other periodicals gave little or no time either to the 1934 Moscow Congress or to the dictates of Socialist Realism. The *New English Weekly*, a self-styled 'Review of Public Affairs, Literature and the Arts', made no mention of the Moscow gathering, though it did report favourably on a less radical 1935 Paris conference in defence of culture, reported on by Stead in *Left Review*. Nor did the specific arguments which animated *Left Review* readers and writers greatly disturb those connected with such periodicals as *The Adelphi, Time and Tide, New Verse* or *Twentieth-Century Verse*. Though these journals were interested in the interplay of politics and literature, they maintained different concerns and emphases. Surprisingly, T.S. Eliot's patrician journal, *Criterion*, did afford the Moscow Congress space, in John Cournos's article 'Russian Chronicle: Soviet Russia and the Literature of Idea'. Cournos eyes the Congress and Soviet literature sceptically, however, arguing that social ideas 'have driven out art, and today only the formula remains, the formula of social reform . . . and we may well ask ourselves: is the wholehearted adoption of the formula by Soviet literature a symptom of a new and rising literature or is it the final symptom of the decline of the old?' (Cournos 1935: 286). He describes Socialist Realism merely as 'a phrase which may mean much or little, according to the definition. But no precise definition has been offered' (p. 289). Finding no novelty in the plea for realism, he judges that the good in recent Soviet literature 'belongs to the old rather than the new, to tradition rather than to Communism' (p. 290).

Even such negative attention was denied by *Criterion*'s chief critical rival, *Scrutiny*. The Moscow Congress generated no comment in *Scrutiny*, and except in book reviews its writers proved indifferent to Socialist Realism and attendant arguments. These reviews almost invariably proved launch pads for antagonism, L.C. Knights dismissing *Literature and a Changing Civilisation* by Philip Henderson with the thought that 'even the Communist cause is not helped by exaltations of this kind' (Knights 1935: 204). Henderson's *The Novel To-Day* drew Q.D. Leavis to remark that '[p]ractically every general position . . . is either arguable, highly questionable or false' (Leavis 1937: 418). Nor did Christopher Caudwell's *Illusion and Reality* fare better, H.A. Mason proclaiming that '[i]t would be difficult to do justice to the unreadability of this book and to the irrelevance of most of the subject matter' (Mason 1938: 432). Spraying his critical fire at Marxist literary interpretation in general, Mason asserts that '[a]s a class these books have no intrinsic interest' (p. 429). Little wonder, then, that *Problems of Soviet Literature* did not rate a review.

Derided though they were by *Scrutiny* reviewers, these and other works indicate the incorporation of Socialist Realist terminology into the discourse of young critics. Caudwell, arguing the need for 'proletarian art', perceives a 'tremendous revolutionary transition' which 'has only begun, but already its effects are felt through the sphere of arts' (Caudwell 1973: 309). Henderson detects in Britain the beginnings of the proletarian novel (Henderson 1936: 258–87), though surprisingly (and incorrectly) he judges that Soviet Socialist

Realism 'inaugurates no particularly new literary method' (p. 298). 'The social organism to which literature has to be related, is humanity in its advance towards socialism', wrote Alick West in *Crisis and Criticism* (West 1975: 103), while Edward Upward restated a key Socialist Realist notion in *The Mind in Chains*, suggesting that for the Marxist critic 'a good book is one that is true not merely to a temporarily existing situation but also to the future conditions which are developing within that situation' (Upward 1937: 46). Ralph Fox set out a more sustained argument in *The Novel and the People*, charting the decline of the novel from being the first 'attempt to take the whole man and give him expression' to a point where the contemporary English novel has 'lost direction and purpose' (Fox 1979: 20). Marxism, Fox argues, offers the novelist the 'key to reality', requiring in turn that the novelist present a 'new realism', 'man in action to change his conditions . . . in harmony with the course of history' (p. 100). Echoing Zdhanov's 1934 demand, Fox states that the novelist must 'become, as Stalin has phrased it, "the engineer of the human soul"' (p. 101).

Storm Jameson favoured the documentary film-maker and the photographer over the engineer in her provocative piece, 'Documents'. Published in the July 1937 issue of *Fact*, a political monthly which occasionally dabbled in the black arts of literature, the essay argues forcefully for socialist literature. Stating that such writing would be the 'literary equivalent of the documentary film' (Jameson 1937: 15), Jameson instructs writers to do away with 'spiritual writings' and to 'go for the *fact*' [original emphasis] (p. 11). As does the photographer, she instructs, 'so must the writer keep himself out of the picture while working ceaselessly to present the fact from a striking (poignant, ironic, penetrating, significant) angle' (p. 15). She sees a 'task of greatest value urgent and not easy, waiting to be done': a task begun, she notes, by George Orwell, in the first half of *The Road to Wigan Pier* (p. 12). Though Jameson's conditional praise highlights the obvious political, if not indeed spiritual, writings of the second half of *Wigan Pier*, her call for the development of socialist literature exemplifies the views of young, politically committed writers and critics, that while such literature was essential, anything approaching Socialist Realism still remained to be written. Not, of course, that literature of a Leftist slant was not being produced (see Croft 1990).

Reasons why Socialist Realism did not take root in British soil are implicit in Randall Swingler's summation of the work of *Left Review*, the final number of which appeared in May 1938. Swingler presents the impetus for the 1934 Writers' International manifesto as 'the understanding that a culture can only make itself safe from Fascist destruction which has rooted itself in the life of the people' (Swingler 1938: 957), significantly failing to mention

the pro-Soviet component which had enthused many *Left Review* supporters at the time. By 1938, the threat of Fascism, it seems, overrode the
defence of the Soviet Union. Swingler argues, questionably, that the periodical had 'established the core of a true social culture, the starting point of
a new phase of literary development – socialist literature' (p. 957), again
signalling that such literature still remained for the most part an aspiration.
In his final comment, Swingler casts his net wide, promising that those
connected with *Left Review* would continue to try to establish in the
popular mind the underlying principle of the journal, 'that the vitality of
a whole culture depends upon the unity of interest of a whole people,
and the opportunity for free expression of their unity and will' (p. 960).
While Swingler situates the vitality of a culture within the interests of its
people, Socialist Realism in its crudest Soviet form reflected the interests
of the ruling party. And not only did it reflect such interests, but it also
drew upon the considerable powers of the state both to promote its ad-
herents and to frustrate and stifle its opponents. The Soviet context demanded and created a particular literary method, and the establishment of
a particular literary culture. No such culture existed in thirties Britain, and
the responses to Alec Brown in *Left Review* make plain that many Left-
leaning British writers found the potential imposition of a literary method
anathema.

It can be argued that in failing to engage with Socialist Realism, British
writers gave up opportunities hinted at by those such as Ralph Fox. The
fact that even *Left Review*'s soil proved too stony for Socialist Realism's
seed, however, underlines the failure of that method to influence thirties
British literature in any significant way. Despite the hopes of those such as
John Cornford, for the most part bourgeois writers did not go over fully
to the side of the workers in the thirties. Though much energy was chan-
nelled by writers into political struggles, most notably in Spain, hard links
between political allegiance and literary method were not forged. Additionally, of course, many writers remained aloof from political engagement,
or became involved only sporadically. Those who did express their opinions in periodicals often did so forcefully, but even within the relatively
circumscribed boundaries of a single journal the variety of positions put
forward signal a plurality of concerns, tactics and attitudes, each liable to
modification in the rapidly changing circumstances of the decade. If the
Speakers' Corner analogy holds good, while debates were often loud and
certainly vigorous, no single voice dominated. Periodicals clearly played a
central role in the formulation and transmission of views on the interaction
of politics and literature in the thirties. Recognising their place and influence provides a key to understanding why, whatever the hopes or fears, the
spectre of Socialist Realism never materialised.

# REFERENCES

'A Note on Poetry and Politics', *Cambridge Left*, Summer 1933: 10

**Aragon L.** 1934 'Waltz', *Left Review*, 1 (1), October: 3–5

**Brown A.** 1934 Response in 'Controversy', *Left Review*, 1 (3), December: 76–7

**Cameron N.** 1934 Reply to 'An Enquiry', *New Verse*, October: 15

**Caudwell C.** 1973 *Illusion and Reality* (London: Lawrence & Wishart; originally published 1937)

**Cornford J.** 1933–34 'Left?' *Cambridge Left*, Winter: 25–9

**Cournos J.** 1935 'Russian Chronicle: Soviet Russia and the Literature of Ideas', *The Criterion*, XIV (LV), January: 283–91

**Croft A.** 1990 *Red Letter Days: British Fiction in the 1930s* (London: Lawrence & Wishart)

**Day Lewis C.** 1932 'The Poet and The Revolution', *The Adelphi*, September: 862–3

—— 1935a 1935 Response in 'Controversy', *Left Review*, 1 (4), January: 128–9

—— 1935b 'Revolutionaries and Poetry', *Left Review*, 1 (10), July: 397–402

**Dimitrov G.** 1935 'Dimitrov to Writers', *Left Review*, June: 343–6

**Ermolaev H.** 1963 *Soviet Literary Theories 1917–1934: The Genesis of Socialist Realism* (Berkeley: University of California Press)

**Fox R.** 1979 *The Novel and the People* (London: Lawrence & Wishart; originally published 1937)

**Gibbon L.G.** 1935 Response in 'Controversy', *Left Review*, 1 (5), February: 179–80

**Gorky M., Radek K., Bukharin N. et al.** 1977 *Soviet Writers' Congress 1934: The Debate on Socialist Realism and Modernism* (London: Lawrence & Wishart; published 1935 as *Problems of Soviet Literature*)

**Graves R.** 1934 Reply to 'An Enquiry', *New Verse*, October: 5–6

**Grigson G.** 1933a 'Why', *New Verse*, January: 1–2

—— 1933b 'Politics: And a Request', *New Verse*, March: 1–2

—— 1934a 'Poetry To-Day: An Enquiry', *New Verse*, August 1934: 1–2

—— 1934b 'An Enquiry', *New Verse*, October: 2–3

**Henderson P.** 1936 *The Novel To-Day: Studies in Contemporary Attitudes* (London: John Lane)

**Hosking G.** 1980 *Beyond Socialist Realism: Soviet fiction since Ivan Denisovich* (London: Granada)

**Jameson S.** 1937 'Documents', *Fact*, July: 9–18

**Knights L.C.** 1935 Review of *Literature and a Changing Civilisation*, *Scrutiny*, IV (2), September: 203–4

**Leavis Q.D.** 1937 Review of *The Novel To-Day*, *Scrutiny*, V (4), March: 418–23

**Lewis W.** 1934 Reply to 'An Enquiry', *New Verse*, October: 7–8

**MacDiarmid H.** 1934 Reply to 'An Enquiry', *New Verse*, October: 18–19

—— 1935 Response in 'Controversy', *Left Review*, 1 (5), February: 182

**MacNeice L.** 1934 Reply to 'An Enquiry', *New Verse*, October: 7

**Madge C.** 1936 Review of *Problems of Soviet Literature*, *Left Review*, 2 (5), February: 228–30

**Mason H.A.** 1938 Review of *Illusion and Reality*, *Scrutiny*, VI (4), March: 429–33

**Muir E.** 1934 Reply to 'An Enquiry', *New Verse*, October: 17

**Murry J.M.** 1932 'The Necessity of Communism', *The Adelphi*, January: 259–67

—— 1933 'Communism and Art: or Bolshevism and Ballyhoo', *The Adelphi*, January: 261–70

**Riding L.** 1934 Reply to 'An Enquiry', *New Verse*, October: 5

**Roberts M.** (ed.) 1935 *New Signatures* (London: Hogarth)

**Scriven M., Tate D.** (eds) 1988 *European Socialist Realism* (Oxford: Berg)

**Spender S.** 1935 'Writers and Manifestos', *Left Review*, 5 (1), February: 145–50

**Stead C.** 1935 'The Writers Take Sides', *Left Review*, August: 453–62

**Swingler R.** 1938 Editorial, *Left Review*, 3 (16), May: 957–60

**Thomas D.** 1934 Reply to 'An Enquiry', *New Verse*, October: 8–9

**Tuck J.P.** 1934 'English Criticism and the Soviet Writers' Congress', *Cambridge Left*, Autumn: 4–13

**Upward E.** 1937 'Sketch For a Marxist Interpretation of Literature' in C.D. Lewis (ed.) *The Mind in Chains: Socialism and the Cultural Revolution* (London: Frederick Muller), pp. 41–55

**West A.** 1975 *Crisis and Criticism and Selected Literary Essays* (London: Lawrence & Wishart; first published 1937)

**Williams-Ellis A.** 1934 Report on Soviet Writers' Conference, *Left Review*, November: 16–28

**Writers' International Statement**, *Left Review*, 1 (1), October: 38

# CHAPTER FOUR

# 'Alien Experiences': Virginia Woolf, Winifred Holtby and Vera Brittain in the Thirties

## Marion Shaw

> But when my mother's son lay dead, had I
> Neglected him and left him there unburied,
> *That* would have caused me grief.
>
> (Sophocles, Antigone)

In 1936, during the closing stages of writing *The Years*, Woolf wrote a brief article on 'Why Art Today Follows Politics' for the *Daily Worker*. She had been asked to explain 'why it is that the artist at present is interested, actively and genuinely, in politics. . . . That the writer is interested in politics needs no saying. Every publisher's list, almost every book that is now issued, brings proof of the fact [that] the novelist turns from the private lives of his characters to their social surroundings and their political opinions' (Woolf 1993: 133). Her explanation is that whilst society is in chaos, the artist cannot remain immune from the conflicts that beset it. The chaos Woolf had particularly in mind concerned the war in Spain and impending war elsewhere in Europe.

Leonard Woolf believed that Virginia Woolf wrote *The Years* 'against her artistic and psychological grain' and in response to the fashion of the time for 'family' novels. He also believed she reacted to criticism which said 'that she could not create real characters or the reality of everyday life. I think that in 1932, beginning *The Years*, at the back of her mind was the desire or determination to prove these critics wrong' (Leonard Woolf 1980: 400–1). He also records its popular success: 'much the most successful of all Virginia's books. It was the only one which was a best-seller in America' (p. 293). The criticism Leonard Woolf had in mind related particularly to *The Waves*. As Woolf herself had predicted, *The Waves*, published in 1931, 'marks my decline in reputation' (*Diary*, vol. 4: 44). The response had been guarded and unwelcoming: 'the myopic observation, the lack of variation in the tension impose a strain on the reader . . . Mrs Woolf has preserved her extraordinary fineness and delicacy of perception at the cost of some cerebral etiolation', wrote the young Muriel Bradbrook (Majumdar and McLauren: 312–13). Edmund Wilson, complaining in 1931 of the poetry scene after ten years of 'depersonalised and over-intellectual verse', included Woolf's fiction in this indictment of pedantry and 'futile aestheticism': it is 'completely self-contained and does not lead to anything beyond itself' (Wilson 1947: 122–3). Such views become widespread in the period to her death and were given summary authority two decades later in Lukács's critique of the ideology of modernism, in lectures first given in 1955, as 'destroying the complex tissue of man's relations with his environment' (Lukács 1963: 28). 'By separating time from the outer world of objective reality, the inner world of the subject is transformed into a sinister, inexplicable flux and aquires – paradoxically, as it may seem – a static character' (p. 39). Lukács's ideal of art rests on 'the Aristotelian concept of man as *zoon politikon* [social animal] [and] displays the contradictions within society and within the individual in the context of a dialectical unity' (p. 31). Although posterity has not concurred with Lukács's verdict on modernism, it has to some extent followed his example in one respect in overlooking Woolf's attempt in *The Years*, according to her own and her husband's testimony, to write more popularly and to provide her characters with 'social surroundings and . . . political opinions'. The context within which she made this switch from the modernist mode, and the character of *The Years* as a social text, are what I wish to explore in this chapter, and to do so by placing Woolf and *The Years* alongside the contrary personalities, experiences and work of two of her contemporaries, Winifred Holtby and, to a lesser extent, Vera Brittain.

Holtby wrote the first book in English on Virginia Woolf in 1932.[1] It was an audacious and unexpected act, to write about a woman whose lifestyle, reputation and work was so different from Holtby's own. This was, of course, the appeal:

> I took my courage and curiosity in both hands . . . and chose the writer
> whose art seemed most of all removed from anything I could ever
> attempt, and whose experience was most alien to my own. . . . I found it
> the most enthralling adventure – to enter, even at second-hand, that
> world of purely aesthetic and intellectual interests, was to me as strange
> an exploration as it would have been for Virginia Woolf to sit beside my
> mother's pie and hear my uncles talk fat-stock prices and cub-hunting. I
> felt I was learning and learning with every fibre of such brain as I have.
> To submit oneself to another person's mental attitudes, to sink oneself
> into their experience – it's almost like bathing in a strange sea.
>
> (Brittain 1980: 308)

Holtby began *Virginia Woolf* in late 1930 but the onset of Bright's disease, which was to kill her in 1935, slowed the work down, so that when she came to complete the book in 1932 her original plan had to be amended to include discussion of *The Waves*, the Introduction to *Life as We Have Known It* ('her furthest incursion into political writing', Holtby says) and *A Letter to a Young Poet*. She described *The Waves* as 'the most delicate, complex and aesthetically pure piece of writing that [Woolf] has yet produced' (Holtby 1932: 186) and she found it the most challenging to her own 'alien' sensibility. Though she greatly admired 'the strange, subtle confusion' of the subconscious world it portrays, a world 'hitherto largely neglected' in English fiction, she concludes with reservations about Woolf's capabilities as a novelist: 'The immense detailed knowledge of the material circumstances of life mastered by Thackeray or Arnold Bennett is beyond her . . . she is unlikely ever to command the allegiance of a wide contemporary public . . . there is still only a minority which prefers *To the Lighthouse*, with its demands upon the reader's intelligence and imagination, to a novel such as [J.B. Priestley's] *The Good Companions*, which tells a pleasant, full and easy tale' (pp. 201–2).

Woolf was always acutely conscious of criticism, and sometimes responsive to it, as happened with Bradbrook's review: 'Now I think the thing to do is to note the pith of what is said – that I don't think – then to use the little kick of energy which opposition supplies to be more vigorously oneself. . . . To investigate candidly the charge; but not fussily, not very anxiously. On no account to go to the other extreme – thinking too much' (*Diary*, vol. 4: 101). Holtby was a different kind of critic from Bradbrook and in some respects less easy to accept and assimilate than the Cambridge set to whom Woolf could respond with robust and straightforward ease, as she would show in her dismissal of Q.D. Leavis's 'wigging' in *Scrutiny* in relation to *Three Guineas* (*Diary*, vol. 5: 165). A generation younger than Woolf, and university-educated, Holtby belonged to the world of journalism, of 'middle-brow' novel-writing, and of political activism. By the early thirties she had come into contact with Leonard Woolf through her attempts to interest the Labour Party in supporting the unionisation of black workers in South Africa; they were both involved with the Labour Party Advisory Committee on Imperial Affairs. She had also come to know him in connection with the League of Nations. As supporters of the League of Nations Union, she and Vera Brittain attended conferences and committee meetings and lectured in towns throughout the country, and as members of the Six Point Group they were also active feminists. These two causes, pacifism and feminism, were what had given substance to their friendship as undergraduates and sustained it during their years as young working women in the early twenties. They were very obviously examples of the new 'woman citizen' of the interwar period, and Holtby in particular was an index of all that was progressive and socially concerned during this time. Brittain's original title for her biography of Holtby had been, appropriately, 'A Woman in her Time'. Holtby's long friendship with Brittain, with its possible lesbian interpretation and its survival of Brittain's marriage, was also a challenging example of an alternative lifestyle. In so many respects, these women were very different from Woolf, not least, as Holtby noted in relation to herself, their different social backgrounds. This class distinction is recorded mockingly by Woolf in relation to Holtby (it seems that she did not during these years meet Brittain, though she would certainly know of her):[2] 'She is the daughter of a Yorkshire farmer and learnt to read, I'm told, while minding the pigs' (*Letters*, vol. 5: 114). Woolf's letters to Holtby (Holtby's letters to her do not survive) ran from the end of January 1931 to the end of January 1933, and she mentions her during that time, and afterwards, in letters to other correspondents and in her *Diary*. Woolf responds to Holtby in nervously disparate styles: letters to her are coyly polite, to the point of condescension and insincerity; in letters to others she is usually rude about Holtby, exaggerating her uncouthness, and she is also dishonest, saying she has not read *Virginia Woolf* when she has, and sometimes she is also grudgingly admiring of her; in her *Diary* she is sometimes cruel ('poor gaping Holtby') but more often simply matter of fact, recording that Holtby has been to tea, that, amongst much adverse criticism, she has praised *The Waves*, and that she has heard that Holtby is dying. She also met Holtby on four occasions, once during the writing of *Virginia Woolf* and three times after it was published. On one of these occasions, in late January 1933, they apparently talked about professions for women. Afterwards Woolf wrote to Holtby:

> I was afraid that Mr Doggett and other interruptions made your visit rather a scramble but it was my fault if we wandered into Yorkshire and professions and so on. I have it at the back of my mind that I will re-write a paper on professions that I read a year or two ago; and thus tend to pick peoples [sic] brains which is a proof that you had the brains – not that you were a moron as you say. It was very good of you to send me the information – I think it will be very useful. I want to keep rather more closely to facts than usual. And I am not at all well up in the subject of professions.
>
> (WHC, 1: 18)

She was referring to a paper read to Philippa Strachey's London branch of the National Society for Women's Service in January 1931, and to the conception of what would become the aborted 'The Pargiters' which would then split into two books, *The Years* and *Three Guineas*: 'I have this moment', she had written on 20 January, 1931, 'while having my bath, conceived an entire new book – a sequel to A Room of One's Own – about the sexual life of women: to be called Professions for Women perhaps – Lord how exciting! This sprang out of my paper to be read to Pippa's society' (*Diary*, vol. 4: 6; and Woolf 1978: xv). The striking conjunction in this diary entry of the sexual life of women and professions for them – as though they are the same, or at least inextricably linked – forewarns of the complex and radical nature of Woolf's conception, and also how difficult it will be to embody. At the time she wrote this entry she was finishing *The Waves* and found the new conception – The Open Door,[3] as she thought of calling it three days later – distracting: 'The didactic demonstrative style conflicts with the dramatic: I find it hard to get back inside Bernard again' (*Diary*, vol. 4: 6). The new project came to mind several times during 1931 and then urgently in February 1932. By February 1933, the day after her letter to Holtby quoted above, she had decided to abandon the original plan of writing a novel-essay; the novel part of it, now called *The Pargiters*, would be developed independently: 'I am going however to work largely, spaciously, fruitfully on that book. Today I finished – rather more completely than usual – revising the first chapter. I'm leaving out the interchapters – compacting them in the text; & project an appendix of dates. A good idea?' (p. 146).

In September of that year, a further impetus was fed into the flow of ideas comprising *The Pargiters*. Woolf read 'with extreme greed' Vera Brittain's *Testament of Youth* published the month before. Woolf didn't like Brittain's 'stringy metallic mind' but conceded that

> . . . her story, told in detail, without reserve, of the war, & how she lost
> lover & brother, & dabbled her hands in entrails, & was forever seeing
> the dead, & eating scraps, & sitting five on one WC, runs rapidly,
> vividly across my eyes. A very good book of its sort. The new sort, the
> hard, anguished sort, that the young write; that I could never write. Nor
> has anyone written that kind of book before. Why now? What urgency
> is there on them to stand bare in public? She feels that these facts must
> be made known, in order to help – what? herself partly I suppose. And
> she has the social conscience. I still have to read how she married the
> infinitely dreary Catlin & found beauty & triumph in poor, gaping
> Holtby. But I give her credit for having lit up a long passage for me at
> least. I read & read & read & . . . But why does my hand shake? Why
> cant I write clearly?
>
> (p. 177)

Leonard Woolf came to believe that the inability of the League of Nations to prevent war stemmed from the 'disastrous' decision of the French and British Governments not to support and encourage 'a pacific, democratic Social-Democrat German government' (1980: 366), and that the two crucial occasions on which a weakened and demoralised League was unable to exert the rights of international collective security over national territorial greed were the Japanese invasion of China in 1932 and the Italian invasion of Abyssinia in 1935. In his view, between these two dates, Hitler's rise to power became unstoppable and war inevitable. No wonder that Virginia Woolf's hand shook in 1933, reading Brittain's 'hard, anguished' account of the slaughter of the previous war in the current context of despair concerning the coming of the next war. But what was the long passage Vera Brittain lit up for her? *Testament of Youth* was the first account by a woman of involvement in the war both as participant, as a VAD, and as a sufferer, through the loss of 'lover and brother'. And because its account of war experience is prefaced by the story of Brittain's feminist struggles for education, it brings together, albeit without theorising the connection, pacifism (and its obverse, militarism) and feminism. It thus added to women's historic role of victim a new role of agent and contained material from which the radical analysis of *The Years* and, even more, *Three Guineas* could grow.

By October 1935, the end of *The Years*, now referred to by its final name, was in sight and the 'essay' parts were demanding to be written: 'Then there's my Next War [*Three Guineas*] – which at any moment becomes absolutely wild, like being harnessed to a shark; & I dash off scene after scene. I think I must do it directly The Years is done. Suppose I finish The Years in Jan: then dash off The War (or whatever I call it) in six weeks: & do Roger. [Fry] next summer' (*Diary*, vol. 4: 348). As it turned out, it was June 1938 that the whole, dual project was completed: '. . . the end of six years floundering, striving, much agony, some ecstasy: lumping the Years & 3Gs together as one book – as indeed they are' (*Diary*, vol. 5: 148). By then Holtby had been dead for nearly three years and the next mention of her was in connection with the publication in 1940 of Vera Brittain's biography, *Testament of Friendship*, which Woolf read and didn't like – '[Holtby] had a good deal more to her than V.B. saw [and] deserved a better' (*Letters*, vol. 6: 379). In the enigmatic and less than honest letter to Brittain thanking her for sending a copy of *Testament of Friendship*, Woolf wrote: 'I was puzzled by something about [Winifred Holtby] when we met . . . I felt she was oddly uncertain about something important . . . I think I see now what it was'. Woolf does not explain what 'it' was but continues that she felt about Holtby 'that she was only at the beginning of a life that held all sort of possibilities not only for her but for all of us' (p. 378). Reading the biography prompted her to read Holtby's *South Riding*:

> I think (so far) she has a photographic mind, a Royal Academicians
> mind. Its as bright as paint, but how obvious, how little she's got
> beneath the skin. Thats why it rattles on so, I think. One's never pulled
> up by a single original idea. She's seen nothing for the first time, for

herself. I feel, as I do when God Save the King strikes up, that I could sing the whole book straight through . . . She's a ventriloquist, not a creator. Sometimes, of course, she has the very words on her lips. But they don't come from the heart.

*(Letters*, vol. 6: 382)

The meetings between Woolf and Holtby after the publication of *Virginia Woolf*, when there was no longer the need for them to meet to discuss it, had been an intriguing development. They seem to have been at Woolf's instigation,[4] and it is tempting to see in Holtby some representative figure of importance for Woolf's writing at this time, particularly in their talk about 'Yorkshire and professions and so on'. Physically, Kitty Malone, in *The Pargiters* and *The Years*, could be modelled on Holtby: five foot nine in height, 'like a cart-horse beside most girls of her own age', her mouth too big and with strong white teeth (Woolf 1978: 94). The Rigby family, Kitty's mother's family, had been 'the wives of Yorkshire squires for generations', and she, Kitty, 'would have liked to know all about Yorkshire; & so something about the lives of English people all through those centuries' (p. 99). Kitty wished to study history, but unlike Holtby's, her father would not permit it: 'he pronounced against Cheltenham, <for one reason> & <against> Somerville Hall for another' (p. 100). Holtby was unusual in being a Yorkshire farmer's daughter who did go to Somerville College and in this respect she marks a profound change in the lives of middle-class women which Woolf is at pains to register in *The Years*. Woolf is also concerned to show a change in the status of unmarried women at the time for which Holtby provided a very satisfying model. In *The Years* Eleanor's busy 'social conscience' work, her full and contented life as a single woman, and particularly her sense of community reflect the kind of woman's life for which Holtby was an exemplar. Holtby's sustaining philosophy was a loss of the individual in the collective self and *The Years* probes this as an alternative to self-assertion and territorial individualism: 'What would the world be, he said to himself – without "I" in it?' (p. 195). 'My life's been other people's lives, Eleanor thought – my father's; Morris's; my friends' lives; Nicholas's' (p. 295). In one of the ways in which texts commune with each other diachronically, these words pick up how Holtby reportedly described her own life: 'I never feel I've really had a life of my own. My existence seems to me like a clear stream which has simply reflected other people's stories and problems' (Brittain 1980: 1) and how she announced her intention in writing *South Riding*: 'we are not only single individuals, each face to face with eternity and our separate spirits; we are members one of another' (p. xii).

These similarities are possibly incidental and certainly speculative. More important was the field of reference that women like Holtby and Brittain created for Woolf as representatives of a linked feminism and pacifism and the radical philosophical and social implications this linkage raised. Holtby was a 'type' for Woolf (*Diary*, vol. 4: 279), a modern, emancipated type, and Woolf's need during the early years of the thirties was to structure the 'novel of facts', or, as it became, the novel *The Years* and its polemical essay *Three Guineas*, to encompass this type and the ideas she embodied: the prevention of war, sexual and professional freedom for women, the responsibility of the writer to society, a refusal of immunity, 'joostice and liberty' as Martin mockingly says in *The Years* (p. 194). It was a new type of female heroism and to give shape to it Woolf chose to invoke a classic heroic text, one she had first briefly used in *The Voyage Out* (1915) and which she was now ready to reshape for contemporary purposes. The text she had nurtured to this point was Sophocles's *Antigone*. As Jane Marcus has said, 'The Pargiters' and all it developed into is 'a kind of Greek opera' (1977: 277)[5] which struggles to resolve conflict and oppression into rebirth, reworking the early drama to provide radical solutions concerning love and war.

   Luce Irigaray, in an essay based on lectures given in Italy in 1986, has commented on the relevance of Antigone to twentieth-century feminism in terms applicable to Woolf's thirties purpose in using Sophocles' play: 'neither an anarchist nor suicidal . . . [Antigone] pits one order against another at the time of the advent of male regal power.' What she stands for is cosmic order, maternal ancestry, and respect for living bodies borne by the mother, which includes the proper burial of the dead. Creon no longer wishes to observe these basic laws but to impose instead a patriarchal law in which the father's authority and word are supreme: 'She says no to men's power struggles, men's conflicts over who will be king, the endless escalation over who will be superior, and at any cost' (Irigaray 1994: 68–70). The cost for Antigone in Sophocles' version is her death. Woolf reverses the direction of the myth; Antigone's love for her brothers, her choice of sibling rather than heterosexual bonds, the hint, in *Oedipus the King*, of forgiveness and affection for her incestuous father, and, above all, her affirmation of the 'unwritten and unchanging laws' of Heaven in opposition to Creon's law of vengeance and male authority, provide Woolf with a schema which she will turn from its tragic, defeatist outcome in Sophocles' play to a dispersed, questioning and, finally, comic subversion in *The Years*: 'what was the difference between Common Law and the other kind of law?' Eleanor wonders: 'She said nothing [and] watched the flame playing on the coals. It was a green flame, nimble, irrelevant' (p. 29). Where *The Years* defers answering this question, *Three Guineas* will develop the myth from its strophic, playful version in the novel to the 'demonstrative didactic' mode of an essay. In either case, the nine million lovers and brothers slain in the last war will be given a kind of ritual burial.

Woolf apparently began her long acquaintance with *Antigone* in 1918 when she discovered her brother Adrian reading it, a scene she transposed into Edward's dalliance with the play in the 1880 section of *The Years*. In 'On Not Knowing Greek' (1925) she commented that although more complicated emotions may be found in, for example, Proust's pages, 'in the *Electra* or *Antigone* we are impressed by something different, by something perhaps more impressive – by heroism itself, by fidelity itself . . . the stable, the permanent, the original human being is to be found there' (Woolf 1992a: 96), rendered in language that is 'spare and bare . . . so clear, so hard, so intense' (p. 104). In 1934, as *The Years* was in the white heat of composition, she wrote: 'Reading Antigone. How powerful that spell is still – Greek. Thank heaven I learnt it young – an emotion different from any other' (*Diary*, vol. 4: 257). This then provided her with a framework of generality in which to write her 'novel of facts' and a different and heroic emotional range in which to broach the radical questions concerning sexual difference and their relationship to war. The first reference to *Antigone* for these purposes is in the third chapter and the fourth essay of *The Pargiters*, and focuses on Edward's reactions to the figure of Antigone and the accompanying erotic reverie involving his cousin Kitty, a reverie both 'bestial' and idealised which results in his writing an inferior poem on 'Persephone'. In *The Years* the episode is considerably shortened and the emphasis moves more quickly to Kitty herself, to her sexual desires and her thwarted wishes to study history. This was, after all, to be a book about the sexual life of women and professions for them, and not about the sexual fantasies of men. When the image of Antigone next occurs it is through Sara's envisioning in *The Years* of the murdered brother and Antigone 'whirling out . . . letting fall white dust over the blackened foot' and then her burial alive by Creon: 'The tomb was a brick mound. There was just room for her to lie straight out' (pp. 110–11). Lying in bed, Sara's body mimics the burial: 'She laid herself out, under the cold smooth sheets, and pulled the pillow over her ears'. But though Edward has given Sara *Antigone*, translated by himself, she resists Antigone's fate to become instead an outsider figure, part seer, part madwoman, wholly a spinster, loving Nicholas, the homosexual, escaping the heterosexual closure. Edward's translation of *Antigone* has failed to bury Sara just as it has failed to bury Kitty, who would not marry him but preferred Lord Lasswade who could give her, as her mother had foretold, 'scope' and the moors near Scarborough where the Rigby girls had been free and where Kitty is reborn, like Persephone, her middle name in *The Pargiters*, each time she travels north away from the dead rituals of social convention. Edward, on the other hand, is buried alive; he will not translate Antigone's words (''Tis not my nature to join in hating, but in loving') for North: 'It's no go, North thought. He can't say what he wants to say; he's afraid. . . . That's what separates us; fear, he thought' (pp. 332–3).

If *The Years* is replete with motifs of burial and rebirth, no less is it obsessed with sibling love. In *Antigone* the dead brother must be buried so that, like all whose death has been accorded due memory and respect, he may be welcomed home by Persephone (Sophocles 1994: l. 894). The fact that he slew his brother, like the millions of Axis and Allied soldiers who slew each other during the 1914–18 war, does not negate for Antigone the duty of love toward both: 'I give both love, not share their hatred' (l. 523). Antigone places love for her brother above that for Haeman, her betrothed, according to the ancient kinship laws of family she opposes to Creon's patriarchal laws of inheritance and contract. It is the irreplacability of the brother that she claims:

> For had I lost a son, or lost a husband,
> Never would I have ventured such an act
> Against the city's will. And wherefore so?
> My husband dead, I might have found another;
> Another son from him, if I had lost
> A son. But since my mother and my father
> Have both gone to the grave, there can be none
> Henceforth that I can ever call my brother.
>
> (ll. 906–13)

Woolf's use of this implacable doctrine in *The Years* thus becomes both an elegy on lost brothers, a celebration of sibling love for its long-memoried but non-appropriative blood ties, and an alternative configuration to marriage and its burial of women, and men, in the 'primeval swamp': 'That was what it came to – thirty years of being husband and wife – tut-tut-tut – and chew-chew chew. It sounded like the half-inarticulate munchings of animals in a stall . . . as they trod out the soft steamy straw in the stable . . . prolific, profuse, half-conscious' (p. 301). Eleanor's love for Morris, the extension of this into the relationship with Morris's children North and Peggy, the incestuous fantasies indulged in by Maggie and Martin, the conspiratorial bond between the sisters Maggie and Sara, constructed over the 'dear little boy [who] died' (p. 22), all make oblique reference to *Antigone* to create a network of the alternative loves and the unwritten laws the novel celebrates. Watching Sara and Nicholas laughing and bickering together, Eleanor thinks, 'This is their love-making. . . . And if this love-making differs from the old, still it has its charm; it was "love", different from the old, perhaps, but worse, was it? Anyhow, she thought, they are aware of each other; they live in each other; what else is love? she asked, listening to their laughter' (p. 297).

If *Antigone* imaginatively structures familial and sexual relations in *The*

*Years*, it is used analytically to explore abstract questions of sexual difference and how these relate to war in *Three Guineas*, the text which at an early stage was going to be called 'The Next War'. The writing of it began in earnest in 1936, and therefore coincided with widespread panic concerning the success of Fascism in Europe, and a corresponding despondency at the failure of the League of Nations. As Woolf worked at the annotations to the book, Hitler invaded Austria: 'last night his army crossed the frontier, unresisted. The Austrian national anthem was heard on the wireless for the last time. . . . Almost war: almost expected to hear it announced' (*Diary*, vol. 5: 129, 131). There had also been the death in Spain of her nephew Julian, Vanessa's son. As the first reviews of *Three Guineas* came in, Woolf talked to Vanessa about Julian: 'She can hardly speak. What matters compared with that?' 'Yet', says Woolf, in self-exculpation, 'I was always thinking of Julian when I wrote' (p. 148), of his glorification of war and his obstinacy in going to Spain – 'wont argue; tight; hard fisted [and] we discussed hand grenades, bombs, tanks, as if we were military gents in the war again. And I felt flare up in me 3 Gs . . .' (p. 80).

For Woolf, Antigone's distinction between the Law and the laws, her insistence on these two kinds of law, the written and the unwritten (and Woolf understands the unwritten laws as the 'private laws that should regulate certain instincts, passions, mental and physical desires' (Woolf 1977: 203)), raises questions about male and female ways of interpreting the world, whether manly and womanly qualities are 'natural' or constructed. Irigaray says that Antigone 'reminds us that the earthly order is not a pure social power, that it must be founded upon the economy of the cosmic order, upon respect for the procreation of living beings, on attention to maternal ancestry, to its gods, its rights, its organisation' (Irigaray 1994: 70). Woolf follows a similar line of argument in which an apparently essential difference between the sexes results in the equation of female with unwritten and male with written laws:

> According to Antigone there are two kinds of law, the written and the unwritten . . . since there are two kinds of body, male and female, and since these two bodies have been proved within the last few years to differ fundamentally, it is clear that the laws that they perceive and respect must be differently interpreted . . . it is clear that the sexes now differ and will always differ. If it were possible not only for each sex to ascertain what laws hold good in its own case, and to respect each other's laws; but to share the results of those discoveries, it might be possible for each sex to develop fully and improve in quality without surrendering its special characteristics.
>
> (Woolf 1977: 203–4)

This sets up a tension in *Three Guineas* between 'the superstructure of intellectual and practical life [which] is essentially the same in both sexes', and is amendable to reason, and the fundamentally different and enduring 'determiners of characters and qualities' according to sex. For if the thrust of the general argument in the essay is towards amalgamation – an extension of the taxi-ride androgyny of *A Room of One's Own* – the details, exemplar and, indeed, the footnotes pull away from this towards separatism. Woolf was only too aware that notions of natural and unalterable sexual difference played into the hands of the dictators: Hitler and Mussolini 'both repeatedly insist that it is the nature of man and indeed the essence of manhood to fight. . . . Both repeatedly insist that it is in the nature of women to heal the wounds of the fighter.' Perhaps the only way forward is to alter the old 'natural and eternal law', and even though this may be 'an affair of millennia, not of decades [it] may be worth attempting' (p. 205). It is an issue Woolf returned to again and again in her late writings: in her last novel, *Between the Acts*, sexual opposition between Giles's 'fierce, untamed masculinity' and Mrs Manresa's powerful femininity is related to one of the most powerful images of the book – a snake choked with a toad in its mouth: 'Birth the wrong way round – a monstrous inversion' (1992: 61). Is it possible to correct the inversion, to make the birth into life rather than into death? In a letter of 1940 she had asked 'Can one change sex characteristics? How far is the women's movement a remarkable experiment in that transformation? Mustn't our next task be the emancipation of man? How can we alter the crest and spur of the fighting cock?' (*Letters*, vol. 6: 379).

This letter was written within weeks of reading *Testament of Friendship*, a work documenting an example of the 'remarkable experiment' of the women's movement and recording love between women. In the title as in much else it also recalled its predecessor, *Testament of Youth*, about the love and grief of women for men. The two *Testaments* make no overt, analytical connection between the two kinds of love but they implicitly raise the question Woolf asks: can the women's movement change and emancipate men?

It was a question central to the debates of the feminist–pacifist movements of the thirties. Vera Brittain, who increasingly embraced extreme pacifist views that under no circumstance was violence justified, believed that '[b]ecause women produce children, life and the means of living matter to them in a way these things can never matter to men' (Berry and Bishop 1985: 218). Her emphasis on the difference between women and men, and this difference as the source of their attraction to each other, is at the heart of conflicting emotions in *Testament of Youth* where, as she admitted, though war is lamented, the virility and romance of men going to war is acknowledged as a proper masculinity. Although she warned of this 'erotic delirium', her next major work, the novel *Honourable Estate*, published in 1936, was unable to avoid a romance element involving a soldier who is killed in battle. *Honourable Estate* is, of course, about marriage, evolving through three generations (one of the 'family' novels Leonard Woolf mentioned) from Victorian tyranny to an impeccably egalitarian interwar partnership. Nevertheless, the most sexually attractive man in the book is not the enlightened husband but the soldier whose fate is part of his erotic appeal.

Winifred Holtby's feminism and her pacifism were slightly different. She was reluctant to believe in an innate femininity and masculinity, adhering instead to an ideal society 'in which there is no respect of persons, either male or female, but a supreme regard for the importance of the human being' (Brittain 1980: 34). Holtby died before disillusionment with the League – 'a reincarnation of the Triple Entente which made the previous war inevitable by dividing Europe into two hostile camps', as Brittain described it (Berry and Bishop 1985: 224) – had forced the peace movement of the thirties into division and polarisation. It is difficult to know how she would have chosen between Brittain's 'no compromise' pacifism and the pragmatic acceptance of the need for violence of many of her contemporaries. Holtby's approach to peace in the early thirties is that of the rationalist's belief in the ability and good sense of individuals to act collectively and effectively in the common good. In her novel of 1936, the posthumously published *South Riding*, there is some loss of confidence in this ability: its protagonist, Sarah Burton, is 'haunted by the spectre of another war' and enraged that 'the greed and arrogance and intellectual lethargy, the departmental pride and wanton folly of an adult world' should endanger the future. But even though Sarah Burton will be a valiant crusader for the women's movement and, herself a 'remarkable experiment', will see that experiment carried forward in the lives of the girls she teaches, she is haunted by another spectre than war. *South Riding* is not a saga novel like *Honourable Estate* or *The Years* but it has the spaciousness that Woolf thought she should aim for and 'the detailed knowledge . . . of material circumstances' that Holtby herself recommended. To structure this also Holtby chose a classic scheme, but in this case, like Brittain's novel, it was the romance story; *South Riding* is a rewriting of *Jane Eyre*. But where *Antigone* seems to liberate Woolf's text into playful subversions of sexual characteristics and alignments, *Jane Eyre* traps Holtby's text into endorsement of sexual stereotypes. Carne, the Rochester figure, dies and this, of course, rewrites the romance conclusion, but his appeal lies in his unmediated masculinity: 'a big dark man on a big dark horse. . . . It was as though some romantic sinister aspect of the snow-scene had taken heroic shape' (Holtby 1988: 119). Holtby places his masculinity in an ironic textual perspective – 'Into Sarah's irreverent and well-educated mind flashed the memory of Jane Eyre and Mr Rochester' (p. 120) – but there is an uneasy sense in which the attractiveness of this man, who has 'a big pale face rather like Mussolini's' (p. 174), depends on an innate masculinity in which sexual difference is marked and unalterable. Is this what Woolf meant when she said of Holtby that 'She's a ventriloquist, not a creator? (*Letters*, vol. 6: 382).

Writing in 1960 Julian Symons described the demand in the mid-thirties, particularly from left-wing readers, that artists should move 'out of the ivory tower of the imagination into the market place' (Symons 1973: 37–8). His comment recalls Woolf's leaning tower in the essay of that name of 1940; the once lofty, remote tower of art is now, she says, forced to lean towards the earth because society, with its dread of war, its increased literacy and consumerism, and its shifting class and gender boundaries, is such that the artist can no longer be immune but longs 'to be put down on the ground with the mass of human kind' (Woolf 1992: 173). 'The Leaning Tower' was written within weeks of Woolf reading Holtby's 'bright as paint' novel, of all novels one which is 'down on the ground with the mass of human kind'. Symons goes on to say that the market-place readers were 'enemies of art, since they were almost always impatient of merely formal considerations' and his implication is that modernism was a dying, guilty mode because it had reneged on its social duty by, in Wilson's words, a 'futile aestheticism' and, to repeat Lukács's charge, had 'destroy[ed] the complex tissue of man's relation with his environment'. In *The Years* and *Three Guineas* Woolf seems to have deliberately leant towards the ground, to have engaged with the complex tissue of men's, and women's, relation with their environment. She did so in terms that Wilson, Symons and Lukács would not have recognised as political, namely, those of family and sexual relations, the unwritten laws of society, which, in her analysis, relate to the wider political relations, including that of war between nations. That she was able to make so complex and radical an analysis in fiction and essay bears its own relation to the work of 'down on the ground' women activists and writers like Holtby and Brittain.

## NOTES

1. I wrote about this book in 'Feminism and Fiction Between the Wars: Winifred Holtby and *Virginia Woolf*' in *Women's Writing: A Challenge to Theory*, ed. Moira Monteith (Sussex: Harvester Press, 1986), pp. 175–91. This chapter is a revisiting and extension of that earlier positioning of the two writers.
2. For instance, they had both been defence witnesses in the prosecution of Radclyffe Hall's *The Well of Loneliness* in 1928 (Berry and Bostridge 1995: 228).
3. Though not active in them, Woolf's attunement to feminist and other radical activities is indicated by the fact that 'Open Door' was the name given to an organisation founded in 1926 to campaign for the removal of all restrictive legislation against women workers. Brittain and Holtby were members.

Note that Woolf punctuated her writing lightly. Quotations reproduced here are as she wrote them, irregularities included.

4. 'My husband says that you are coming to see him on Tuesday afternoon. I wonder if it would suit you to come after dinner on Tuesday instead? . . . I should like so much to see you, but can't be in that afternoon', Woolf wrote in early 1933 (unpublished letter, Winifred Holtby Collection).

5. Marcus valuably correlates Woolf's use of *Antigone* with her use of Wagner's *Ring of the Niebelung*. She also comments on the influence during these years of the classical scholar Jane Harrison, whose ideas on the decay of the patriarchal family are particularly relevant to *The Years*.

# REFERENCES

**Berry Paul** and **Bishop Alan** (eds) 1985 *Testament of a Generation* (London: Virago Press)

**Berry Paul** and **Bostridge Mark** 1995 *Vera Brittain: A Life* (London: Chatto & Windus)

**Brittain Vera** 1980 [1940] *Testament of Friendship: The Story of Winifred Holtby* (London: Virago Press)

**Holtby Winifred** 1932 *Virginia Woolf* (London: Lawrence & Wishart)

―――― 1988 [1936] *South Riding* (London: Virago Press)

**Irigaray Luce** 1994 'Civil Rights and Responsibilites for the Two Sexes' in *Thinking the Difference for a Peaceful Revolution*, trans. Karin Montin (London: The Athlone Press)

**Lukács Georg** 1963 *The Meaning of Contemporary Realism*, trans. J. and N. Mander (London: Merlin Press)

**Majumdar Robin** and **McLauren Allen** (eds) 1975 *Virginia Woolf: The Critical Heritage* (London: Routledge & Kegan Paul)

**Marcus Jane** 1977 '*The Years* as Greek Drama, Domestic Novel, and Gotterdammerung', *Bulletin of New York Library*, 80 (II), Winter: 276–301

**Sophocles** 1994 *Antigone, Oedipus the King, Electra* (Oxford: Oxford University Press, World's Classics)

**Symons Julian** 1973 [1960] *The Thirties: A Dream Revolved* (Westport, Connecticut: Greenwood Press)

**WHC** Unpublished letters of Virginia Woolf to Winifred Holtby, Hull Public Library, Drawer 1 File 18. Permission to quote from the letters is kindly given by Mr Nigel Nicolson.

**Wilson Edmund** 1947 [1931] *Axel's Castle: A Study in the Imaginative Literature of 1870–1930* (London: Charles Scribner & Son)

**Woolf Leonard** 1980 [1964] *Autobiography*, vol. 2, 1911–69 (Oxford: Oxford University Press)

**Woolf Virginia** 1968 [1937] *The Years* (London: Penguin)

―――― 1977 [1938] *Three Guineas* (Harmondsworth: Penguin)

―――― 1979–85 *The Diary of Virginia Woolf*, ed. in five volumes by Anne Olivier Bell (London: Penguin)

―――― 1978 *The Pargiters*, ed. Mitchell A. Leaska (London: The Hogarth Press)

—— 1980 *The Letters of Virginia Woolf*, ed. Nigel Nicolson in six volumes, vol. 6 1936–41 (London: The Hogarth Press)

—— 1992a *A Woman's Essays: Selected Essays*, vol. 1, ed. Rachel Bowlby (London: Penguin)

—— 1992b [1941] *Between the Acts* (London: Penguin)

—— 1993 *The Crowded Dance of Modern Life: Selected Essays*, vol. 2, ed. Rachel Bowlby (London: Penguin)

# CHAPTER FIVE

# *Remembering Bryden's Bill: Modernism from Eliot to Auden*

Stan Smith

Tom Driberg introduced Auden to *The Waste Land* in the summer of 1926, in the wake of the General Strike.[1] Auden was immediately impatient to take Eliot's poetic revolution further, linking it to the social upheaval he had just lived through, reading the poem's hysteric iconoclasm as a directly political statement – a *literal* account of contemporary Britain. 'Whatever its character', he was to write in America in the summer of 1940, 'the provincial England of 1907, when I was born, was Tennysonian in outlook; whatever its outlook the England of 1925 when I went up to Oxford was *The Waste Land* in character.'[2] The implications for Auden were immediate. To Nevill Coghill, his tutor at Oxford, he confided: 'I've been reading Eliot. I now see the way I want to write.'[3]

Writing Auden, that is, had become inseparable from reading Eliot. In late 1931 Auden sent to Eliot at Faber & Faber a draft of *The Orators: An English Study*. In Eliot's opinion 'The second part to me seems quite brilliant though I do not quite get its connexion with the first.' Early in 1932 Auden therefore forwarded a preface which apologised for the obscurity and explained that 'The central theme is a revolutionary hero. The first book describes the effect of him and his failure on those whom he meets; the second book is his own account; and the last some personal reflections on leadership in our time.'[4] Within a few months Faber had published the book under Eliot's own avuncular direction. On the tenth anniversary of *The Waste Land*'s publication, in October 1932, Eliot's friend and confidant John Hayward welcomed it in Eliot's journal *The Criterion* as 'the most valuable contribution to English poetry since "The Waste Land"'; noting, also, that 'Mr Auden is profoundly dissatisfied with the present state of civilisation in this country.'[5]

*The Orators* is an odd kind of book, a surreal mish-mash of prose and verse nebulously linked by a mysterious Airman who seems to be plotting a *coup d'état* in a state which is also a public school in a small provincial town. The discourses of education, politics and a military campaign are constantly overlaid in the text. Though there is no coherent, developing storyline, it endlessly hints at a secret narrative that the reader is duty-bound to track down, like the famous fictional detectives invoked in an opening prayer. The book's ambiguous politics was early acknowledged by Auden, who wrote to a reader shortly after publication that the book was 'far too obscure and equivocal. It is meant to be a critique of the fascist outlook, but from its reception among some of my contemporaries, and on rereading it myself, I see that it can, most of it, be interpreted as a favourable exposition. The whole Journal ought to be completely rewritten.'[6]

In fact, the text perpetually subjects itself to such re-reading and re-writing, its verbal obscurities and equivocations mirroring the politically ambivalent mentality it evokes. Auden was to admit in the Preface to the revised, third edition in 1966: 'My name on the title-page seems like a pseudonym for someone else, someone talented but near the border of sanity, who might well, in a year or two, become a Nazi.' It is precisely this which gives strength and importance to the work. For it offers an autocritique of the social and cultural ambivalence of such would-be revolutionaries as Auden in the England of the early 1930s. In the process, it also offers perhaps the first postmodernist exposé of the hidden agenda of modernism, a sly Oedipal deconstruction of its pretensions to universality and timelessness.

The modernist orthodoxy Eliot initiated in 'Tradition and the Individual Talent' casts Tradition as pure impersonal utterance in some synchronic present removed from origins and ends, from interests and partisanship. Eliot's Tradition constitutes a space like that theatre in *Four Quartets* where 'the distant panorama / And the bold imposing façade are all rolled away'. This panorama, Eliot's famous remarks on *Ulysses* make clear, is 'the immense panorama of futility and anarchy which is contemporary history', from which a universalising 'mythical method' will redeem us.[7] But the young Auden discerned that the exhilarating, dissolute polyphony of Eliot's poem denied any special authority to the Individual Talent that sought to impose authorial coherence on it (and on contemporary history) in the name of Tradition. The 'Police' it mimics in its 'different voices' are always elsewhere, displaced beyond the poem into the babble of that history. For all the desperate insistence of the Notes, Tiresias is not 'the most important personage in the poem, uniting all the rest', but only one more voice competing for authority. There is no voice of power, no ultimate signifier waiting at the Chapel Perilous to make the fragments whole again.

From *The Waste Land* Auden learnt that all utterances are transactions, oratorical performances with an end in view – that they are 'interested' rather than disinterested, intended to persuade, whether as prophecy, indictment, seduction, conversion, greeting, insult, reproach, complaint, confession or whatever. All the voices of *The Waste Land* imply at least two interested parties, and refer or defer to an absent third, whether Mrs Equitone, Lil, or Christ. Even the 'inviolable voice' of the traditionally disinterested night-ingale denounces her violator.[8]

A passage in the 1932 text of *The Orators* announces this realisation as its theme with characteristic opacity, in a rambling, inconsequential anecdote where one unidentified person addresses another, beginning, abruptly, *in medias res*: 'To return to the interest we were discussing', and ending, in two voices: 'I should have said the word by now to have convinced you. / 'Yes, but the interest.' (The phrase, which Auden also uses elsewhere, derives from Henry James.) Even in ordinary conversation, the passage suggests, there is no such thing as a disinterested utterance, and if we look back over it we see that the conversational stops and starts, the candid editorial admissions ('But I shall have to leave that out. / The point I want to make clear is . . .') all conspire to persuade – are, that is, oratorical acts.

Edith Sitwell, contrasting Eliot and Auden in her book *Aspects of Modern Poetry* (1934), saw, without approving, what Auden was doing. The terms of her analysis correspond closely to those we have subsequently come to associate with the distinction between modernism and 'post-modernism'. Eliot's poetry, Sitwell claimed, had 'an integral being, an intense visual and tactile sense, had depth, wisdom and passion'. By contrast Auden's work is all surface. Its rhythms communicate the 'sensation of running away':

> Mr Auden's greatest danger, in his longer poems, is that he is led towards disintegration, not cohesion, of matter and manner. A certain critic said of him that 'we must wonder if Book II, the "Journal of an Airman", is perhaps a kind of life of Lawrence, reduced to elements and then built up again.' I find that whereas Mr Auden frequently reduces his subject to fragments, he does not always reduce them to elements (the latter at times being a valuable process). Mr Auden does not organize his experience. It must be said, too, that his material is too often of a purely temporary interest, has no universal significance. And in this failure to sift, and then reorganize the experience, lies one of the major dangers of the poetry of our time. It is especially Mr Auden's danger. In the power of assimilating details into a whole, in the visual and the tactile sense, Mr Auden is, at the moment, almost entirely lacking. 'The Orators', for instance, is not an organic whole. It may be claimed that it represents the disintegration of the world in its present state, but it shows merely lack of fusion, looseness of interest, 'the belief', to quote Mr John Sparrow, 'that experience hitherto taken to be the raw material of art, should be accepted as its finished product'.[9]

For all her disdain, Sitwell identifies the main innovative thrust of Auden's text, which, in deconstructing the strategies of power in *The Waste Land*, opens up the central contradiction of modernism – that 'original meaning' which, a year or so earlier, in his Norton Lectures, Eliot had spoken of 'forgetting'.

In 1932, ten years after the publication of *The Waste Land*, Eliot was himself nervously alert to contemporary re-readings of his poem. In the Charles Eliot Norton Lectures, which he gave at Harvard University during the winter and spring of 1932–33, subsequently published as *The Use of Poetry and the Use of Criticism*, Eliot acknowledged that 'what a poem means is as much what it means to others as what it means to the author; and indeed, in the course of time a poet may become merely a reader in respect to his own works, forgetting his original meaning – or without forgetting, merely changing'.[10] Though he is here ostensibly responding to I.A. Richards' recent account of *The Waste Land*,[11] it is Auden's re-reading of the poem – a re-reading inscribed in that book Eliot had just seen through the press – which constitutes his real concern throughout these lectures.

Auden was much in his mind at the time. Harry Levin, then an undergraduate in the audience, records that in conversation 'Eliot was warm in his commendation and recommendation' of Auden's *Poems* (1930) and of *The Orators*, while 'his predictions for Auden's future virtually constituted a laying on of hands'.[12] Both these volumes must be among 'the work of some of the more interesting younger poets today' the lectures describe as influenced by Pound's 'Seafarer'. But, closer to home, as *The Orators* re-read and rewrote the poem Eliot had half forgotten, it exposed the extent to which it subverted the very critical orthodoxy its author had proposed in 'Tradition and the Individual Talent', and carried even further the poetic revolution initiated by *The Waste Land*.

What Auden's re-reading represented for Eliot may be deciphered from another forgetful moment of some curiosity in Eliot's work. When his *Selected Essays* were first published in 1932, in the same season as *The Orators*, their subtitle indicated a very clear *terminus a quo*: *1917–1932*.[13] In fact only one essay in the 1932 volume is dated 1917 – the essay placed first, as a keynote for the critical practice of the whole. In the rest of the text the essays, though dated, are arranged not chronologically but thematically, as if to reinforce that claim for the synchronicity of 'Tradition' described in this opening essay. That essay is of course 'Tradition and the Individual Talent'. In the 1951 edition of *Selected Essays*, however, the subtitle *1917–1932* is dropped, and the essay is correctly ascribed to 1919. (It first appeared in two parts in *The Egoist* in September and December 1919.)

Now any critic, particularly one as prolific as Eliot, can misremember the date of an essay. But few would knowingly institutionalise that mistake in the title of a definitive collection. Eliot, however, compounded the error thirty years later, in the Preface to the 1964 reissue of *The Use of Poetry and the Use of Criticism.* There he describes 'Tradition' as 'perhaps the most juvenile and certainly the first to appear in print' of all his essays, and evinces some embarrassment at its role in fathering a critical tradition. He is sure, nevertheless, about when it was written: 'That, the best known of my essays, appeared in 1917, when I had taken over the assistant editorship of *The Egoist* on Richard Aldington's being called up for military service, and before I had been asked to contribute to any other periodical.'

This persistent mis-dating suggests that, in Eliot's symbolic calendar, 1917 is remembered as a date when, in Auden's words, 'one did something slightly unusual'. What might this be, in the retrospect of 1932? The answer is suggested by the Norton Lectures themselves. Discussing I.A. Richards' 'shrewd' identification of Canto XXVI of the *Purgatorio* as an intertext of *The Waste Land*, Eliot rejects Richards' claim that sex has replaced religion in modern literature, with the retort that 'My contemporaries seem to me still to be occupied with it [religion], whether they call themselves church-men, or agnostics, or rationalists, or social revolutionists.'

The apparently gratuitous gesture towards a younger generation of writers is in reality part of a continuous subtext to the lectures: Eliot's somewhat embarrassed acknowledgment that he and Pound are now seen as the makers of a poetic revolution identified, in its second wave, with political revolution. But he is also aware of standing rebuked as the 'Lost Leader' of that revolution, as Shelley had reproached Wordsworth and Coleridge in an earlier era. (Both Auden and Spender were variously identified with Shelley in the thirties.)

His comments on these three Romantics then become a surrogate dis-course negotiating his own relations with his estranged heirs. Wordsworth and Coleridge, Eliot insists, were 'not merely demolishing a debased tra-dition, but revolting against a whole social order'. Again, 'If Wordsworth thought he was simply occupied with reform of language, he was deceived; he was occupied with revolution of language.' (The 'revolution of language' is what Eugene Jolas had declared to be modernism's legacy, in the journal *transition* in 1928.)[14] Somewhat superfluously, Eliot hastens to assure his audience that he does not intend to associate himself with any particular tend-ency of modern criticism, 'least of all the sociological'. Elsewhere, however, we find him trying on the part, responding for example in the hard-boiled tones of thirties Leftism, 'Tell that, we might add, to the Unemployed.'

Bemused by the revolutionary lineage to which Auden has conscripted him, Eliot admits the link precisely as he disentangles himself. It is a characteristic Eliot ploy, involving both memory and forgetfulness. 'I myself can remember a time', he says, considering an analogy with Coleridge and Wordsworth, 'when he [Pound] and I and our colleagues were mentioned by a writer in *The Morning Post* as "literary bolsheviks" and by Mr Arthur

Waugh . . . as "drunken helots".' But, he says, both he and Pound believed that they were 'affirming forgotten standards, rather than setting up new idols'. Shortly afterwards, an aside about the rejection of 'Wordsworth as the *original* Lost Leader' (my emphasis) carries an equally strong personal charge. Critics, he says, 'should make pause and consider that when a man takes politics and social affairs seriously the difference between revolution and reaction may be by the breadth of a hair . . . it is Wordsworth's social interest that inspires his own novelty of form in verse . . .'. Yes, but the interest – the social interest?

In 1932 Eliot dated 'Tradition' to 1917, I would suggest, because, startled by the radical new talent which had turned up on his doorstep, demanding its inheritance, he remembered the literary revolution he and Pound initiated as complicit with that which, in October 1917, had broken out in Petrograd. That this connection is in his mind is confirmed later, when he refutes Richards with an *obiter dictum* 'on the relation of the poet to his environment' from no less an authority than Leon Trotsky, an improbable rabbit plucked with evident approval from Mr Eliot's bowler hat.

For all his admiration for Auden, Eliot insisted on making a divorce between his renewed linguistic revolution and his political views. As early as 1930 he wrote to Herbert Read that 'I chiefly worry about Auden's ethical principles and convictions, not about his technical ability; or rather I think that if a man's ethical and religious views and convictions are feeble or limited and incapable of development, then his technical development is restricted.'[15] *The Orators* wickedly reveals the inseparability of these two elements, and it does this by developing the insights lurking in the blind spots not only of *The Waste Land* but of Eliot's Tradition-bound criticism.

*The Orators* probably gets its title from Eliot's claim in his 1923 essay, 'The Function of Criticism', that 'criticism, far from being a simple and orderly field of beneficent activity, from which impostors can be readily ejected, is no better than a Sunday park of contending and contentious orators.'[16] Certainly Ode IV depicts the workers 'Sloping up the hill . . . / To the park and the platforms where the windbags blow', in an apparent echo of this passage. But whereas *The Waste Land* indicts the reader as an 'hypocrite lecteur' and criminal, planter of corpses, from the security of a prophetic soapbox, *The Orators* encourages the reader to resist any complicity with the text. There is no point of absolute authority such as that deputed to Tiresias. The Airman appears *in propria persona* only in his fragmentary Journal entries. The author is himself converted to a mere reader in the first of Book III's six Odes, urged by a passing and casual prophetic voice, along with his friends ('Wystan, Stephen, Christopher, all of you') to 'Read of your losses'.

At the beginning of *The Orators* the old boy delivering an 'Address for a Prize-Day' speaks of a 'Divine Commission' of Angels sent out to survey the British Isles, one of whose members will 'take all rain-wet Scotland for his special province'. Their task will be completed only 'when every inch of the ground has been carefully gone over, every house inspected' and 'a complete report' filed. The report will include statistics on 'the average number of lost persons to the acre'. (There was in fact a National Census in 1931.)

Unlike Eliot, whose 'unreal city' is London and nowhere, on the shores of Asia and in the Edgware Road, Auden chose to specify a real time and a place for his survey of lost persons: 1931, Helensburgh, situated on the Clyde twenty miles downstream from Glasgow, but a world away in time and space. Auden wrote the book, and saw it through the press, during his time as a master at the Larchfield School, Helensburgh, from 1930 to 1932. Like *Ulysses* and *The Waste Land*, it derives much of its formal coherence from the physical and social geography, the 'maps and chaps', of an actual community. Unlike them, however, Auden's Ordnance Survey treads deliberately unfamiliar ground. In doing so, it makes a political point about the metropolitan, universalising pretensions of modernism.

That this study of Englishness should be undertaken in Scotland is part of the point. One theme of the book is 'the gradual abdication of central in favour of peripheral control'. Helensburgh, 'a provincial town' squarely centred in itself, infected by what the book calls 'the mass hatred of the villas', lies on many peripheries, in a Scotland itself in turn marginalised by London and the culture of 'Englishness'. *The Orators* looks in on a self-regarding English culture from what that culture considers the margins, to deconstruct the whole centre–periphery model upon which Englishness is constructed. The text repeatedly attempts to create between 'a centre and a circumference . . . awareness of interdependence – sympathy'; whereas 'The enemy attempts to disturb this awareness by theories of partial priority.' Against the partial priorities of a hegemonic culture, *The Orators* affirms that, in the words of one of the Odes, 'The marginal grief / Is source of life.'

The metropolitan voices of *The Waste Land* constantly disperse into a dream landscape. Auden's locations, however, grow more tangible and consistent the more we set the text against the topography and demography of Helensburgh. Ode IV names the town itself, together with its Tower cinema, Hermitage Park and Greenock across the river. Other local places named include Sinclair Street and Ardencaple, Clydebank, with its derelict ship cranes, Cardross Golf Club and Craigendoran Pier – the transfer point from rail to steamer for Clydeside's day-trippers, where on the second day of the revolution 'packed excursions, jumping the points, enter the sea from Craigendoran Pier'. On the same day, the regular 'nine o'clock business train' is diverted on 'a mystery trip through the more remote upland valleys'. This train took the fathers of Larchfield's pupils to their offices in the engineering, shipping and insurance companies of Glasgow. Since the diversion would reroute them north up the West Highland Line to Fort William, it is an effective piece of economic sabotage.

The text is full of such local knowledge, repeatedly naming or alluding to real people who wielded authority, actual and oratorical power, in contemporary Helensburgh: teachers, JPs, provosts, doctors, clerics, mediocrats. In contrast to what Donald Davie has called Eliot's 'pseudo-references', Auden's technique is that of an inverted *roman à clef*: the names of actual people known privately are not disguised for decoding but are paraded instead as references the readers feel they ought to recognise but fail, pathetically, to do so. Thus, we hear out of the blue of a 'whist-drive at the Stewarts' on Wednesday', but do not connect this with the house called 'The Hollies' later, though the *Helensburgh Directory* for 1930 records that this was the name of its residents. Indeed, two of the sons were Auden's pupils and their father, who refereed the school rugby matches, had offended Auden by mocking his appearance as games master. Again, what is certainly the first literary reference to television ('My first memories of my Uncle were like images cast on the screen of a television set, maternally induced') seems less egregious when one discovers that its inventor, Logie Baird, was an old boy of the Larchfield School, whose progress in the United States was proudly charted in almost every issue of the local newspaper, *The Helensburgh and Gareloch Times*.

Such local references are unimportant in themselves. It is what they *signify* that counts. For they represent a knowledge which is *ordinary*, available to every inhabitant of Helensburgh in 1931, but to which London publishers, poets and critics can have no access, unless specifically initiated (Book I is called 'The Initiates'). It is in this light that we should look at *The Orators* as a critique of Eliot's idea of Tradition — in particular, its use of allusion as a technique of exclusion, a social as well as a literary strategy.

*The Orators* was *intended* to be obscure, but with an obscurity that could not be reassuringly cleared up by reference to any Great Tradition of literary touchstones. The private allusions reveal that Eliot's 'Tradition' is really a question of *privileged access*. In cocking a snook at the metropolitan high priests of culture, the whole book is one of those postmodern 'practical jokes' which the Airman argues are weapons against the Enemy.

The Enemy, he says, exercises his power through 'private associations': 'but note that he is serious, the associations are constant. He means what *he* says.' The Enemy has the power to make his private associations public, to institutionalise them, as Eliot contrived to place some of his own idiosyncratic preferences at the centre of the English literary canon. But 'practical jokes', according to the Airman, 'consist in upsetting these associations.

They are in every sense contradictory and public, e.g. my bogus lecture to the London Truss Club. Derek's seduction of Mrs Solomon by pretending to have been blessed by the Pope.' Auden's practical joke on his publisher/ mentor and his literary public says: 'Anyone can play exclusion games. Read of your losses.' The power of the orator resides as much in that which is withheld, as in that which is uttered. The book demonstrates how much of the 'obscurity' of the modernist 'tradition' is what Auden apologised for in his own suppressed preface: 'mostly swank'.

The obscurity of *The Orators* thus offers an intimidatingly *democratic* critique of the knowing allusiveness with which Eliot's poem reprieves itself from political and cultural anarchy. We can see this at work in its treatment of Eliot's great cultural icon, Dante. For Eliot, Dante consistently represents the universalising power of art, as in his 1929 essay on the poet, which reconsiders the Ulysses passage from Canto XXVI of the *Inferno* he had first discussed in 'Tradition'. Dante, Eliot says,

> has been reproved or smiled at for satisfying personal grudges by putting
> in Hell men whom he knew and hated; but these, as well as Ulysses, are
> transformed in the whole; for the real and the unreal are all
> representative of types of sin, suffering, fault and merit, and all become
> of the same reality and contemporary.[17]

This picks up a point already made in 1927 in 'Shakespeare and the Stoicism of Seneca', which extends the same argument to that pillar of the English Tradition:

> Dante's railings, his personal spleen – sometimes thinly disguised under
> Old Testamental prophetic denunciations, – his nostalgia, his bitter regrets
> for past happiness – or for what seems happiness when it is past – and
> his brave attempt to fabricate something permanent and holy out of his
> personal animal feelings . . . can all be matched out of Shakespeare.
> Shakespeare, too, was occupied with the struggle – which alone
> constitutes life for a poet – to transmute his personal and private agonies
> into something rich and strange, something universal and impersonal.[18]

Dante figures largely in 'Address for a Prize Day', where the pompous old boy evokes the *Purgatorio*'s observations on perverted, excessive and defective love, to browbeat the boys – we can infer – about homosexuality and masturbation. He is invoked, that is, not as cultural touchstone, but as a spiritual policeman, his public face poked into their private places.

When Auden cited Dante again, at the start of *The Ascent of F6*, it was explicitly to repudiate Eliot's 'Dante' essay. Here, Dante's Ulysses is simply another oily orator, 'a crook speaking to crooks'. But Dante himself is tarred with the same brush, another self-regarding, self-deluding cultural con-man. Exiled from Florence, he may have thought that he wrote the *Divine Comedy* to celebrate the love of God revealed through the beauty of Beatrice.

But in fact he was driven by a desire for 'absolute revenge' on the people who had exiled him, whom he delights to place in hell (as Auden revenges himself on his Helensburgh tormentors). He may have spoken of 'Virtue and Knowledge', but 'It was not Virtue those lips, which involuntary privation had made so bitter, could pray for; it was not Knowledge; it was Power.' 'Address for a Prize-Day' is recalled in all its phrases:

> Virtue. Knowledge. We have heard these words before; and we shall hear them again – during the nursery luncheon, on the prize-giving afternoon, in the quack advertisement, at the conference of generals or industrial captains: justifying every baseness and excusing every failure, comforting the stilted schoolboy lives.[19]

Eliot's canonisation of Dante lies behind two of *The Orators'* most private practical jokes – jokes which make it difficult to look 'Tradition' in the face ever again. Norman Wright, who was in 1932 a ten-year-old pupil of Auden's at Larchfield, tells me that Auden 'introduced a reading book for our English tutelage which, when I took it home, my father banned and as he was a Director of the school he had it withdrawn. I do not remember what it was – perhaps something like Dante's Inferno'. This is what the grand discourses of 'civilisation' come down to, in the parishes and classrooms of Britain.[20]

But *The Orators* has an even better practical joke on the poet whose mock-scholarly Notes shored up *The Waste Land* with the authority of anthropology. On 30 December 1931, the 'Diary of Events' for the previous year in the *Helensburgh and Gareloch Times* reports that in June (while, that is, Auden was drafting 'Address for a Prize Day'), 'At Larchfield School Speech Day, an address was given by Sir James Frazer, O.M., the author of "The Golden Bough" and other works, and Larchfield's most distinguished former pupil.'[21]

Such localised and specific data are central to *The Orators'* postmodern assault on the universalist pretensions of modernism. In 'Journal of an Airman', the revolution comes to a head in the last week of August 1931. The entry in the Airman's Journal for 26th August contains the cryptic instruction which provides the title of this essay: 'Remember to pay Bryden's bill.' No one, to my knowledge, has yet tracked down the meaning of this memorandum, probably because they were looking in the wrong place. The place to look is not in Dante, or any other more immediately available literary source. The place to look is in the *Helensburgh and Gareloch Times*. On that same day, 26 August 1931, almost a whole page of the newspaper was taken up with an obituary for its founder, the eighty-year-old Samuel Bryden, JP, complete with a striking photograph of a white-bearded patriarch accompanied by his faithful dog, straight out of His Master's Voice advertisements.

The obituary records just how extensive was Samuel Bryden's influence in the community, not only as editor and columnist for forty years, but in particular in his control over the means of communication, 'the business of bookselling and stationery . . . taking up property agency and valuation work and printing and publishing'. In short, he occupied locally the same near-monopoly position that on the national scene was filled by the press-barons Beaverbrook and Rothermere, lampooned as the composite 'Beethameer, Beethameer, bully of Britain' a few pages earlier. He is an enemy orator *par excellence*, and even his 'social and philanthropic works' recorded in the obituary complement his business activities in terms which reflect the 'Enemy Gambits' listed in the attack on Beethameer: 'Hygiene against the aware-ness of likeness. Newspapers against the awareness of difference'.[22]

The Airman's decision to publish his lampoon on the press-barons by dropping it from his plane ('10,000 Cyclostyle copies of this for aerial dis-tribution') places him in a double bind. For in order to duplicate his propa-ganda against the Enemy, he will have to use the Enemy's facilities. For who controls the means of communication in Helensburgh but the firm of Macneur and Bryden? Each week the *Helensburgh and Gareloch Times*, owned by the Bryden family, carried on its front page Macneur and Bryden's advertisement for the 'latest in duplicating machines', 'to undertake the reproduction of Testimonials, Estimates, Specifications, Schedules, Circular Letters, etc.'. Even, perhaps, seditious lampoons. Bryden's bill, which the Airman guiltily recalls he has not yet paid, is actually for the 10,000 cyclo-styled sheets he intends to drop on Helensburgh (according to the *Helensburgh Directory* for 1930, population: 9,703).[23] Thus the Enemy dictates even the terms of the struggle against him.

There are other dates in the Airman's Journal which register the inex-tricable intertwining of private and public lives in the summer of 1931. The key dates here just precede Bryden's obituary. The entry for 23rd August records, cryptically, 'We are lost. A cart has just passed carrying a plaster eagle. The enemy are going to attack.' Whether the plaster eagle is an allusion to Eliot's image of himself, in the recently published *Ash-Wednesday*, as an 'aged eagle' (albeit for Auden a plaster saint with feet of clay), is a matter for conjecture. But the importance of the occasion is clear, as the next item discloses, referring to 'The enemy orders commun-icated tonight of August 23rd–24th' – orders of extensive troop move-ments. These are not arbitrary dates. The Enemy was massively on the move in the real world of 23–24 August 1931. The significance of the dates has already been indicated, in that passage about 'the interest' which immediately follows the lampoon on Beethameer. This is 'The week the Labour Cabinet resigned'.

Ramsay MacDonald's Government resigned on 24 August 1931, and on the 25th he formed a National Goverment of Conservative, Labour and Liberal MPs, which went on to obtain a massive majority in the elections of October 27th. We don't have to look far to see how the Enemy subverts one's deepest self, in August 1931: a Scottish Labour Prime Minister's abject surrender to the English establishment is its glaring epitome. When the Airman writes, on 25th August, that 'Conquest can only proceed by absorption of, i.e., infection by, the conquered', his conclusions reflect the immediate events of that day, though it still remained obscure who precisely had conquered whom, as it must have seemed at the time.[24]

That 'infection' metaphor recalls the rhetorical question of 'Address for a Prize Day': 'What do you think about England, this country of ours where nobody is well?' This is no Groddeckian invention of Auden's. On 27 October 1931, the tone of Britain for the whole of the thirties was set by a General Election which returned a 'National' Government to power with 554 seats to fifty-two for Labour. After this MacDonald became no more than His Master's Voice for the British establishment, shortly to be replaced by Stanley Baldwin. The old boy's question alludes directly to the campaign slogan adopted by the National leaders on 5th October. The slogan was endorsed, in an editorial headed simply 'Loyalty', in the *Helensburgh and Gareloch Times* six days before that election: 'the Government must be returned with a "doctor's mandate" to examine and correct each contingency as it arises.'[25]

The editorial called up the sacrifices of the Great War, shortly to be commemorated in Hermitage Park on Remembrance Day, to support a plea to forget sectional interest in the name of national unity. Its terms directly recall the moral manipulations of 'Address for a Prize Day': 'This particular period in the life of our country calls for loyalty of the highest degree – a loyalty that forgets self and party and thinks first and only of country and the great tradition of our race.' Eliot's timeless 'Tradition' here finds its timebound equivalent, in the far from disinterested rhetoric, the convenient rememberings and forgettings, of provincial newspaper editors.

'Everyone knows that the only emotion that is fully developed in a boy of fourteen is the emotion of loyalty and honour', Auden was to write in 'Honour', his 1934 essay on his old school, originally called 'The Liberal Fascist':

> For that very reason it is dangerous. By appealing to it, you can do
> almost anything you choose . . . like a modern dictator you can defeat
> almost any opposition from other parts of the psyche, but if you do, if
> you deny these other emotions their expression and development,
> however silly or shocking they may seem to you, they will not only
> never grow up, but they will go backward, for human nature cannot stay
> still; they will, like all things that are shut up, go bad on you.[26]

This, then, is the diagnosis *The Orators* offers of England's collective sickness: emotional retardation, loyalty inturned and gone bad on itself, political introversion, orchestrated by a dishonest and bankrupt oratory. It is this that persuaded the electorate to vote for the 'doctor's mandate' of the National Government, in which the remedy for Depression and unemployment is more of the same, as the Airman's Journal slyly observes in speaking of the doctor's cure for 'arsenical poisoning': 'a tablespoonful of . . . arsenic three times a day'.

Ode IV of Book III, completed during the course of the General Election campaign, offers a rather different diagnosis of the British sickness, extending its critique to all classes, including a Laodicean intelligentsia, amongst whom Eliot himself is singled out as a Lost Leader, unresponsive to the arrival of the English Lenin:

> Hearing the arrival of his special train,
> Hearing the fireworks, the saluting and the guns . . .
> Where is Eliot? dreaming of nuns.
> Their day is over, they shall decorate the Zoo
> With Professor Jeans and Bishop Barnes at 2d a view,
> Or be ducked in a gletcher, as they ought to be,
> With the Simonites, the Mosleyites and the ILP.

Humphrey Carpenter comments that the Ode 'takes a . . . neutral and mocking attitude to politics; among those it attacks are not only Oswald Mosley's extreme right-wingers but also "the ILP" – the Independent Labour Party, a breakaway group from the main Labour movement. Auden as yet made no distinctions; all politics appeared equally absurd to him.' Similarly, Carpenter argues that in lampooning both MacDonald and Stanley Baldwin in a related Helensburgh poem from 1932, 'Happy New Year', 'Auden is being a buffoon rather than a satirist. Certainly he takes no positive political line, but presents all the politicians as equally ridiculous.'[27]

This is politically illiterate in a familiar English mode. Since 26 August 1931, the day when the Airman was reminded to pay Bryden's bill by a death notice in the local paper, MacDonald and Baldwin had been not political opponents but partners in the same, supposedly 'National', Government. *Pace* Carpenter, the postures of *The Orators* evince a very specific politics. They are those of the British Communist Party, in the ultra-left Third Period of the Comintern, which ran from its Sixth Congress in 1928 until Hitler's accession to power in 1933 forced a rethink. In this disastrously doctrinaire reading of contemporary history, both the rump Labour Party, and its ILP left-wing, which in 1932 split off to form a separate party, were no more than 'false Lefts', 'social Fascists' as untrustworthy as those Mosleyites who in February of 1931 had deserted Labour to form the New Party, itself originally intended as a left-wing formation, or the Simonites, a Liberal faction within the National Government.[28]

Opportunistically grafted on to Auden's anarchism here are the *idées reçus* of orthodox Stalinism he would have heard from Gabriel Carritt, the dedicatee of his second Ode, and already a member of the inner councils of the CPGB, at whose Pembrokeshire home occurred that conversation about 'the interest' in 'The week the Labour Cabinet resigned'. From the same source Auden may have derived the contempt for the Scottish National-ists in the Envoi to Ode IV: 'Scotland is stirring: in Scotland they say / That Compton Mackenzie will be king one day.' Mackenzie had recently scored a *succés de scandale* by giving a Nationalist inaugural address at Glas-gow University, where the students had elected him Rector. Auden wrote to Naomi Mitchison, around September 1931, 'I don't think any of the Scottish nationalists are of any use. McDiarmid is such a fearful intellectual snob and prig.'[29]

Ode IV proper ends with the mock-heroic promise of renewal:

> This is the season of the change of heart,
> The final keeping of the ever-broken vow,
> The official remarriage of the whole and part,
> The poor in employment and the country sound,
> Over is the tension, over the alarms,
> The falling wage, and the flight from the pound. . . .
> A birthday, a birth
> On English earth
> Restores, restore will, has restored
> To England's story
> The directed calm, the actual glory.

But the supposed 'saviour' (as Auden pointed out in his 1966 Preface) is Rex Warner's day-old son, and the next Ode, 'To My Pupils', returns to the *Kulturkampf* as a guerrilla war, ending in a renewed emergency, the ever-broken vow broken again, all leave cancelled, as 'We entrain at once for the North . . . / The headlands we're doomed to attack . . . / We shall lie out there.' The remaining two poems struggle to a conclusion through the rhetoric of war, defeat, blockade, disease and horror. Auden's text, that is, refuses the restoration of which one of its moments speaks exultantly, but also whimsically and fatuously.

Rightly so: the same page of the *Helensburgh and Gareloch Times* that carries the Bryden obituary reports that Anchor Lines of Glasgow planned to ter-minate its employees' contracts on 30th September, offering re-engagement the next day 'on certain conditions, including reduced salaries'.

In 1942, in time of another war, a naturalised Englishman offered a rather different vision of English restoration in 'Little Gidding'. Eliot's pastoral is

chocolate-box-full of the rhetoric of reconciliation, speaking of a new cultural unity in which tradition may be restored, 'but not in time's covenant',
for the compromised historical moment is 'only a shell, a husk of meaning'.
The present time and place, 'Now and in England', generate a discourse
of Englishness which, when grasped, becomes 'England and nowhere' – a
'nowhere' remote from Morris's socialist utopia, but, 'transfigured in another
pattern', returning as 'a pattern of timeless moments'.

History as social and political conflict, revolution, civil war and foreign
war, all those forces which actually shaped the seventeenth-century settle-
ment the poem addresses, are transitory: 'We cannot revive old factions /
We cannot restore old policies / Or follow an antique drum.' What abides
is a unitary Englishness, as in that Restoration where regicide and time-
server, Milton and Dryden, parliament and monarchy, were 'United in the
strife which divided them'. In this 'constitution of silence', where all factions
and interests are 'folded in a single party', Eliot finds a persuasive model
for wartime Britain, the prototype for a new and permanent – what else?
– National Government.

It is moving oratory. But what the poem fails to remember are the
'twenty years largely wasted', the years *entre deux guerres*, 1919, 1926, 1929,
1931, 1935, 1939, when the British establishment and its orators bullied,
cajoled and blustered the working classes through Demobilisation, General
Strike, Wall Street Crash, Slump and Depression, National Governments,
Means Tests, mass unemployment, the falling wage and the flight from the
pound, to the threshold of another war to end all wars – a shameful and
shabby history to which a 'timeless' modernism maintained a full-fed,
equable indifference.

Three years before, as war had rumbled into place, on time, in 1939,
Auden had left for the United States. In 1963, he revealed that his decision
to leave England had already been made in 1936, and his reason, even in
postwar retrospect, is significant: '*F6* was the end. I knew I must leave
when I wrote it. . . . I knew it because I knew then that if I stayed, I would
inevitably become a member of the British establishment.'[30]

Eliot's vision of England in 'Little Gidding' is posited on a series of
incorporating conditionals ('If you came this way . . .') which defer true reconciliation to that site exterior to the text, 'the place where a story ended'.
*The Orators*, however, disowns such grand narrative accommodations in an
act of postmodern renunciation, riding 'Out of this house', abandoning the
fearful reader to the horror that is seeking him out, warning that ' "They're
looking for you" . . . / As he left them there, as he left them there.' Auden's
postmodern 'English Study' had known all along where the story would end.
Bryden's bill would finally have to be paid – 'Every farthing of the cost /
All the dreaded cards foretell' – and paid on both sides.[31]

NOTES

This essay originally appeared in the Auden special issue of *Critical Survey*, 6 (3), 1994. Acknowledgment is made to Oxford University Press for permission to reprint it here. The Eliot material extends an argument advanced in my *Origins of Modernism: Eliot, Pound, Yeats and the Rhetorics of Renewal* (Hemel Hempstead: Harvester/Wheatsheaf, 1994).

1. Tom Driberg, *Ruling Passions* (London: Jonathan Cape, 1977), p. 58.
2. W.H. Auden, in *Southern Review*, Summer 1940: 83.
3. Nevill Coghill, in Richard March and Tambimuttu (eds), *T.S. Eliot: A Symposium* (London: Editions Poetry London, 1948), p. 82.
4. W.H. Auden, *The Orators: An English Study* (London: Faber & Faber, 1932). A second edition appeared in 1934, with significant cuts and alterations. A new edition in 1966 further emended the text, and added a disclaiming preface. The most reliable accessible edition is that provided by Edward Mendelson (ed.), *The English Auden* (London: Faber & Faber, 1977), but since Mendelson silently restores some of Auden's changes, but retains others, it should be read with care, and only in conjunction with his remarks in the introduction and the appendices, which contain material dropped in 1934. Mendelson's introduction quotes the correspondence with Eliot, pp. xiv–xv. See also Humphrey Carpenter, *W.H. Auden: A Biography* (London: George Allen & Unwin, 1981), pp. 120–30.
5. John Hayward, *Criterion*, October 1932: 131–4.
6. Carpenter, *W.H. Auden*, p. 130.
7. T.S. Eliot, 'Tradition and the Individual Talent', in *The Sacred Wood: Essays on Poetry and Criticism* (London: Methuen & Co., 1920); *Four Quartets* (London: Faber & Faber, 1944); 'Ulysses, Order, and Myth', *The Dial*, November 1923: 480–3.
8. Auden wrote about language in just such oratorical–functionalist terms in 'Writing, or the Pattern Between People', Naomi Mitchison (ed.), *An Outline for Boys and Girls and Their Parents* (London: Gollancz, 1932). A section of the essay theorises communication in terms of actual and intended meaning-effects in differing purposive contexts, and illustrates its argument by reference to a 'Mr Snig'. In *The Orators* 'Offal and Snig' are the proprietors of a hardware shop on the seafront at Helensburgh. Such a shop, under a different pair of names, existed in 1930–32, and has continued to the present day.
9. Edith Sitwell, *Aspects of Modern Poetry* (London: Duckworth, 1934), pp. 238–40.
10. T.S. Eliot, *The Use of Poetry and the Use of Criticism* (London: Faber & Faber, 1993; new edn 1964), p. 130.
11. I.A. Richards' critical writings in the twenties, *The Principles of Literary Criticism* (1925), *Science and Poetry* (1926) and *Practical Criticism* (1929), were massively influential in mediating the first generation of modernists, particularly Eliot, to their successors in the 1930s. On this, see Valentine Cunningham, *British Writers of the Thirties* (Oxford: Oxford University Press, 1989), pp. 58–9.
12. Harry Levin, 'W.H. Auden, 1907–1973', *Harvard Advocate*, 108 (2/3): 38.
13. T.S. Eliot, *Selected Essays: 1917–1932* (London: Faber & Faber, 1932).
14. Eugene Jolas, 'The Revolution of Language and James Joyce', *transition*, 11, February 1928.
15. Letter to Herbert Read, 11 December 1930, quoted in Carpenter, p. 137.

16. Eliot, *Selected Essays*, p. 25.
17. Eliot, 'Dante', *Selected Essays*, pp. 209–10.
18. Eliot, 'Shakespeare and the Stoicism of Seneca', *Selected Essays*, p. 137.
19. W.H. Auden and Christopher Isherwood, *The Ascent of F6* (London: Faber & Faber, 1936), Act I, scene i.
20. Norman Wright, private letter, 20 May 1988. See also Stan Smith, 'A Manuscript Poem to Norman Wright', *W.H. Auden Society Newsletter*, 1, 1988: 3–4; 'Two Unknown Holograph Poems by W.H. Auden and C. Day Lewis', *Notes and Queries*, June 1989; Donald MacLeod, 'Recollections that throw an ironic light on Auden', *The Scotsman*, 21 June 1988. I am sad to record here Norman Wright's death in Helensburgh on 16 February 1994.
21. There is a full report of Frazer's speech, and of the Speech Day, in the *Helensburgh and Gareloch Times*, 1 July 1931. For a further discussion of the relevance of this event to Auden's text, see Stan Smith, 'Dog Days: Plays and Other Dramatic Writings by W.H. Auden', *London Review of Books*, 11 January 1990: 9–11; and 'Loyalty and Interest: Auden, Modernism and the Politics of Pedagogy', *Textual Practice*, Spring 1990: 54–72. According to the *Roll of Larchfield Club 1933–4* (Helensburgh: Macneur & Bryden, ?1934), Sir James George Frazer, DCL, LLD, OM had been President of the Club in 1923.
22. Samuel Bryden, although clearly a patriarch, seems to have been an admirably socially-conscious citizen of Helensburgh. Auden deploys the name primarily to identify a site in a system of power and patronage. His grandson, W.S. Bryden (in 1988–89, when I talked to him, a sprightly man in his mid-eighties), appears in the columns of the *Helensburgh and Gareloch Times* in the winter of 1931–32 as a successful golf- and badminton-playing associate of several of Auden's closest Helensburgh friends. While texts are the carriers of history, they carry it with a certain insouciance.
23. *The Helensburgh Directory*, 37th edn (Helensburgh: Macneur & Bryden, 1930). The figures are those of the 1921 census. The new national census in 1931, widely reported in the local press, may have given Auden his idea for the angelic survey in 'Address'. The *Directory* for 1931–32, published after Auden's book, gives the results of this census as pop. 8,893.
24. On the crisis years of 1929–31, see Sean Glynn and John Oxborrow, *Interwar Britain: A Social and Economic History* (London: George Allen & Unwin, 1976), particularly pp. 67–83 and 178–85.
25. David Thomson, *England in the Twentieth Century* (Harmondsworth: Penguin, 1965), pp. 129–51, provides a brisk survey of events, apposite profiles of Macdonald and Baldwin and an account of the 'doctor's mandate'. For a further consideration of Auden's poetry in this context, see Stan Smith, 'The Dating of "Who will endure" and the Politics of 1931', *Review of English Studies*, 41 (163), 1990: 351–62.
26. W.H. Auden, 'Honour', in Graham Greene (ed.), *The Old School* (London: Jonathan Cape, 1934).
27. Carpenter, *W.H. Auden*, pp. 133–4. The poem is 'A Happy New Year', which appeared in *New Country* in 1933. It is reprinted in a disassembled form in Mendelson, *The English Auden*, pp. 115–16, 420–1, and 444–51. In other stanzas the poem casually juxtaposes Sir Montagu Norman, then Governor of the Bank of England, and 'Unhappy Eliot choosing his words'.
28. On the politics of the Third Period, see James Joll, *Europe Since 1870: An International History* (Harmondsworth: Penguin Books, 1976), Chapter xii,

'Fascism, Communism and Democracy, 1929–37', particularly pp. 327–30. There is a characteristically perspicacious account of the Comintern line, and its appalling practical consequences, in Isaac Deutscher, *The Prophet Outcast: Trotsky 1929–1940* (Oxford: Oxford University Press, 1970), pp. 38–42. Deutscher (p. 39) paraphrases Third Period policy as follows:

> Because they concealed their 'true nature' under the paraphernalia of democracy and socialism, the Social Democrats were an even greater menace than plain fascism. It was therefore on 'social fascism' as 'the main enemy' that communists ought to concentrate their fire.
> Similarly, the left Social Democrats, often speaking a language almost indistinguishable from that of communism, were even more dangerous than the right-wing 'social fascists', and should be combated even more vigorously.

This is not to say that *The Orators* is politically coherent. It is in fact a second-hand mish-mash of fashionable leftist attitudes. But when it comes to assuming overt political postures, it espouses the prevailing Communist orthodoxy. The politics of *Look Stranger* (1936) and *Spain* (1937), later follow the CPGB's 'Popular Front' line with equal consistency.

Carpenter, along with most critics, dates Auden's adoption of a thoroughly Leftist position to somewhat later than 1932, but on my reading he had already acquired the groundworks at least by 1929, and probably in Berlin. See Stan Smith, 'Ruined Boys: Auden in the 1930s', in Gary Day and Brian Docherty (eds), *British Poetry 1900–50: Aspects of Tradition* (London: Macmillan/Lumière, 1995), pp. 109–30, in particular the discussion of the poem later called '1929'; and, on 'A Communist to Others', written in August 1932 at the end of his Helensburgh period, 'Auden's Others', in Katherine Bucknell and Nicholas Jenkins (eds), *W.H. Auden: 'The Map of All My Youth'*, *Auden Studies*, vol. 1 (Oxford: Clarendon Press, 1989), pp. 186–91.

29. Naomi Mitchison, *You May Well Ask: A Memoir 1920–1940* (London: Fontana/Collins, 1986), p. 122.
30. BBC television interview, 28 November 1965, quoted in Carpenter, *W.H. Auden*, p. 195.
31. W.H. Auden, 'Lullaby' (1937), *Another Time* (London: Faber & Faber, 1940).

CHAPTER SIX
# Believing in the Thirties

PETER MCDONALD

More than many literary periods, the thirties in Britain is a decade defined
by its conclusion: the meaning of the thirties was of course at issue in that
very conclusion, and in the quick construction of literary history by which
the period was given a parabolic function. Samuel Hynes's important study,
*The Auden Generation* (1976) was the first major critical work to attempt an
assessment of the 'Myth' of the thirties, but the myth-making began during
the decade itself, and entailed at every stage a self-historicising habit of
interpretation and presentation. As the thirties ended, the many statements
of conclusion and retrospect which came from writers tended to suggest
that work of the period had a worth and distinctiveness which made its
interpretation significant; specifically, this significance was presented in terms
of the relation between the writer and society, the individual and history,
art and commitment. It will be one purpose of this essay to suggest ways
in which such constructions of parable significance were successful, in so
far as they projected into the future a paradigm still invoked and played up
to in contemporary literature and criticism. A secondary purpose will be
to question such a paradigm, by looking into the ways in which its found-
ational assumptions are both touched by and dependent on certain issues
more often considered separately by critics of literary modernism.

As anyone who has studied the thirties knows, the decade ended early
and often: conclusions, of sorts, were provided by the Spanish Civil War
and the Munich agreement, with the result that the outbreak of the Second
World War came as an event so thoroughly anticipated that, for writers at
any rate, there was little left to say on the subject. One of the many acts of
literary stocktaking from the younger generation of British poets was Louis
MacNeice's *Autumn Journal* (1939), which charted the public landscapes of
later 1938 from the perspective of a privately troubled observer, without
influence on the wider scene of catastrophe. When, in section VIII of his
poem, MacNeice comes to the days of the Munich agreement, it is a voice
of mundane impotence which speaks bitterly of the politics involved:[1]

> And the next day begins
> Again with alarm and anxious
> Listening to bulletins
> From distant, measured voices
> Arguing for peace
> While the zero hour approaches,
> While the eagles gather and the petrol and oil and grease
> Have all been applied and the vultures back the eagles.
> But once again
> The crisis is put off and things look better
> And we feel negotiation is not vain –
> Save my skin and damn my conscience.
> And negotiation wins,
> If you can call it winning,
> And here we are – just as before – safe in our skins;
> Glory to God for Munich.
> And stocks go up and wrecks
> Are salved and politicians' reputations
> Go up like Jack-on-the-Beanstalk; only the Czechs
> Go down and without fighting.

This is tensed, combative verse; its satiric bite is a strong one, with the descent of the last line to an unrhymed close a cruelly exact enactment of the dying fall it observes. Yet the poetry is also functioning by being powerless, in the sense that the speaking voice registers a profound helplessness before the events which – at second hand – it witnesses. In its way, and in the context of retrospect which the poem sets up, this is itself a conclusion which plays a part in the wider movement of summary and assessment going on in poetry and writing about poetry at the time. Here, in 1938, the 'thirties', as a literary period encapsulating certain literary and political assumptions, are certainly already over. MacNeice's irony is at the expense of the kinds of commitment which were already being absorbed into the thirties 'Myth'; at the same time, the simple individualism of 'Save my skin and damn my conscience' is put on display as another element in the catastrophe which is by now past avoiding. The very language of the events is tainted by the situation – 'Go up' builds a momentum which the answering 'Go down' halts, shifting abruptly from metaphoric ascent of already metaphoric categories ('stocks', 'reputations') to the literal fall of 'Go down'. The poetic voice is positioned as the agent of exposure here, an intelligence able to insist on the unsatisfactoriness of available language – 'And negotiation wins, / If you can call it winning.' Beyond that, the voice is unable to *do* anything: it does not urge, condemn directly, moralise or exhort. This, too, is an important aspect of the poem's involvement with conclusions, setting the seal (like Auden's poetry at the same time) on a period of literary contact with the 'political' which does not just admit failure, but rather *insists* upon its failure in certain respects.

MacNeice's position has sometimes been read as more idiosyncratic than it is, and the complexity of *Autumn Journal*'s engagement with the thirties 'Myth' has been overlooked in favour of more narrowly biographical interpretations. Poems like 'September 1, 1939' or 'In Memory of W.B. Yeats' by Auden seem to make explicit the predicaments which MacNeice's poem experiences with regard to the poetic 'voice' in a time of crisis, but comparison with another voice in the aftermath of the Munich agreement is also instructive, suggesting as it does that the issues at stake go beyond those of the success of one local phenomenon in literary history. T.S. Eliot's lectures on *The Idea of a Christian Society*, delivered at Cambridge in March, 1939 and published in October of the same year, were, like *Autumn Journal*, directed to the moment, and were explicitly the products of a personal voice seeking to make sense of the apparent helplessness of any merely individual voice in the face of national and international crisis. The conclusion to the last lecture situates itself at the same moment of historical realisation of impotence from which MacNeice reported:[2]

> I believe that there must be many persons who, like myself, were deeply shaken by the events of September 1938, in a way from which one does not recover; persons to whom that month brought a profounder realization of a general plight. It was not a disturbance of the understanding: the events themselves were not surprising. Nor, as became increasingly evident, was our distress due merely to disagreement with the policy and behaviour of the moment. The feeling which was new and unexpected was a feeling of humiliation, which seemed to demand an act of personal contrition, of humility, repentance, and amendment; what had happened was something in which one was deeply implicated and responsible. It was not, I repeat, a criticism of the government, but a doubt of the validity of a civilization. We could not match conviction with conviction, we had no ideas with which we could either meet or oppose the ideas opposed to us. Was our society, which had always been so assured of its superiority and rectitude, so confident of its unexamined premises, assembled round anything more permanent than a congeries of banks, insurance companies and industries, and had it any beliefs more essential than a belief in compound interest and the maintenance of dividends?

Publishing the lectures, Eliot appended a note dated '6 September 1939' which could do no more than register the formal, historical conclusion already anticipated. The reflection that 'We could not match conviction with conviction' is, of course, in key with the theme of the lectures themselves, but it is also close to the kinds of verdict being returned on the thirties at the time by men much younger than Eliot, MacNeice among them, whose closing accounts of a period and a literary movement were much possessed by the inadequacy of convictions to events. Eliot's final question about the society he and the younger writers shared, 'Had it any beliefs?', is close to

MacNeice's bitter 'Save my skin and damn my conscience' in the justified bleakness of its assumptions.

Long afterwards, Christopher Isherwood recalled his reactions to Munich in the third person, as a crisis of postponement:[3]

> As far as Christopher was concerned – I won't venture to speak for anybody else – this post-Munich autumn of 1938 was a period of relief disguised as high-minded disgust. Like all his friends, and thousands of other people, Christopher declared that England had helped betray the Czechs. He meant this. It seemed to him absolutely self-evident. Yet his dead-secret, basic reaction was: What do I care for the Czechs? What does it matter if we are traitors? A war has been postponed – and a war postponed is a war which may never happen.

There is more than narrative distancing involved here, and even the 'honesty' of the passage may be a function of the retrospective construction in which it takes part. Nevertheless, the recollection may serve to strengthen the case for taking Eliot's 1938 remarks more seriously as a criticism of the assumptions by which writers in the thirties – like other people – made provisional sense of their situation. Eliot's question about contemporary society, 'Had it any beliefs?', seems to receive a negative reply in Isherwood's retrospect, as it does in MacNeice's *Autumn Journal*, and the air of dishonesty with oneself detected by both Isherwood and MacNeice is wholly in tune with the articulate despair of Eliot's closing remarks. Another factor silently at work in all three accounts is the awareness that the thirties possessed any number of beliefs – indeed, by this stage, an embarrassment of beliefs of one kind or another; the trouble was that they were all implicated in the general failure for which Munich became, like defeated Spain, an instant symbol.

In this reading, the 'beliefs' common in the thirties are on the way out 'As the clever hopes expire / Of a low dishonest decade' in Auden's 'September 1, 1939';[4] they are not what T.S. Eliot had in mind, but are certainly closer to the kinds of belief espoused earlier in the decade by young writers full of the excitement of discovering what seemed to be their own significance. An objection soon arises to this kind of elision: to equate Eliot's 'belief' with the forms of political commitment involved in, for example, Communism from the early thirties onwards, is surely to yoke together two scarcely comparable kinds of intellectual devotion. However, the separation of 'religious' from 'political' commitment obscures the degree to which the issues at stake in the thirties (and the issues fundamental to the inscription of the thirties as a literary/critical 'Myth') are carried over from arguments central to the development and survival of modernism. Eliot's role here is a significant one: as publisher to Auden, Spender, MacNeice and others of the 'thirties poets', he was in a position of some real involvement with

British writing of the period, while his critical preoccupations in the decade relate in various ways to the issues debated through the thirties. Of course, it is more than a generation gap which divides Eliot from these writers, since the political difference would seem to be that between (in however broad terms) Right and Left. Yet such distinctions may not be as adequate as they at first appear, and the issue of 'belief', especially, is one where the thirties 'Myth' converges very closely with Eliot's concerns.

Stephen Spender, one of the most industrious contributors to the initial formation of the 'Myth', had consistently seen the question of political commitment as a pressing aspect of a larger problem of 'belief'. His critical study *The Destructive Element* (1935) was subtitled *A Study of Modern Writers and Beliefs*, and included Eliot, along with Yeats, in its roll of figures of special relevance in relation to this question:

> He [Eliot] and Yeats are the first English poets of this century who seem to have realized that if the beliefs which govern a poet when he is writing are hopelessly removed from the beliefs on which contemporary society and the law are based, then his poetry will seem remote from the life around him. The poet is driven either into an attitude of eccentric and defiant individualism, or else he must try and work out his ideas and relate them to society.[5]

This enterprise answers very closely to the business upon which Eliot was engaged often in the thirties, though the resulting articles, commentaries and lectures were hardly in accord with the ideas of Spender and many of his contemporaries. Even so, the tone of Eliot's 1935 'Religion and Literature' is far from incompatible with the calls for commitment coming at the time from the younger, politically engaged writers:

> It is not that the world of separate individuals of the liberal democrat is undesirable; it is simply that this world does not exist. For the reader of contemporary literature is not, like the reader of established great literature of all time, exposing himself to the influence of divers and contradictory personalities: he is exposing himself to a mass movement of writers who, each of them, think that they have something individually to offer, but are really all working together in the same direction. . . . Individualistic democracy has come to a high tide: it is more difficult today to be an individual than it ever was before.[6]

The end of the individual is a common theme in much left-wing writing of the thirties, but the creative problems inherent in the theory are particularly the domain of writers like Spender, and they become central elements in the creation of the parable-charged 'Myth' of the thirties, in the sense that they are finally seen to be guarantees of the integrity of the artist when faced by the anti-individualist demands of political dogma. Yet here is Eliot (speaking from the 'Right', of course, rather than the 'Left') announcing the demise of the 'individual' in the perceived collapse of political Liberalism: in this sense, at least, Eliot in 1935 is in accord with Spender's 1935 analysis, despite apparently polarised political positions.

Four years later, in his pamphlet *The New Realism. A Discussion*. (1939), Spender is able to convert the dilemma of individualism into a condition of artistic integrity and literary/historical significance, discussing the Marxist critique of thirties literature as offered in Christopher Caudwell's *Illusion and Reality* (1937):

> The fundamental weakness of Caudwell's position is in assuming that the writer who is in a divided position is not in a position to portray historic truth. Surely, the fact that he derides, the 'illusionment' that makes these writers 'pathetic' is precisely that thing in their historic situation which makes them interesting and valuable. The divisions in their interests is [*sic*] a fact, one of the most significant facts in the history of our time.[7]

Spender's 'divided position' is still roughly equivalent to the dilemma identified by Eliot, but now it has been transformed into an aspect of literary and historic virtue. There is more than a hint of self-approval here, and it is at this point that the mythologising activities of Spender and others start to be problematic. In fact, Eliot's gloomy insistence on the intense difficulty of any individualism at all makes individualism, as more commonly understood, exactly the 'illusion' diagnosed by Caudwell, for whom 'the bourgeois poet sees himself as an individualist striving to realise what is most *essentially* himself by an expansive outward movement of the energy of his heart'.[8] 'Individualism' for Caudwell is illusory, because it attests to a failure of belief, or a failure to believe enough; while Communism was far from being Eliot's notion of the object of belief, he also saw 'individualism' as the unsatisfactory consequence of failed, inadequate, or missing belief. Spender's attempts to make the 'divided position' of the writer a touchstone of integrity satisfy Eliot's demands no more than they do those of Caudwell's analysis, but they become very important in the transformation of the thirties into a period of parable significance, for which divided interests are of great importance.

An issue arising here is that of the meaning and construction of the realm of the 'political' in the thirties. Two caveats are necessary: first, the function of the term 'political' needs to be considered as of a particular kind in relation to the writers (and it is, effectively, a small group of writers) who belong to the canonical 'club' of the thirties literary 'Myth' – it does not serve the same function in this context which it does for a political historian of the period; second, the 'political' may be playing a part in the evaluative strategies of canon-formation during and after the thirties – it is a term called upon to do critical service. Attempts to use 'political' in other (and perhaps more usual) ways in relation to thirties writers put these special functions of the word into a clearer light: the proposition that W.H. Auden becomes a politically preoccupied writer in the later decades of his career, for example, is entirely tenable, but also looks undeniably odd, given his canonically 'political' significance in the thirties. In terms of the 'Myth' and its canon, questions of evaluation are connected to measurements of 'political' commitment and detachment which describe degrees of involvement during the decade, then allow for honourable distancing in the interests of artistic integrity afterwards.[9] If Auden himself provides the best example for this kind of pattern, it could be seen also in Spender's career and reception, in Isherwood's, or MacNeice's. If certain writers, such as Edward Upward, seem to skew the picture by persisting in their 'political' commitment when others had taken stock of a 'division in interests', then they can be processed by the 'Myth' into the artistic victims of that commitment. Similarly, certain figures who die young during the decade (such as Caudwell, or Julian Bell) become frozen in the literary history as examples of the real dangers of the 'political' when imported into the artist's life; this, certainly, is the tendency of many of Spender's late-thirties retrospective accounts.

Is it possible, then, to take seriously an equation between 'commitment' in the political sphere in its thirties sense, and Eliot's thirties thinking on the issue of 'belief'? Eliot himself perceived affinities, though he was of course unwilling to see these as in any way satisfactory. In his Commentary in the April 1932 *Criterion*, Eliot took stock of the rising levels of 'political' enthusiasm: 'I find that younger people with whom I talk have, not exactly revolutionary ideas, but rather a yearning towards revolutionary ideas of some kind.'[10] The apparently casual insistence on imprecision amongst those with 'revolutionary yearnings' allows Eliot to define the present levels of 'interest' in revolution 'of some kind' as something 'which may easily be a muddle, of economic theory, humanitarian enthusiasm, and religious fervour'. As far as the preliminary analysis of the state of society is concerned, Eliot is happy to agree with the younger enthusiasts: 'The present system does not work properly, and more and more people are inclined to believe both that it never did and that it never will.' Generous observations on Karl Marx follow this: 'He is, of course, much more cited than read; but his power is so great, and his analysis so profound, that it must be very difficult for anyone who reads him without prejudice on the one hand, and without any definite religious faith on the other, to avoid accepting his conclusions.' All this rather edgy fellow-travelling has been to a certain purpose, however, as Eliot's next paragraph reveals:

> But those who are in this way converted to Marxism must also become converts to the religion to which it has given rise; it is the absence of the religious fervour, the complete gentility, which makes the Fabians look today so antique. And it is exactly in its religious development that

77

Communism seems to me to collapse and to become something both ludicrous and repulsive.

Eliot's use of the vocabulary of religious enthusiasm seems to insist that, if Communism presents itself as 'scientific', then it is no less a system of quasi-religious 'belief', and it is ultimately an inadequate one. A year later, also speaking as editorial voice of *The Criterion*, Eliot elaborated on this same serious irony of political belief:

> Communism − I mean the ideas of communism, not the reality, which would be of no use in this way − has come as a godsend (so to speak) to those young people who would like to grow up and believe in something. Once they have committed themselves, they must find (if they are honest, and really growing) that they have let themselves in for all the troubles that afflict the person who believes in something. I speak of those who are moved by the desire to be possessed by a conviction, rather than by the obvious less laudable motives which make a man believe that he has a belief.[11]

The subtlety of this lies in its caution with regard to the vocabularies of commitment: the 'godsend (so to speak)' is registered by Eliot as a beginning, though no more than that, in the process of learning which issues in an awareness of the inadequacy of 'belief' when used to express a finally contingent enthusiasm. And for Eliot, in the end all *merely* 'political' beliefs are matters of unsatisfactory contingency. The sting of the observation (how 'obvious' is it, exactly?) of the 'motives which make a man believe that he has a belief' is of some importance, and it makes contact directly with the younger generation of thirties writers.

Eliot's prose throughout the thirties (and later, it could be argued, his poetry of *Four Quartets*) makes a point of language's inadequacy in the matter of 'belief', and insists upon the extreme difficulty of an intellectual commitment to any religious or 'political' system of value. This seemed uncongenial at the time; it is revealing that it seems just as uncongenial now, *several generations later*, in the various adaptations of the thirties 'Myth' which literary history continues to find useful. A basic question which faces the literary critic dealing with the thirties is, of course, how to interpret the kinds of 'political' enthusiasm which are so often and so stridently expressed, and may now have a distinctly period air. Julian Bell's writings pose the problem of embarrassment in this respect, as for example in this statement of position:

> It is frankest to start with this political label; like nearly all the intellectuals of our generation, we are fundamentally political in thought and action: this more than anything else marks the difference between us and our elders. Being socialist for us means being rationalist, common-sense, empirical; means a very firm extrovert, practical, commonplace sense of exterior reality. It means turning away from mysticisms, fantasies, escapes into the inner life.[12]

In fact, Bell is here intoning a litany of his own mysticisms, and is clearly exposed to the kind of criticisms Eliot was making at the time of the younger generation; his term 'political' is an essentially narcissistic marker, and his repeated verb 'means' is markedly emptied of meaning by the brisk listing of desired labels. The remarks are in a language drained of self-doubt, which has renounced any suspicion of its inadequacy to give an account of what is being offered as a crucially significant conviction. Any student of the periodical literature of the thirties will recognise Bell as something more than a lonely voice, and the problem of interpretation of such strident confessions of faith is one which cannot really be avoided.

Addressing this very difficulty was an important part of the consolidation of the thirties 'Myth', in which such enthusiasms were deplored (for their artistic shortcomings), while their historical placing, and even their inevitability were granted a degree of value. As often, Stephen Spender plays a significant part in this interpretative turn. In 1938, speaking of poets' 'reaction' against the environment provided by society, he notes how 'they join the communist party, they deliberately cut themselves off from the roots of their own sensibility, which derive from a life they have come to despise, and then they either stop writing or they produce stuff in which new and undigested material is imposed on a medium which was adapted to quite different material'.[13] This is the distance of critical analysis, but it is hardly disinterested. By 1939 Spender was firmly entrenched on the cultural high ground, expressing his hope that:

> writers would write about the kind of life they know best, learning as
> much about it as possible and saying what they believe to be true of it,
> without airing too much their opinions. Far too many writers and artists
> have been driven away from the centre of their real interest towards some
> outer rim of half creating, half agitation. A great deal is said about saving
> culture, but the really important thing is to have a culture to save.[14]

Sure enough, Spender's 1939 volume of poems, *The Still Centre* (with its loudly Eliotic title) begins with the announcement that 'a poet can only write about what is true to his own experience, not about what he would like to be true to his experience'.[15] The contact with 'belief' in its 'political' form is at once admitted as inevitable for the writer, and at the same time declared to be inevitably limiting, so that the good writer progresses from a binding commitment towards an individual artistic independence. Figures like Bell, and even more so John Cornford, become for Spender martyrs to 'commitment', and thus take up an extremely important position in the thirties 'Myth', adding a tragic lustre to its staged conflict between art and beliefs.

Such patterns of interpretation can be rejected, of course; but their pervasiveness in the literary history of the thirties makes it extremely difficult to shake them off altogether. Merely reversing Spender's value-terms is of little help: by defining the 'political' as artistically positive, and the 'individual' as negative, all that results is a literary map on which different names are highlighted for different reasons, and the claims of literary value which may be made for those names will inevitably be deeply problematic, conditioned by political feeling of an unignorably provincial tinge. Eliot's more thoroughgoing critique, because it is unable to take comfort from whatever sense it might have of its own 'political' position, exposes the essential problems more clearly, and brings those problems into the compass of the kinds of anxiety and perplexity which run from modernist writing through the thirties and beyond.

In his 1933 *Criterion* 'Commentary', Eliot develops his observations on 'belief' in a way which reflects the kind of profound dissatisfaction it recommends:

> For the smaller number, the first step is to find the least incredible belief and live with it for some time; and that in itself is uncomfortable; but in time we come to perceive that everything else is still more uncomfortable. Everyone, in a sense, believes in something; for every action involving any moral decision implies a belief; but a formulated belief is better, because more conscious, than an unformulated or informulable one. And, on the other hand, a belief which is *merely* a formulation of the way in which one acts has no validity; unless it turns and compels action of certain kinds in certain circumstances it has no status.[16]

Again, Eliot goes a considerable way with the young literary Communists here – further, certainly, than Spender will go by the end of the decade. The 'action' mentioned by Eliot was a standard feature of Leftist vocabulary, and Eliot agrees that it is in terms of 'action', finally, that commitment must be judged, rather than in terms of the individual's needs and desires. As he concludes his editorial, Eliot pushes things to extremes:

> I have, in consequence of these reflexions, much sympathy with communists of the type with which I am here concerned; I would even say that, as it is the faith of the day, there are only a small number of people living who have achieved the right *not* to be communists. My only objection to it is the same as my objection to the cult of the Golden Calf. It is better to worship a golden calf than to worship nothing; but that, after all, is not, in the circumstances, an adequate excuse. My objection is that it just happens to be mistaken.

If this lacks the patina of strenuous, no-nonsense revolutionary discourse, as exemplified by some of the younger writers, its self-consciously unreasonable solemnity and its grim sense of amusement are nonetheless offered seriously by Eliot as the ironic consequences of rejecting any easy or self-satisfied individualism. At bottom, the joke concerns the potential farce of 'belief' when conjoined with a purely individual frame of reference and value, a self-declared freedom to make words 'mean' things. The same kind of farce is conjured up for Eliot in 1927 when he considers the critical position of I.A. Richards and 'a poetry of the future detached from all belief': 'If he is right, then I think that the chances for the future are not so bright as he hopes. Poetry "is capable of saving us", he says; it is like saying that the wallpaper will save us when the walls have crumbled.'[17] This ludicrous trust in the wallpaper, like the sudden appearance of the Golden Calf at a Party meeting, directs its irony towards the hopes for literature as a guide to 'action', hopes which were common amongst more writers than Julian Bell in the thirties. Auden's wish for someone to 'Make action urgent and its nature clear'[18] is well-known, and even Spender in 1933 could announce that 'A kind of poetry must be written which is complementary to action', and yearn for a 'simple, clear, and definite statement or command' in poems.[19]

Eliot's thirties irony, and the scepticism with regard to the currency of 'belief' which lies behind it, derive directly from modernist arguments of the twenties on the relation between poetry and belief. While these arguments may well be said themselves to derive from the problems of reception posed by modernist writing, especially that of Yeats, Pound and Eliot, they are crucial also in the transmission of modernism in the thirties. The significance of I.A. Richards for the younger writers of that decade is widely acknowledged, especially his reading of *The Waste Land* in *Science and Poetry* (1926), where Eliot is praised for 'effecting a complete severance between his poetry and *all* beliefs', and the 'sense of desolation, of uncertainty, of futility . . . are the signs in consciousness of this necessary reorganization of our lives'.[20] The ways in which Richards filtered through to the thirties writers are in fact complicated, involving a degree of determined misreading, and need to be distinguished from the ways in which Eliot thought and argued through the problems of 'belief' raised by Richards' remarks. One possibility, for the committed, was to dismiss altogether the notion of a poetry uncoupled from beliefs ('beliefs', after all being so necessary and urgent): thus, Cecil Day Lewis stated the common sense that 'One can neither write nor exist completely severed from all beliefs, and the beliefs which a writer holds or against which he is reacting are bound to affect his writing', but found himself obliged in consequence to declare *The Waste Land* 'chiefly important as a social document', a poem to which there had been given 'a terribly inflated value'.[21] More stridently, Alick West noted that 'Dr Richards is trying to isolate himself from whole-hearted social action',[22] and Philip Henderson asked of Richards' championing of Eliot, 'Are we, then, to follow a saviour in whom we do not believe?'[23]

Writers more intelligent (if less 'committed') than these understood the

Eliot–Richards disagreements on the question of belief as being of fundamental importance, and were not willing to dismiss *The Waste Land* as simply a decadent bourgeois phenomenon. For Michael Roberts in 1934, '*The Waste Land* for many readers fulfils the functions of myth: because that poem was possible, life is valuable'; furthermore, 'the terminology of Mr I.A. Richards was particularly suited to the elucidation and discussion of such poetry.'[24] The poem's importance for poets like Auden and MacNeice is evident, and both writers were well-informed on the details and implications of Richards' theories. Eliot's dissent from Richards was also part of the currency of literary theory in the thirties, and this too is significant in the process of engagement with and disengagement from 'beliefs' for the younger writers. In *The Use Of Poetry And The Use Of Criticism* (1934), Eliot summarised a debate between himself and Richards which had been in progress since 1926:

> I will admit that I think that either Mr Richards is wrong, or I do not understand his meaning. . . . It might also mean that the present situation is radically different from any in which poetry has been produced in the past: namely, that now there is nothing in which to believe, that Belief itself is dead; and that therefore my poem is the first to respond to the modern situation and not call upon Make-Believe. . . . We cannot, of course, refute the statement 'poetry is capable of saving us' without knowing which one of the multiple definitions of salvation Mr Richards has in mind. (A good many people behave as if they thought so too: otherwise their interest in poetry is difficult to explain.)[25]

Here it is possible to catch the contemporary turn of Eliot's remarks as he contemplates the evolution of his own place in literary history; the 'interest in poetry', about which he is both laconic and caustic, is an interest in poetry *for the wrong reasons*, and must be taken here to include 'political' interests. There is a shrewdly far-reaching footnote also on offer, provided by Eliot as a further possible elucidation of 'Poetry is capable of saving us': 'There is of course', Eliot points out, 'a locution in which we say of someone "he is not one of *us*": it is possible that the "us" of Mr Richards's statement represents an equally limited and select number.'

It is evident that Eliot is not at this stage, as far at least as the thirties poets are concerned, entirely 'one of *us*'; in his disagreement with Richards, he disagrees also with influential arguments about the potential function of poetry. Essentially, the argument hinges upon what beliefs 'mean' for poetry, and what poetry 'means' for beliefs. Richards had made the notion of 'meaning' in literature a point of critical debate: yet the kind of literature so ardently desired by many younger writers on the Left in the thirties required 'meaning' to be more or less transparent as a term. Richards' distinction between 'scientific' and 'emotive' meaning in *The Principles of Literary Criticism* (1929) haunted a great deal of thirties writing on literature:

A statement may be used for the sake of the *reference*, true or false, which it causes. This is the *scientific* use of language. But it may also be used for the sake of the effects in emotion and attitude produced by the reference it occasions. This is the *emotive* use of language. The distinction once clearly grasped is simple. We may either use words for the sake of the references they promote, or we may use them for the sake of the attitudes and emotions which ensue.[26]

It is worth remembering that Richards produces this distinction immediately after a consideration of 'make-believe' in modern writing, 'Mr Yeats trying desperately to believe in fairies or Mr Lawrence impugning the validity of solar physics'. Here, Richards provides a good example of the wariness with regard to the directions of modernism which strikes a chord with thirties writers, and his warning that 'To be forced by desire into any unwarrantable belief is a calamity'[27] seems to sum up many of the verdicts returned upon Yeats and others during the decade. Of course, those deploring such a calamity were perhaps too confident in the warranted nature of their own 'beliefs'. Still, Richards provided useful terminology for the critique of bourgeois modern literature from a Marxist point of view; Edward Upward in 1937 could report that 'so-called eternal realities can be, as Mr I.A. Richards has admirably demonstrated, defined in almost as many different ways as there are different literary critics', and this exposure of the need for 'objective' terms of reference allows Marxism to step into the ring in full 'scientific' regalia: 'The more nearly a critic succeeds in ignoring the objective world, the more limited and irrational will his practical criticism be. The more closely he approaches to the Marxist practice of explaining spiritual realities (i.e., nature and human society) the fuller and more scientific will his criticism be.'[28] Where Upward lays emphasis on the 'scientific' meaning available to the Marxist as a result of his warranted beliefs, a critic like Christopher Caudwell stresses Marxism's access to the right kinds of *emotive* meaning:

> The emotions of poetry are *part* of the manifest content. They seem to be in the emotional reality as it appears in the poem. We do not appear to take up an emotional attitude to a piece of reality; it is there, given in the reality: that is the way of emotional cognition. In poetic cognition, objects are presented already stamped with feeling-judgements. Hence the adaptive value of poetry. It is like a real emotional experience.[29]

In this kind of derivation from Richards, literary meaning can be scientific *and* emotive, given of course that it is in the right relation to 'reality'; and 'reality' is defined by the beliefs of Marxist analysis. This amounts to a sustained rejection of Richards' point that 'The bulk of the beliefs involved in the arts are . . . provisional acceptances, holding only in special circumstances . . . made for the sake of the "imaginative experience" which they make possible.'[30] For the literary critics of the thirties Left, Richards' diagnosis of the failings of modernism was necessary, and much of his theoretical terminology was serviceable, even though his conclusions could not take account of the 'scientific' knowledge of the realm of the 'political' vouchsafed to a later generation.

Eliot's scepticism with regard to the claims of the 'scientific' often came into play in his writing on Richards and the problem of belief, and it is present in his reactions to the claims of Marxism in the thirties, when assertions of 'objectivity' are repeatedly re-described as quasi-religious 'conversion' phenomena. In his 1937 contribution to a volume entitled *Revelation*, Eliot chooses a French convert, André Gide, as an illustration of something observable also closer to home:

> It will be observed that although Communism does not attempt to answer the question: what is the end of man? and would I presume affirm such a question to be meaningless, it does offer an answer to another question: what is the end of the individual man or woman? and to many people this answer seems good enough. It is this answer which Communism is able to give to the question: what is the end of the individual? which goes to account for the 'conversion' of some notable individualist intellectuals, such as M. André Gide.[31]

Eliot alludes discreetly here (or at least, to adopt one of his own devices, discreetly *enough*) to the voluminous discourse on the British literary Left in the thirties on 'individualism', and the doctrine that the end of any individual was to recognise that the concept of the individual was at an end. This large-scale earnest punning on ends makes the Christian answer 'meaningless', but Eliot's scepticism about the general sufficiency of an understanding of 'meaning' is operative here in his own insistence on such determination of 'meaning' as an act of faith rather than a scientific phenomenon. As Gide's case is considered further, this insistence on 'conversion' becomes more important:

> I cannot help believing that M. Gide's motive was largely the *desire for his individual salvation* – which can remain a desire of something for oneself, even when it is a desire to escape from oneself. I am the more inclined to this belief because M. Gide's writings have always seemed to me to belong to a class of literature of which they are neither the first nor the last example: that in which the author is moved partly by the desire to justify himself, and partly by the desire to cure himself.

Eliot chooses to mix the vocabulary of psychology here with the register of religion, and in the process brings the 'conversion' to Communism into line with the kinds of 'desire' for a personal 'cure' which feature in British thirties writing, most notably in the earlier poetry of W.H. Auden. 'Belief' is thus functioning in Eliot's argument as something which, when understood in political or psychological terms, defines ends in terms of the needs and desires of the individual artist, the 'meaning' of which is conditioned, and limited, by such requirements. In speaking from the position of one whose beliefs rendered his understanding of 'the end of the individual' 'meaningless' in terms of other conceptions of that end, Eliot registers here a profound wariness of any 'meaning' too easily accounted for in a 'scientific' model, whether that of Richards, or those of his younger, 'political' successors.

Richards had made the concept of 'meaning' in literature a notion requiring consideration, definition and defence; in recognising this, Eliot insisted on the very thing which remained as a stumbling-block in theories of 'statement' and 'pseudo-statement' or 'scientific' and 'emotive' meaning: that is, the untenable nature of any finally relativistic 'belief', and the role which this plays inevitably in the creation of the categories of 'meaning' themselves. In his debate with Richards, Eliot returned, with Arnold-like persistence, to certain 'touchstone' lines of poems which seemed to him to exemplify the problem of poetry and beliefs in its starkest terms: Shakespeare's 'Ripeness is all', for example, or Dante's 'in la sua voluntate e nostra pace'. It is no accident that when, in 1937, Stephen Spender struggles with the problem of the meaning of poetry in his *Forward From Liberalism*, he has recourse to these same lines, already marked by the stress put on them by Eliot in the debate:

> Thus the poetic truth working through the poetic logic, does not propagate an impulse, it plants a seed . . . poetry may plant the seed of revolution because the truth which the poet conveys may be a nucleus for the truths of political justice.
>   There are occasions, of course, where poetry rises to the heights of bare statement – 'Ripeness is all', 'In his will is our peace.' Here indeed the truth is naked and the poet by leaving it unconditioned, claims that it is absolute. So that such statements – which are equally statements in prose – have a significance in poetry far greater than their prose meaning.[32]

The very deep critical confusion of this is clear enough, but the significance of such confusion has to do centrally with the problems of belief in the thirties which Eliot's writing brings into focus. Spender accommodates Eliot's touchstones, and attempts to reconcile them with what he understands of Richards' theories by acknowledging what he calls their 'truth'; but in order to do this, he has to accept a relativistic scheme in which, effectively, poetry conditions truth. 'For the poets to forsake poetic truth would be a betrayal not only of themselves but of society' is wholly in line with Spender's statement a few pages earlier that 'I believe that the revolution must be an example of poetic justice',[33] but it provides an excellent example of what Richards called an 'unwarranted belief' in personally-angled definitions of meaning and truth. Bernard Bergonzi's statement of 1978 is pertinent here: 'Spender soon disowned *Forward From Liberalism*. It is one of the texts of the time that illustrate the melancholy paradox that literary men, when seized by political passions, can often use words without knowing what they mean.'[34] Yet this is in many ways the crux of the problem of belief in the thirties: as the heading for the final part of Spender's book, 'Ends and Means', makes obvious, for a confusion about 'meaning' to lead to a casually metaphorical understanding of the means to ends is a cruel pun, however unintended.

Arguments about meaning in the thirties, involved as they were with arguments about belief, issued by the close of the decade in arguments about ends. Again, one could say that the purposive end of the literary thirties in the 'Myth' was to make sense of its historical end, its coming to conclusion. The outlines of the resultant literary history are familiar, as are the degrees of value accorded to different writers in its canonical constructions. It is vital to understand, however, that the construction of the 'Myth' of the thirties as a literary period made the best of a series of confusions, compromises, and inconsistencies from which the writers put together narratives of coherence for each other. Thus 'commitment', of some kind or other, became a justified artistic impulse to be balanced, in retrospect, by an equally justified disengagement from commitment; to put the matter crudely, individualism was salvaged from politics, keeping the liberal conscience intact. The blunders, crassnesses and intellectual squalor of a generation could be processed into something of historical interest and significance, 'one of the most significant facts in the history of our time'.[35] The thirties, in this interpretation, end when an awareness of its own significance in the parable of art and commitment dawns on (most of) the generation.

More than self-respect is preserved by the 'Myth', for the retrospective readjustments and interpretations leave the literature itself insulated from the demands of any criteria for 'truth' other than its own. By making mistakes into significant virtues, the authors of the 'Myth' salvaged a place for 'belief' as something relative, with different facets and functions at different times, something finally invested in the individual. Similarly, the problem of literary 'meaning' could be defused by putting the individual artist back at the centre of concern, and allowing his beliefs their own significance. Writing in America in 1940, Louis MacNeice, like W.H. Auden, was trying to come to terms with the prevalence of endings which were beginning to place and define his own poetic achievements. 'In the long run', MacNeice reflected, 'a poet must choose between being politically ineffectual and poetically false', and continued:

For the younger English poets the choice has now been simplified. A poet adopts a political creed merely as a means to an end. Recent events having suggested that there are too many slips between certain means and certain ends, the poet is tending to fall back on his own conscience. . . . And to shun dogma does not mean to renounce belief. I.A. Richards wrote in the twenties, in *Science and Poetry*: 'It is never what a poem says which matters, but what it *is*.' This may be a half-truth but it is nowadays worth emphasizing, the poets of the thirties having been so much concerned with what they were saying, and to whom, and with whose approval. Not that I accept Richards's complete severance of poetry from beliefs; a poem flows from human life with which beliefs are inevitably entangled. But to let beliefs monopolize poetry is to be false not only to poetry but to life, which is itself not controlled by beliefs.[36]

MacNeice here refuses the easy course of accepting that poetry and beliefs are utterly distinct, at the same time rejecting the idea that beliefs can simply produce poetry. There is a kind of humility implied here – one akin to the awareness of the inadequacy of language to the magnitude of events in *Autumn Journal* – but also a determination to make secure an area of artistic control. As MacNeice wrote in the same year, in a review of Auden's *Another Time*, poets would be now 'at the same time more humble and more arrogant'.[37]

Eliot's formula in the wake of Munich, that of 'humility, repentance, and amendment' also, in its way, preserves a space for the alert conscience. In Auden's career after the thirties, it is possible to see a mixture of humility and arrogance similar to that perceived in 1940 by MacNeice: there is 'humility' in Auden's acceptance that beliefs are not casually relative things, combined with an apparent 'arrogance' in the freedom with which Auden felt able to put into practice an often drastic process of 'repentance and amendment' in the matter of his own past writings. For both MacNeice and Auden, as for Eliot, the responsibility of literary language was the unavoidable consequence of the kind of 'freedom' which the writer both experiences and questions. A belief which is 'personal' means nothing, for it serves really to support a sense of individuality which desires only the freedom to define its own kinds of 'meaning'. Auden's stern suppression of 'lies' in his poetry, much lamented in the thirties 'Myth', declares his distance from the kinds of retrospective self-evaluation upon which the 'Myth' itself depended.

It is true, nevertheless, that the thirties still have a function to perform in many critics' understandings of British literary history, and that function is to do with the possibilities of art's working alongside political commitment. If the 'Myth' as constructed in the forties and after, by Spender and others, encouraged a safely liberal object lesson in the ultimate incompatibility of literature and politics, the more recent attempts to turn the 'Myth' through 180 degrees, thus demonstrating the viability (for however short a time, and in however straitened circumstances) of an art that can have a political significance, are no less in thrall to an illusion of value which sees 'belief' as something available for easy definition. From whatever angle it is regarded, the 'Myth' of the thirties cannot accommodate the kinds of critique represented by Eliot; nor, of course, can it quite come to terms with the presence of modernism in the period as much other than a political liability, nor with the possibility that the very definition of a thirties canon has ignored, not just much of value from Britain, but contemporaneous American achievements of relevance and value. Finally, such a critical paradigm believes that literary language can do a great deal, believes that the 'political' can be easily defined, and that value can be declared rather than proven. Remaining true to what was most false in the bourgeois (and 'emotive') intellectual modes of the thirties, this critical paradigm can issue in rhetoric and wishful judgements which are themselves soon (and all too easily) 'dated'.[38] It is this paradigm which comes into play in the various modes of condescension or condemnation practised on the later Auden: in the attempts to argue away or marginalise the significance of writers like Eliot, Yeats or Pound on modishly political grounds; even in the positive reception of some contemporary poets on account of their apparently easy combination of political with artistic intensity, as though the literary thirties might somehow be made good in a later generation. It is possible, of course, that the use of this critical paradigm will be offered as a rejection of the kinds of thinking exemplified by the Eliot of the thirties, and such a rejection is, to invoke the 'political' criterion, at present a reassuring gesture of orthodoxy; it might be worth thinking of it, however, not as a rejection, but as a retreat from a powerful and uncomfortable challenge. Literary criticism and theory remain parasitic upon beliefs of various kinds, and have grown confident of their scepticism with regard to 'meaning', but are no closer than in the thirties to asking what 'belief' means. The more closely the ramifications of belief in the thirties are studied, the stronger the case becomes to give up believing in the thirties.

## NOTES

1. Louis MacNeice, *The Collected Poems of Louis MacNeice*, ed. E.R. Dodds (London: Faber & Faber, 1979), pp. 116–17.
2. T.S. Eliot, *The Idea Of A Christian Society and Other Writings* (London: Faber & Faber, 1982), p. 82.
3. Christopher Isherwood, *Christopher and his Kind* (London: Eyre-Methuen, 1977), p. 241.
4. W.H. Auden, 'September 1, 1939', *The English Auden: Poems, Essays and Dramatic*

*Writings 1927–1939*, ed. Edward Mendelson (London: Faber & Faber, 1977), p. 245.

5. Stephen Spender, *The Destructive Element: A Study of Modern Writers and Beliefs* (London: Cape, 1935), p. 156.

6. T.S. Eliot, 'Religion and Literature', *Selected Essays* (London: Faber & Faber, 1951), pp. 397–8.

7. Stephen Spender, *The New Realism. A Discussion.* (London: Hogarth Press, 1939), p. 21.

8. Christopher Caudwell [Christopher St John Sprigg], *Illusion and Reality: A Study of the Sources of Poetry* (London: Macmillan, 1937), p. 58.

9. See Stan Smith, *W.H. Auden* (Oxford: Basil Blackwell, 1985), pp. 1–2 for two versions of 'a moral fable called "W.H. Auden"'. As evidence of the continuing potency of such a 'fable', see Terry Eagleton, 'And the poetry he invented was easy to understand', *Poetry Review*, 73 (4), January 1984: 61: 'When capitalism hits a severe crisis, one of its major ideological motifs – liberal humanism – is regularly deflected into an idealist brand of Marxism. When capitalism recovers, liberal humanism disentangles itself from these materialist trappings and resumes its proper role as the impotent conscience of bourgeois society. W.H. Auden has been one of several proper names for that process in our own epoch.'

10. T.S. Eliot, 'A Commentary', *The Criterion*, 11 (44), April 1932: 467–8.

11. T.S. Eliot, 'A Commentary', *The Criterion*, 12 (48), April 1933: 472.

12. Julian Bell, *Essays, Poems and Letters*, ed. Quentin Bell (London: Hogarth Press, 1938), p. 259.

13. Stephen Spender, 'The Left-Wing Orthodoxy', *New Verse*, 31–2 (Autumn 1938): 13.

14. Spender, *The New Realism*, p. 24.

15. Stephen Spender, 'Foreword', *The Still Centre* (London: Faber & Faber, 1939), p. 10.

16. Eliot, 'A Commentary', *The Criterion*, 12 (48), April 1933: 472–3.

17. T.S. Eliot, 'Literature, Science, and Dogma', *The Dial*, March 1927: 243.

18. W.H. Auden, 'August for the People and their Favourite Islands', *The English Auden*, p. 157.

19. Stephen Spender, 'Poetry and Revolution', *New Country*, ed. Michael Roberts (London: Hogarth Press, 1933), p. 63. The paragraph from which these remarks are drawn was cut from the version of this essay reprinted by Spender in *The Thirties and After* (London: Macmillan, 1978).

20. I.A. Richards, *Science And Poetry* (London: Kegan, Paul, French, Frubner, 1926), p. 64. For a discussion of the relevance of Richards to the thirties writers, see Samuel Hynes, *The Auden Generation: Literature and Politics in England in the 1930s* (London: Bodley Head, 1976), pp. 28–9, and Valentine Cunningham, *British Writers of the Thirties* (Oxford: Clarendon Press, 1988), Chapter 3, 'Destructive Elements', passim.

21. Cecil Day Lewis, *A Hope for Poetry* (Oxford: Basil Blackwell, 1934), pp. 22–3.

22. Alick West, *Crisis And Criticism* (London: Lawrence & Wishart, 1937), p. 79.

23. Philip Henderson, *The Poet and Society* (London: Secker & Warburg, 1939), p. 22. Henderson's further remarks are of some interest: 'If the poet cannot any longer believe in the validity and importance of his experience, why should he bother to write at all, or why should we read him?' (ibid., p. 23).

24. Michael Roberts, *Critique Of Poetry* (London: Cape, 1934), pp. 208–9, 163.

25. T.S. Eliot, *The Use of Poetry and the Use of Criticism: Studies in the Relation of*

*Criticism to Poetry in England* (London: Faber & Faber, 1933), pp, 130–1. For a detailed discussion of the Eliot–Richards debate, see John Constable, 'I.A. Richards, T.S. Eliot, and the Poetry of Belief', *Essays in Criticism*, 40 (3), July 1990: 222–43, which draws upon Richards' notes and correspondence in Magdalene College, Cambridge to illustrate the progress of a disagreement in which the two men seem to have remained locked in earnest incomprehension of each other's arguments.

26. I.A. Richards, *Principles Of Literary Criticism* (London: Kegan Paul, 1924; 2nd edn 1926), p. 211.
27. Ibid., p. 210.
28. Edward Upward, 'Sketch for a Marxist Interpretation of Literature', *The Mind In Chains*, ed. C. Day Lewis (London: Frederick Muller, 1937), p. 45.
29. Caudwell, *Illusion and Reality*, p. 243.
30. Richards, *Principles Of Literary Criticism*, p. 220.
31. T.S. Eliot, contribution to *Revelation*, ed. John Baillie and Hugh Martin (London: Faber & Faber, 1937), repr. in *The Idea Of A Christian Society and Other Writings*, pp. 175–6.
32. Stephen Spender, *Forward From Liberalism* (London: Gollancz, 1937), pp. 197–8.
33. Ibid., p. 196.
34. Bernard Bergonzi, *Reading the Thirties: Texts and Contexts* (London: Macmillan, 1978), p. 144.
35. Spender, *The New Realism*, p. 21.
36. Louis MacNeice, 'The Poet in England Today: A Reassessment', *New Republic*, 102 (March 1940), repr. in *Selected Literary Criticism of Louis MacNeice*, ed. Alan Heuser (Oxford: Clarendon Press, 1987), pp. 113–14.
37. Louis MacNeice, 'Not Tabloided in Slogans', *Common Sense*, 9 (4), April 1940, repr. in Alan Heuser (ed.), *Selected Literary Criticism*, p. 114.
38. See, for example, the conclusion of Stan Smith's *W.H. Auden*, p. 216:

I write at the beginning of the ninth month of the Miners' Strike, on a day when a British state apparatus unequivocally committed to the victory of *its* working class has brought the full weight of the law to bear on that [class] struggle, through its courts appointing an official receiver to take over the assets of the NUM. Fifty years after Auden the Yorkshireman wrote those lines, that 'old heroic battlefield' is still the front line. Whatever the outcome of this dispute, one thing is sure: there can be no 'final solution' for the ruling class, as long as it continues to rule. For where there is power there will always be resistance.

# CHAPTER SEVEN

# 'A Marvellous Drama out of Life': Yeats, Pound, Bunting and Villon at Rapallo

## STEVEN MATTHEWS

It often seems to be the case that, in thinking of 'the thirties' as a professional literary-critical category, critics tend to forget that those features which we might choose to associate with the period of 'high' modernism – a reaction against vague, 'Victorian' rhetoric; formal and technical experimentalism – continued to be reflected upon and reviewed across the decade itself. The figures normally associated with that international modernist moment immediately after the First World War continued to write and significantly to develop their craft and aesthetic at this time. Joyce was still labouring at the 'Work in Progress' which was eventually to become *Finnegans Wake* in 1939. Virginia Woolf was, more adamantly than ever in *The Waves* (1931) and *The Years* (1937), turning her own formal experiment towards an ever-closer engagement with sexual politics. The results of T.S. Eliot's 1927 acceptance into the Anglo-Catholic Church and gaining of British citizenship were not revealed until *Ash-Wednesday* of 1930 and the first two of the *Four Quartets*: *Burnt Norton* (1935) and *East Coker* (1940). Ezra Pound did not publish the first full section of his fifty-year odyssey, *The Cantos* until 1930, when a small-scale operation in Paris, the Hours Press, brought out *A Draft of XXX Cantos.*[1] Between 1930 and 1940 W.B. Yeats produced three volumes of poetry: *The Winding Stair and Other Poems* (1933), *A Full Moon in March* (1935) and the posthumous *Last Poems and Plays* (1940), as well as eight plays, many essays and introductions and his last volume of memoirs, *Dramatis Personae* (1936).

Yet the predominant critical focus when discussing the thirties has been on writers as different in themselves as Auden, Isherwood, Jean Rhys, and Stevie Smith, writers who were under the anxiety of modernist influence, but who were often split in their attitudes towards the political and aesthetic responsibilities of form. This focus has tended to obscure, though, the later developments within the 'high' modernist writers themselves, the debates with each other in which they engaged at that time. It has also obscured their more direct influence upon a generation of writers who have never achieved the critical prominence of the Auden–Isherwood line, but who might be said to have wrestled with the modernist inheritance more directly than those whose concerns were, however tentatively, revisionist and political.

In this chapter I want to pursue one such interchange of ideas and influence as it confirms and gives substance to the ideas and aesthetic of Yeats as well as re-energising his poetry of the thirties. It is an interchange which continues an earlier conversation between Yeats and a member of the next generation, Ezra Pound. But the encounter shows Yeats also founding his own poetic through resistance to the ideas of a poet from the next-but-one generation, the English writer Basil Bunting, as he in turn took on the insights of his mentor, Ezra Pound, and sought to adapt them to his own poetic purposes.

After several visits from 1923 on, Ezra Pound, who had become as bored with Paris as he had been with London at the end of the First World War, established himself in a flat on the seafront of Rapallo on the Italian Riviera in February 1925. The resort had for some while been a retreat for writers and artists, and at the time of the Pounds' arrival Thomas Mann, Oskar Kokoschka, Gerhart Hauptmann and Max Beerbohm lived in or near the town. This cosmopolitan character meant that the town was something of a remote haven, remote even within Italy itself, and – tellingly, given Pound's later political wrongheadedness and misapprehension – was disengaged from the upheavals caused by the early years of Mussolini's rule. A resident who knew Pound in the late twenties and early thirties emphasised the Arcadian nature of existence in Rapallo: 'It was an unproblematic world, not yet bombarded by daily news of catastrophes. The radio had only just started; newspapers were read absent-mindedly because they always promised fair weather. And they were usually right.' For Pound himself the town clearly represented a literary paradise, where at the lunch table he might get drawn into 'a good three-cornered discussion of the respective merits of Horace and Catullus'.[2]

In these early years the Pounds were visited by friends from both London and Paris – Ernest Hemingway came before they were finally settled in residence, T.S. Eliot visited at the end of 1925. Other friends came and decided to live in the town themselves (Richard Aldington in 1928, George Antheil, the American composer with whom Pound had collaborated in Paris), and, in the late twenties and early thirties, a stream of younger poets including George Oppen, Louis Zukofsky and the poet-publisher James Laughlin, drawn by Pound's influence – all came to visit him there.

Having suffered congestion of the lungs the previous winter and having been advised to seek some sunshine, W.B. Yeats moved to the town in 1928, also attracted by the presence of the Pounds. Ezra had been the best man at Yeats's wedding in 1917 and Yeats's wife George was a close friend of Pound's own wife, Dorothy. The Yeatses spent the winter of 1929–30 in the town, and returned again briefly in 1934.

In making the move, Yeats was clearly trying to recapture an impetus gained at an earlier crisis in his career. His physical problems at this time were exacerbated by years of overwork in trying to combine his writing with his duties as a Senator in the Irish Free State. Now his time in the Senate was over, and he suffered some kind of nervous crisis while being forced to review the future course of his writing career. At a similar crisis moment in 1912, Pound had helped to re-energise Yeats's work by going through his earlier writing and removing its nineties archaicisms, while urging the older poet to 'make it new', to write in a more 'modern' manner. The three winters which the two poets spent together at Stone Cottage during 1913–15, when Pound acted as Yeats's live-in secretary, had crucial effects on the style and manner of both poets' work.[3]

Now, the congenial setting provided by Rapallo and the proximity of Pound, with whom he had daily meetings, again released something in Yeats: as early as 29 March 1929, he was proclaiming in a letter to Olivia Shakespear that 'I am writing more easily than I ever wrote and I am happy, whereas I have always been unhappy when I wrote and worked with great difficulty.'[4] The poems he started to work on also represented something of a new departure, as he reported in a letter to Olivia Shakespear earlier in the same month:

> I am writing *Twelve poems for music* – have done three of them (and two other poems) – not so much that they may be sung as that I may define their kind of emotion to myself. I want them to be all emotion and all impersonal. One of the three I have written is my best lyric for some years I think. They are all the opposite of my recent work and all praise of joyous life.[5]

Yeats worked on the sequence between 1929 and 1932, when they were published as *Words for Music Perhaps* in a separate pamphlet by the Cuala Press, Dublin. They were then included in *The Winding Stair and Other Poems* in the next year. In the Introduction to *The Winding Stair*, Yeats reiterated the importance of the move to Rapallo which had been expressed in his private letters, whilst somewhat conflating the chronology of the sequence's production:

> . . . in the spring of 1928 during a long illness . . . a Cannes doctor told me to stop writing. Then in the spring of 1929 life returned as an

impression of the uncontrollable energy and daring of the great creators; it seemed that but for journalism and criticism, all that evasion and explanation, the world would be torn to pieces . . . I wrote . . . almost all that exultant group of poems called in memory of those exultant weeks 'Words for Music Perhaps'.

Much of the 'impersonality' which goes with this vigour, as he described it in the letter to Olivia Shakespear, is derived from the fact that most of the sequence is 'sung' by various personae, of whom the most prominent is Crazy Jane. Crazy Jane was based on an old woman who lived near Lady Gregory, as Yeats told Mrs Shakespear in a letter of November 1931:

> She has just sent Lady Gregory some flowers in spite of the season
> and [has] an amazing power of audacious speech. One of her great
> performances is a description of how the meanness of a Gort shopkeeper's
> wife over the price of a glass of porter made her so despair of the human
> race that she got drunk. The incidents of the drunkenness are of epic
> magnificence.[6]

His recourse of seeking to write a poetry which could capture something of that 'amazing power of audacious speech' taps into Yeats's sense both early and late that poetry must be an inherently dramatic force. As early as 1913, just before his first winter at Stone Cottage, he had written to J.B. Yeats that

> Of recent years instead of 'vision', meaning by vision the intense
> realization of a state of ecstatic emotion symbolized in a definite imagined
> region, I have tried for more self portraiture. I have tried to make my
> work convincing with a speech so natural and dramatic that the hearer
> would feel the presence of a man thinking and feeling. There are always
> two types of poetry – Keats the type of vision, Burns a very obvious
> type of the other, too obvious indeed. It is in dramatic poetry that
> English is most lacking as compared with French poetry. Villon always
> and Ronsard at times create a marvellous drama out of their own lives.[7]

Something of what Yeats meant by the 'marvellous drama' is contained in a piece written in 1919, when again it is Villon who forms one of the main exemplars of a poetry which goes against the grain of post-Romantic expectation, of a poetry which, it seems suggested, Yeats himself would wish to write:

> When we compare any modern writer, except Balzac, with the writers
> of an older world, with, let us say, Dante, Villon, Shakespeare,
> Cervantes, we are in the presence of something slight and shadowy.
> . . . The strength and weight of Shakespeare, of Villon, of Dante, even of
> Cervantes, come from their preoccupation with evil. In Shelley, in
> Ruskin, in Wordsworth . . . there is a constant resolution to dwell upon
> good only; and from this comes their lack of the sense of character,
> which is defined always by its defects or its incapacity, and their lack of
> the dramatic sense; for them human nature has lost its antagonist.[8]

For Yeats later in his career, then, drama comes out of recognition and expression of that essential struggle of good and evil which is paradoxically the true expression of human character. It is the opposite of the unmediated expression of experience which in the late twenties and throughout the thirties Yeats came to associate with the generation of writers after him, including Pound. This philosophical, even religious argument forms the basis of Yeats's increasingly explicit arguments for the retention of a traditional form over and against the developments of 'modern' experiment. Once again this argument is involved with his feeling for the need to create a drama out of life rather than to write a poetry which is only self-expression. As he put it in the 1937 'A General Introduction to My Work':

> Because I need a passionate syntax for passionate subject-matter I compel myself to accept those traditional metres that have developed with the language. Ezra Pound, Turner, Lawrence wrote admirable free verse, I could not. . . . If I wrote of personal love or sorrow in free verse, or in any rhythm that left it unchanged, amid all its accidence, I would be full of self-contempt because of my egotism and indiscretion, and foresee the boredom of my reader. I must choose a traditional stanza, even what I utter must seem traditional.[9]

The *Words for Music Perhaps* sequence which Yeats started soon after his arrival at Rapallo represents his most sustained attempt in the later work to write poems that fulfil this prescription for the dramatic. The 'amazing power of audacious speech' remembered from the old woman who lived near Coole Park is translated into the passionate lyricism of Crazy Jane. And Villon, the consistent exemplar for Yeats of that marvellous dramatic expression which is lacking in post-Romantic English poetry, overshadows many of Crazy Jane's speeches, attitudes, or songs perhaps.

He is present in 'Crazy Jane Talks With the Bishop', for instance, one of the later-written poems in the sequence, which A. Norman Jeffares dates to November 1931:[10]

> I met the Bishop on the road
> And much said he and I.
> 'Those breasts are flat and fallen now,
> Those veins must soon be dry;
> Live in a heavenly mansion,
> Not in some foul sty.'
>
> 'Fair and foul are near of kin,
> And fair needs foul,' I cried.
> 'My friends are gone, but that's a truth
> Nor grave nor bed denied,
> Learned in bodily lowliness
> And in the heart's pride.

> 'A woman can be proud and stiff
> When on love intent;          ·
> But love has pitched his mansion in
> The place of excrement;
> For nothing can be sole or whole
> That has not been rent.'[11]

There is an echo in the Bishop's words in the first stanza which provides
a curious gloss on Yeats's classic statement of the dilemma of the artist in
'The Choice' which had been written earlier in 1931 – 'The intellect of
man is forced to choose / Perfection of the life, or of the work, / And if
it take the second must refuse / A heavenly mansion, raging in the dark.' The
division between heaven and sty which the Bishop seeks to enforce is not
one which Crazy Jane as a liver of life in all its degrees chooses to recognise, since 'Love has pitched his mansion in / The place of excrement'. For
the Bishop the choice is no choice, as he seeks to define character 'by its
defects or its incapacity', to adopt Yeats's 1919 phrase; whereas Crazy Jane's
reply, which takes up the chant of the witches in *Macbeth*, is the expression
of a full dramatic sense of life. Crazy Jane recognises the soiled nature of
all abstract ideals such as 'Love', their dependence on worldly experience.
In other words, in a moment of crazy afflatus, she utters the philosophy of
Berkeley as Yeats came to see and depend upon it in the later twenties, a
philosophy which is defined against the drift of English thought as Villon's
poetic is defined for him against the later history of English poetry: 'Born in
such [Irish] community Berkeley with his belief in perception, that abstract
ideas are mere words . . . found in England an opposite that stung [his] own
thought into expression and made it lucid.'[12]

Crazy Jane's reproof of the Bishop contains, then, many of the strands
of Yeats's own thinking both poetically and in the version of an Anglo-
Irish tradition which he was anxious to establish throughout the thirties. A.
Norman Jeffares relates the impetus of the poem to Synge's translation of
Villon's 'Les Regrets de la belle Heaulmière' as 'An Old Woman's Lam-
entation', but the lament at ageing and the loss of a lover which the poem
contains does indeed run through the sequence, from 'Crazy Jane and the
Bishop' through 'Crazy Jane and Jack the Journeyman' to 'Crazy Jane on
God', 'Crazy Jane Grown Old Looks at the Dancers', 'Young Man's Song',
'Love's Loneliness' and 'Three Things'.

This last is that 'best lyric' Yeats felt he had written for some years, as
he put it in his early letter from Rapallo to Olivia Shakespear:

> 'O CRUEL Death, give three things back,'
> *Sang a bone upon the shore*;
> 'A child found all a child can lack,
> Whether of pleasure or of rest,
> Upon the abundance of my breast':
> *A bone wave-whitened and dried in the wind* . . .[13]

The image of the singing bone here looks forward to Yeats's 1936 Introduction to *The Oxford Book of Modern Verse, 1892–1935*, where he proves himself curiously attentive to the 'persistent image' of bones in modern poetry ('That's what's left over from the beauty of a right woman – a bag of bones', Synge's translation of Villon's 'Les Regrets' goes):[14]

> . . . it seems most persistent amongst those who . . . seek something somebody has called 'essential form'. . . . Does not intellectual analysis in one of its moods identify man with that which is most persistent in his body? The poets are haunted once again by the Elizabethan image, but there is a difference. Since Poincaré said 'space is the creation of our ancestors', we have found it more and more difficult to separate ourselves from the dead when we commit them to the grave; the bones are not dead but accursed, accursed because unchanging. . . . Perhaps in this new, profound poetry, the symbol itself is contradictory, horror of life, horror of death.[15]

Such contradictions are, of course, the stuff of this sequence as of much of the later poetry: 'A woman can be proud . . . But Love has pitched' here, for example; 'I know / That out of rock, / Out of a desolate source, / Love leaps upon its course' ('His Confidence'); 'Bodily decrepitude is wisdom' ('After Long Silence'). The 'preoccupation with evil' and its essential struggle with 'good' emerges in this as a Villonesque assertion of energy against worldly disappointment and the woe in ageing; the virtues of memory in sparking a song without regret or despair.

What I want to suggest, however, is that Yeats would not have had to remember back to the distant version of Villon by Synge to underpin the character of Crazy Jane; that it was the move to Rapallo which restirred some of these meditations and which confirmed the philosophical and religious course, as well as the 'persistent images', of Yeats's poetry through the thirties. Later in the 2nd March letter to Olivia Shakespear (which I quoted from above) he wrote:

> Tonight we dine with Ezra . . . Auntille – how do you spell him? – and his lady will be there and probably a certain Basil Bunting, one of Ezra's more savage disciples. He got into jail as a pacifist and then for assaulting the police and carrying concealed weapons and is now writing up Antille's music. George and I keep him at a distance and yet I have no doubt that just such as he surrounded Shakespeare's theatre, when it was denounced by the first puritans.
> . . . I have come to fear the world's last poetic period is over
>
> > Though the great song return no more
> > There's keen delight in what we have –
> > A rattle of pebbles on the shore
> > Under the receding wave.
>
> The young do not feel like that – George does not, nor Ezra – but men far off feel it – in Japan for instance.[16]

The generational consciousness revealed in this letter's first version of his poem 'The Nineteenth Century and After'[17] became hardened throughout Yeats's stay in Rapallo, and the evidence suggests that it was Bunting's presence which sparked some of the more sharply defined recognitions of the contradiction between his own poetic and that of his juniors.[18] Bunting had known Pound in Paris in the early twenties and had followed him to Rapallo. He left in 1925 to return in 1929 and to live there for fairly long periods up until 1934. In 1925 Pound had performed the same editorial function for him which he had for T.S. Eliot on *The Waste Land* a few years earlier, and Bunting's first 'Sonata' (as he called his longer poems), 'Villon', which dates from then shows the results of Pound's red pen. Bunting's use of the French poet as a persona at this time also seems to have rekindled Pound's own interest in the poet to whom he had devoted a chapter in his first critical book, *The Spirit of Romance* (1910), as his opera, *Le Testament de Villon* received its first performance on 29 June 1926.

Bunting's 'Villon' did not receive a wide circulation, though, until it was published in the frivolously-titled pamphlet which Bunting had privately printed in Milan in 1930 – *Redimiculum Matellarum* ('A Necklace of Chamberpots'). This pamphlet is then almost immediately mentioned in a footnote to one of Yeats's 'Pages from a Diary of 1930', and Bunting's views launch Yeats into an amazing meditation upon his own philosophical, religious and poetic opinions:

> A poet whose free verse I have admired★ rejects God and every kind of unity, calls the ultimate reality anarchy, means by that word something which for lack of metaphysical knowledge he cannot define. He thinks, however, that a baptismal and marriage service and some sort of ceremonial preparation for death are necessary, and that the Churches should stick to these and be content.
>
> He now writes in the traditional forms because they satisfy a similar need. But why stop at the metrical forms? It has always seemed to me that all great literature at its greatest intensity displays the sage, the lover, or some image of despair, and that these are traditional attitudes. . . . All these have collapsed in our day because writers have grown weary of the old European philosophy and found no other. . . . When the image of despair departed from poetical tragedy the others could not survive, for the lover and the sage cannot survive without that despair which is a form of joy and has certainly no place in the modern psychological study of suffering. Does not the soldier become the sage, or should I have granted him a different category, when some Elizabethan tragedy makes him reply to a threat of hanging: 'What has that to do with me?' . . .
>
> I find among some of the newer school of poets hatred of every monotheistic system.

---

★ Basil Bunting, *Redimiculum Matellarum* (Milan 1930).[19]

Crazy Jane's lament in *Words for Music Perhaps*, despite its recognitions of contradiction and of the transitory nature of things, does not question the traditional monotheistic system:

> That lover of a night
> Came when he would,
> Went in the dawning light
> Whether I would or no;
> Men come, men go;
> *All things remain in God.*
>
> ('Crazy Jane on God')[20]

A similar wearied yet laconic recognition informs also Yeats's sense of the 'despair that is a form of joy', which had been developed in the mid-twenties, when he worked on his versions of Sophocles' *Oedipus* plays for the Abbey Theatre. He seems particularly taken with the stoical joy discovered by the Chorus in *Oedipus at Colonus*. He published his version of the full play in 1934, but the Chorus had been reprinted as the concluding poem of the 1926–27 sequence 'A Man Young and Old', a more humanistic earlier version of the Crazy Jane idea which until this final poem had lacked the Villonesque philosophical range of the later work:

> Never to have lived is best, ancient writers say;
> Never to have drawn the breath of life, never to have looked
>     into the eye of day;
> The second best's a gay goodnight and quickly turn away.[21]

The fluidity of Bunting's 'Villon', its determined setting of one theme against another in the manner of the sonata-based musical method which he adopted for all his longer poems, does not allow for such a declarative, settled sense of tragedy or of turning away. His use of Villon as a persona paradoxically enables him to include some of his own experience in the poem as Yeats's more dramatic poetic does not. Bunting had read Villon's laments from prison while he was himself doing time for conscientious objection during the First World War. The opening of his 'Sonata' broods upon that 'persistent image' which Yeats notes in his Introduction to *The Oxford Book of Modern Verse*, but does so in a way which seeks to establish the direct imaginative parallel between the French poet and the modern poet-narrator languishing in his cell, rather than out of a sense of 'contradiction':

> He whom we anatomized
> 'whose words we gathered as pleasant flowers
> and thought on his wit and how neatly he described things'
> speaks
> to us, hatching marrow,
> broody all night over the bones of a dead man.[22]

Bunting immediately opens the debate between Art and Life which Yeats takes up in 'The Choice': the critically approved, aesthetically pleasing 'anatomised' words of Villon hide the physical actuality of his death and the lived experience upon which his poetry is grounded. It is out of this experience, which he 'shares' with Bunting, that the persona in the poem 'speaks'. 'Vision is lies', that persona asserts in the next line to these, strikingly taking up a similar idea to that which seems implicit in Yeats's 1913 letter to J.B. Yeats which lauded Villon's 'marvellous drama' over Keats's 'vision'.[23] It is 'lies' because, as the lyrical parody of Villon's 'Ballade des dames du temps Jadis' later in the first section of Bunting's poem has it, 'We are less permanent than thought':

> Remember, imbeciles and wits,
> sots and ascetics, fair and foul,
> young girls with little tender tits,
> that DEATH is written over all.
>
> Worn hides that scarcely clothe the soul
> they are so rotten, old and thin,
> or firm and soft and warm and full –
> fellmonger Death gets every skin.[24]

The first stanza here is surely a more direct source for the crucial Crazy Jane poem, 'Crazy Jane Talks with the Bishop', written in 1931, the year after the first publication of Bunting's 'Sonata', than the more distant Synge version of Villon. 'Fair and foul are near of kin, / And fair needs foul', Crazy Jane cries in retort to the Bishop who has used the fact that 'Those breasts are flat and fallen now' to chide her for her continued wallowing in the 'foul sty' of lust. Further, Bunting opens the second section of his poem with a rant against the person responsible for his imprisonment which is not made explicit in Villon's *Grand Testament*, but which might have spurred the antagonist in Yeats's sequence: 'Let his days be few and let / his bishoprick pass to another.'

Yet the use of the Macbeth witches' 'fair and foul' by the two poets tellingly reveals much about the interaction between their two contradicting poetics. Bunting's 'sots and ascetics, fair and foul' performs the cataloguing of those subject to Death's dominion; but the sense is that Bunting is simply seeking to fill out his traditional stanza, needing to find a rhyme word for 'all' the 'fair and foul' suggested itself to his ear. He is mimicking the ballad form of Villon's great lament, but remains more concerned with the 'ceremonial' (to adopt Yeats's troubled term from the 'Pages from a Diary in 1930') than with the 'assertion of the eternity of what Nature declares ephemeral' (to adopt Yeats's definition of the lover in his description of the 'traditional attitudes' he laments the passing of from poetry). By contrast, Yeats's Crazy Jane asserts the unity, the proximity and interdependence of 'fair and foul' which opens the poem to that metaphysics and monotheism which he recognises that Bunting's poetry lacks, and which he was throughout the thirties increasingly to assert against the next generation's sense of drift and flux. This feeling is enhanced by the relish and prurience with which Bunting envisages the doom of the 'young girls', a relish which exacerbates the connection between poet and 'persona' rather than encapsulating the metaphysical 'truth' of its subject – as Yeats's more matter-of-fact vocalisation would do.

The remainder of Bunting's 'Sonata' restlessly shifts backwards and forwards ('hither and thither scurrying as the wind varies' as one line has it) between the life, the filthy reality in the prison, and the art or vision which has been seemingly rejected near its beginning, but which seems increasingly necessary to the survival of anything against the impermanence so strongly captured in the lyric parody of Villon in the first section. The third section opens with a surprising, classical, unpunctuated, sunlit vision of freedom:

> Under the olive trees
> walking alone
> on the green terraces
> very seldom
> over the sea seldom
> where it ravelled and spun
> blue tapestries and green . . .

But even this seemingly seamless interweaving of nature and art soon mutates into a sense of fragility and impermanence, of the war into which perhaps the greatest vision of beauty soon lapsed:

> silverplated in silk and embroidery
> with offerings of pictures
> little ships and arms
> below me the ports
> with naked breasts
> shipless spoiled sacked
> because of the beauty of Helen[25]

The 'Sonata' ends by abstractly and rather yearningly recounting its ambitions, suggesting that they cannot be enacted within the poem itself but that they demand statement. Those ambitions are Poundian and sculptural, setting up an analogy between carving and writing which was to continue throughout Bunting's life:[26]

> precision clarifying vagueness;
> boundary to a wilderness
> of detail; chisel voice
> smoothing the flanks of noise . . .

The sense in the concluding metaphor of the work is, however, that all experience simply runs together indistinguishably, and that it therefore defeats lyrical expression:

> The sea has no renewal, no forgetting,
> no variety of death,
> is silent with the silence of a single note.
>
> How can I sing with my love in my bosom?
> Unclean, immature and unseasonable salmon.[27]

The obscure way in which the last two lines are set the one against the other is symptomatic of Bunting's poetic and of the Villon who emerges from the poem, one in which the 'uncleanliness' of experience is ultimately all that the poet can struggle to sing. Given the transitoriness of experience from this perspective, the poetry is doomed to drift and imprecision. It is this version of Villon who seems to have shaped Bunting's poetic throughout his life, from the further parody of 'Les Regrets de la Belle Heaulmière' in the 1935 'The Well at Lycopolis' ('I had them all on a string at one time, / lawyers, doctors, businessmen') to the lament for lost love which forms the keynote of the 1965 *Briggflatts* ('It is easier to die than to remember. / Name and date / split in soft slate / a few months obliterate').[28] Life and art seem mutually and irredeemably contradictory as they do in Yeats's 'The Choice' – but not in the older poet's actual enactment of poetry as the creation of a 'marvellous drama' out of life.

In a striking passage from his 1934 *Wheels and Butterflies* Yeats develops the sea image used by Bunting in this 'Sonata' and further elaborates on the argument developed in the pages of the Diary:

> Certain typical books – *Ulysses*, Virginia Woolf's *The Waves*, Mr Ezra Pound's *Draft of XXX Cantos* – suggest a philosophy like that of the *Samkara* school of ancient India, mental and physical objects alike material, a deluge of experience breaking over us and within us, melting limits of line or tint; man no bright hard mirror dawdling by the dry sticks of a hedge, but a swimmer, or rather the waves themselves. In this new literature announced with much else by Balzac in *Le Chef d'oeuvre inconnu*, as in that which it superseded, man in himself is nothing.[29]

After his re-encounter with the man 'whose art is the opposite of mine, whose criticism commends what I most condemn'[30] at Rapallo, it was Pound who throughout the thirties proved the interlocutor and antagonist against whom Yeats constantly weighed and redefined his later ideas on poetry. His statements about *The Cantos* reveal that his own criticism of Pound is very close to that offered of Bunting in the 'Pages from a Diary in 1930'; it is a criticism which he is content to apply to all the poets of the generations succeeding his own:

When I consider [Pound's] work as a whole I find more style than
form; at moments more style, more deliberate nobility and the means to
convey it than in any contemporary poet known to me, but it is
constantly interrupted, broken, twisted into nothing but its direct
opposite, nervous obsession, nightmare, stammering confusion. . . . Style
and its opposite can alternate, but form must be full, sphere-like, single.
Even where there is no interruption he is often content, if certain verses
and lines have style, to leave unbridged transitions, unexplained
ejaculations, that make his meaning unintelligible. He has great influence,
perhaps more than any other contemporary except Eliot, is probably the
source of that lack of form and consequent obscurity which is the main
defect of Auden, Day Lewis, and their school.[31]

Here again is that appeal to singleness which was there in the criticism of
Bunting, a singleness related to 'traditional attitudes', 'intensity' and tragic
joy. Yeats's criticism heralds the lament which Pound was himself exhaustedly
to write out over twenty years later, a lament that 'I cannot make it cohere.'
The transitory moments cannot be brought into any pattern; finally, Pound's
is a poetic which works by rejection of certain rhetorics and forms of 'knowledge' but which is unable to discover its own unity.

This becomes clear in the poem from *Words for Music Perhaps* in which
Yeats most directly addresses himself to Pound's agenda. 'Those Dancing
Days Are Gone', which was first published in 1930, quotes, as Yeats pointed
out at the time, 'a line from somewhere in Mr Pound's "Cantos"' as the
first line of its refrain:

> Come, let me sing into your ear;
> Those dancing days are gone,
> All that silk and satin gear;
> Crouch upon a stone,
> Wrapping that foul body up
> In as foul a rag:
> *I carry the sun in a golden cup,*
> *The moon in a silver bag* . . .[32]

The source of the quotation is near the opening of 'Canto XXIII', in
which Pound weighs the worth of modern scientific knowledge against the
mythical view of Nature contained in the classics, so making the implicit
conclusion that the modern quest is fruitless. Yeats might have been lured to
this particular 'Canto' by the fact that it opens with a quotation from the
Byzantine philosopher Michael Constantine Psellus: the 1930 Diary records
a 'subject for a poem' which has 'been in my head for some time', and gave
a prose draft of 'Byzantium' which was written in September 1930. The
quotation from Psellus confirms that sense of flux which is the basis of the
poem's method, 'Et omniformis . . . omnis / Intellectus est.'[33] Pound's poem
proceeds with an example of science in action which comes from Pierre
Curie's experiment in placing some radium on his arm, before the 'Canto'

launches into a poetic paragraph derived from Johannes Schweighaeuser's Greek and Latin *Athenaeus* about the journeying of the sun around the earth into night:

> La Science ne peut pas y consister.     'J'ai
> Obtenue une brulure' – M. Curie, or some other scientist
> 'Qui m'a couté six mois de guérison'
>       and continued his experiments.
> Tropismes! 'We believe the attraction is chemical.'
>
> With the sun in a golden cup
>       and going toward the low fords of ocean
> Ἄλιος δ' Ὑπεριονίδας δέπας 'εσκατέβαινε χρύσεον
> Ὄφρα δί ὠκεανοῖο περἀσας
>       ima vada noctis obscurae
> Seeking doubtless the sex in bread-moulds . . .[34]

Yeats in 'Those Dancing Days Are Gone' shares the sense that a golden past has gone, the sense that 'the great song [will] return no more' as he put it in 'The Nineteenth Century and After'. But this leads to none of the satiric bitterness of the Pound, the tone which is there in Bunting's 'Villon' also. Yeats's truly dramatic lyric continues to assert the persistence of the lyric gift itself against the debilities of age and belatedness:

> I thought it out this very day,
> Noon upon the clock,
> A man may put pretence away
> Who leans upon a stick,
> May sing, and sing until he drop,
> Whether to maid or hag:
> *I carry the sun in a golden cup,*
> *The moon in a silver bag.*[35]

Again, Yeats writes out of that 'form of joy' which can be discovered in the note of despair which inhered in his revaluation of 'traditional attitudes' in the encounter with Pound and Bunting at Rapallo; again it is in the interpretation of that preoccupation of Villon's with age and 'les neiges d'antan' that the renewed vigour and drama of Yeats's poetry derives.

What I want to suggest is that the self-lacerating voice of Yeats's later poetry does not only depend on that *saeva indignatio* which he was discovering in the Swift works he was concurrently reading at Rapallo. It is confirmed by the renewed energy he found there in the challenging encounters with Pound and Bunting, and in the reading of the latter's 'Villon', which got filtered into the 'all emotion, all impersonal' lyrics of *Words for Music Perhaps* that he began writing soon after his arrival. The encounter reinforced his notion that there was a dramatic lyricism which could survive even within the sense of drift that the next generation felt so strongly, that only by confronting evil and despair fully could there remain a sense of pattern ('can such a poem have a mathematical structure?' he asked of *The Cantos*[36] and of the persistence of (perhaps joyful) song. This is the burden of 'The Gyres' from *Last Poems 1936–1939*: 'Irrational streams of blood are staining earth; / Empedocles has thrown all things about; / Hector is dead and there's a light in Troy; / We that look on but laugh in tragic joy.'[37] It is the burden also of the more 'personal' late lyrics, in which it is possible to see the mask of la belle Heaulmière tighten on to Yeats's own face – where, as in 'The Spur', the 'horrible' lust and rage of old age are turned into a source of inspiration, for 'What else have I to spur me into song?'[38]

## NOTES

1. The volume was not taken up by the larger publishers of Farrar & Rinehart in America and Faber & Faber in England until 1933. An earlier 'draft', of XVI Cantos, appeared in 1925, but it was the XXX Canto 'section' which Pound retained in all the collected versions of the work.

2. Quoted by Humphrey Carpenter, *A Serious Character: The Life of Ezra Pound* (London: Faber & Faber, 1988), p. 447.

3. It is symptomatic of how even those most concerned with charting the history of modernist debate tend to ignore the later encounter that James Longenbach, whose excellent *Stone Cottage* (Oxford: Oxford University Press, 1988) traces the history of this earlier one, claims 'When Pound stationed himself in Rapallo, he became the member of a secret society of one. The dream of community and collaboration, embodied in Stone Cottage, was rejected in Pound's later career' (p. 267).

4. *The Letters of W.B. Yeats*, ed. Allan Wade (London: Rupert Hart-Davis, 1954), p. 761. Hereafter identified as *Letters*.

5. 2 March 1929. *Letters*, p. 758.

6. Quoted by A. Norman Jeffares, *A Commentary on the Collected Poems of Yeats* (Stanford: Stanford University Press, 1968), p. 371.

7. *Letters*, p. 583. George J. Bornstein and Hugh H. Witemeyer have argued that it is in his later sense of Villon as a dramatic and philosophical poet that Yeats's poetic differs most from Pound's. Pound admired poets like Villon who succeeded in 'living their verse', but knew that he was himself unable to do so. As a result he made Villon one of the many dramatis personae in his early work as he felt unable to achieve 'sincere self-expression'. For the later Yeats, however, Villon is always much more of an impersonal poet, using the actual facts of his life as the ground upon which to wrestle with more eternal themes. See 'From *Villain* to Visionary: Pound and Yeats on Villon', *Comparative Literature*, XIX (4), Fall 1967: 310–20.

8. *Explorations*, selected by Mrs W.B. Yeats (London: Macmillan, 1962), p. 316.

9. *Essays and Introductions* (London: Macmillan, 1961, repr. 1974), p. 522.

10. Jeffares, *A Commentary on the Collected Poems of Yeats*, p. 375.

11. *The Collected Poems of W.B. Yeats* (London: Macmillan, 1933 repr. 1979), pp. 294–5.

12. *Essays 1931–1936* (Dublin: Cuala Press, 1937), p. 36.

13. *Collected Poems*, p. 300.

14. *Poems and Translations* (Dublin: Maunsel, 1912), p. 44.

15. Oxford: Clarendon Press, 1936, p. xx.

16. *Letters*, pp. 758–9.

17. In the *Collected Poems* the only change from the version in *Letters* is that 'A rattle' becomes 'The rattle'.

18. There is even some early suggestion of the impact of Bunting's literary discussion on Yeats in an image used in the second (29 March) letter to Olivia Shakespear from Rapallo, in the sentence succeeding the one describing his new-found ease and delight in writing – 'I feel like one of those Japanese who in the middle ages retired from the world at 50 or so – not like an Indian of that age to live in jungle but to devote himself "to art and letters" which was considered sacred.' It is just one such Japanese who forms the persona in Bunting's 1932 'Sonata', 'Chomei at Toyama'.

19. *Explorations*, pp. 295–6. Yeats so admired Bunting's poetry at this time that he learnt some of it by heart and recited it at a dinner party, recited it 'so dramatically, in fact, that the author did not even recognize it'. Victoria Forde, *The Poetry of Basil Bunting* (Newcastle upon Tyne: Bloodaxe, 1991), p. 31.

20. *Collected Poems*, p. 293.

21. *Selected Poems*, p. 255. Yeats's liking for his version of this Chorus and his sense that it encapsulated his later philosophy was such that he made it the final poem in his selection from his own work in the *Oxford Book of Modern Verse*.

22. *Collected Poems* (Oxford: Oxford University Press, 1978), p. 3.

23. Notably Yeats's own description of the genesis of his *A Vision*, first published in 1925 but revised throughout the thirties until the second edition of 1937, fulfils his later philosophy:

> my Christ, a legitimate deduction from the Creed of St Patrick
> as I think, is that Unity of Being Dante compared to a perfectly
> proportioned human body, Blake's 'Imagination', what the
> Upanishads have named 'Self': nor is this unity distant and therefore
> intellectually understandable, but imminent, differing from man to
> man and age to age, taking upon itself pain and ugliness, 'eye of
> newt, and toe of frog'.
>
> Subconscious preoccupation with this theme brought me *A
> Vision*, its harsh geometry an incomplete interpretation.
>
> ('A General Introduction to My Work',<br>*Essays and Introductions*, p. 518)

24. *Collected Poems*, p. 4.

25. *Collected Poems*, pp. 6–7.

26. See, for example, the description of Pound's poetic in Donald Davie's *Ezra Pound: Poet as Sculptor* (Manchester University Press, 1965). Bunting uses a stone mason as figure of the artist in his last 'Sonata', *Briggflatts*: 'Pens are too light. / Take a chisel to write. / Every birth a crime, / every sentence life' (*Collected Poems*, pp. 41–2).

27. *Collected Poems*, p. 7.

28. Ibid., pp. 17, 42.

29. *Explorations*, p. 373.

30. 'A Packet for Ezra Pound', first published by Cuala Press 1929, then used as Preface to *The Vision* (London: Macmillan, 1937, 1981 edn), p. 3.
31. Introduction to *The Oxford Book of Modern Verse*, p. xxv.
32. *Collected Poems*, p. 302.
33. Pound's scepticism about the advances of modern science had, significantly, been the subject of a passage in his 'savage disciple' Bunting's 'Villon' when the method of Bertillon, the Paris police chief who invented anthropometrics (a system of identifying suspects by measuring their features), comes under question as another of the threats to art which the 'Sonata' registers:

> What is your name? Your maiden name?
> Go in there to be searched. I suspect it is not your true name.
> Distinguishing marks if any? (O anthropometrics!)
> Now the thumbprints for filing.
> Colour of hair? of eyes? of hands? O Bertillon!
> How many golden prints on the smudgy page?
> Homer? Adest. Dante? Adest.
> Adest omnes, omnes et
> Villon.
> Villon?
>
> (*Collected Poems*, p. 6)

34. *The Cantos of Ezra Pound* (London: Faber, 1975), p. 107. The Greek and Latin translates as 'The sun, Hyperion's child, stepped down into his golden bowl / and then after crossing the stream of the ocean / the depth of black night.'
35. *Collected Poems*, p. 303.
36. Introduction to *The Oxford Book of Modern Verse*, p. xxiv.
37. *Collected Poems*, p. 337.
38. Ibid., p. 359.

CHAPTER EIGHT

# Thirties Poetry and the Landscape of Suburbia

SIMON DENTITH

I start in a familiar place – but a place still new for J.B. Priestley when he wrote about it in *English Journey* in 1934. At the end of the book he is stuck in a traffic jam in a fog, crawling back through North London, and reflecting on the different Englands he has seen on his journey:

> There was, first, Old England, the country of the cathedrals and minsters and manor houses and inns, of Parson and Squire; guide-book and quaint highways and byways England. . . . Then, I decided, there is the nineteenth-century England, the industrial England of coal, iron, steel, cotton, wool, railways; of thousands of rows of little houses all alike, sham Gothic churches, square-faced chapels, Town Halls, Mechanics Institutes, mills, foundries, warehouses. . . .

Priestley extends this list with some panache. But the third England that Priestley had found is the now familiar place that is the topic of this chapter. This is how he describes it:

> The third England . . . belonged far more to the age itself than to this particular island. America, I supposed, was its real birthplace. This is the England of arterial and by-pass roads, of filling stations and factories that look like exhibition buildings, of giant cinemas and dance-halls and cafés, bungalows with tiny garages, cocktail bars, Woolworths, motor-coaches, wireless, hiking, factory girls looking like actresses, greyhound racing and dirt tracks, swimming pools, and everything given away for cigarette coupons. If the fog had lifted I knew that I should have seen this England all round me at that northern entrance to London, where the smooth wide road passes between miles of semi-detached bungalows, all with their little garages, their wireless sets, their periodicals about film stars, their swimming costumes and tennis rackets and dancing shoes.
>
> (Priestley 1984: 297–301)

This is an England that is the subject of polarised cultural debate in the thirties – though perhaps that word 'debate' is to dignify too much the various kinds of name-calling performed with some of the items on Priestley's list, many of which were made into icons of a new degeneracy. For Priestley at least, this new England was 'essentially democratic'. Making that characteristic thirties gesture towards a transformed future, he adds, 'After a social revolution there would, with any luck be more and not less of it.' This is, of course, the democracy of the market-place, and this is the area of most difficulty for the Left, both then and now, in coming to terms with this third England. But this is not a problem for Priestley:

> Notice how the very modern things, like the films and wireless and sixpenny stores, are absolutely democratic, making no distinction whatever between their patrons; if you are in a position to accept what they give – and very few people are not in that position – then you get neither more nor less than what any body else gets, just as in the popular restaurants there are no special helpings for favoured patrons but mathematical portions for everybody. There is almost every luxury in this world except the luxury of power or the luxury of privacy.
>
> (p. 301)

One does not have to accept the full logic of this to be impressed by its generosity of spirit, especially when compared to most other accounts, in the thirties, of this particular version of modernity (shortly I shall try to disentangle more carefully the various connotations of the sheerly contemporary, the modern, and – another key thirties word, the 'new'). Before leaving Priestley's account, however, I wish to draw attention to two further aspects of it, which are closely related in his thinking on this topic. Firstly he notes how unpropitious this England is for novelistic treatment, compared to the strongly marked individualities of Dickens's England. He is prepared to tolerate this – 'After all, the world does not exist simply for creative writers who happen to like strong effects.' Nevertheless . . . 'I cannot help thinking that this new England is lacking in character, in zest, gusto, flavour, bite, drive, originality, and that this is a serious weakness.' This apparently professional complaint – how might this new England form the subject of artistic treatment? – now modulates into an overtly political worry: 'Monotonous but easy work and a liberal supply of cheap luxuries might between them create a set of people entirely without ambition or any real desire to think and act for themselves, the perfect subject for an iron autocracy' (p. 303). We shall see both of these worries appearing elsewhere in the thirties. What is an appropriate manner for writing about the landscape of the suburbs? – a question of genre that intrudes itself especially awkwardly for poets. And are the inhabitants of this landscape indeed the 'perfect subject for an iron autocracy'? This too, with different inflections, will be a question that other writers will be asking.

The generosity of Priestley's response can be rapidly gauged by a comparison with Stephen Spender, normally, one would have thought, the most readily sympathetic and generous of writers. Where Priestley anticipates that after a social revolution there will be more of this England, just such a vision forms part of a brief dystopian moment in *Forward from Liberalism*. Spender is mounting an argument against private ownership and production, and gives an example demonstrating the necessity of public ownership and planning:

> Suppose everyone in England received a national dividend of £300 a
> year, then, within a few months, the whole countryside would, except
> for certain reserves, be built over with small houses. Property must
> belong to the whole people, since it is to the interest of the whole
> people that they should not be allowed to destroy each other's view.
> Instead of living in semi-detached bungalows, it will be the pride of the
> whole people to live in towns that are planned as towns, in a country of
> electric power and air transport. Don't imagine that I think there will be
> no mistakes, no ugliness: but our mistakes will be generous, not mean;
> they won't be the mistakes of shopkeepers who put up buildings built in
> the most florid and extravagant of styles at the least possible expense.
> (Spender 1937: 190–1)

This is a vision of England entirely covered by Peacehaven, emblematic image for many in the thirties of private fantasy made manifest in jerry-building and a despoiled 'view'. We might read such a passage in two ways – and indeed, two unresolved impulses in Spender's sensibility are present in it, the Georgian and the modernist, both of which are hostile to the sub-urban landscape. There is the countryside, of course, as a value to be pre-served; but there is also, sitting oddly with this, that futurist vision of a 'country of electric power and air transport'. This strange doubleness is just the combination out of which emerges, with differing emphases, the poetry of 'The Pylons', 'The Express', and 'The Landscape Near an Aerodrome'.

It is much easier to provide other examples of Spender's antipathetic response than it is to find other writers prepared to echo Priestley's nuanced but finally accepting attitude. Staying for a moment only in the area of utopian or dystopian anticipations, it seems to me to be possible to read the whole of *Brave New World* as a negative vision of a world given over to suburbia:

> Lenina looked down through the window in the floor between her feet.
> They were flying over the six kilometre zone of parkland that separated
> Central London from its first ring of satellite suburbs. The green was
> maggoty with foreshortened life. Forests of centrifugal Bumble-puppy
> towers gleamed between the trees. Near Shepherd's Bush two thousand
> Beta-Minus mixed doubles were playing Riemann-surface tennis. A
> double row of Escalator-Fives Courts lined the main road from Notting
> Hill to Willesden. In the Ealing stadium a Delta gymnastic display and
> community sing was in progress.
> (Huxley 1971: 58)

The place names, of course, are significant: from Shepherd's Bush and Notting Hill out to Willesden and Ealing, the landscape reproducing the social zoning of thirties London; while the games – tennis and community singing rather more, perhaps, than fives and gymnastics displays – are the games of Priestley's third England. *This* dystopian vision, taken up at least by Orwell in, for example, *Road to Wigan Pier*, associates the suburbs with a horrified account of modernity as the world of planning, efficiency, glass and steel. There is something odd about this, given the overwhelming cultural conservatism of the new suburbs. But against this dominant dystopian account of the suburbs, it is hard to find many utopian projections to set beside Priestley's. I am happy to include the Auden of 'Spain' – and here I am conscious of finally quoting an actual poem:

> Tomorrow for the young the poets exploding like bombs
> The walks by the lakes, the winter of perfect communion
> Tomorrow the bicycle races
> Through the suburbs on summer evenings . . .
>
> (Skelton 1979: 136)

I am impressed by the happy ordinariness of these anticipations (excluding, perhaps, the poets 'exploding like bombs'); but I am not sure how typical they are of Auden. When he writes at the end of 'Sir, no man's enemy'

> . . . look shining at
> New styles of architecture, a change of heart,

I don't suppose he has suburban Jacobethan in mind.

So if one is addressing the question of the thirties and modernity, it seems important to consider responses to the very visible indications of the modern world represented by the new suburbs. It is worth recalling just how extraordinary was the transformation of the landscape effected by suburban growth between the wars – four million houses built between 1918 and 1939; the surface area of London doubling in the same period; around London alone, at the height of the building boom in the early thirties, houses being built at the rate of 65,000 and 70,000 a year. But the problem for people like Spender – in his futurist aspect, at least – was just that, as symbols of the modern world, these were not modern at all; on the contrary, these suburbs drew upon an eclectic range of revival styles which included Queen Anne as well as the most immediately recognisable Tudor. In the dominant view, these suburbs were merely contemporary, not modern; modernity was represented by the modern style: '. . . cities / Where often clouds shall lean their swan-like neck'. As we shall see, where the landscape of suburbia is not offered as exemplary of the horrors of contemporaneity, it appears simply as the doggedly mundane, the plain dull ordinariness of the contemporary world which greets us all on our travels. At all events it is not *new* in the excited sense of that word which appears in *New Country*, *New Signatures*, ironically even in *Brave New World*. (There's a footnote here on the suburban house in the modern style – people come from all over to Southport, near Liverpool, to see such houses, where there are more than most. The Ideal Home exhibition of 1933 featured all its specially built exhibition houses in this style. But of course it didn't really catch on, except in its attraction to builders as a way of simplifying the elevations, and in the common feature of later thirties houses: sun-catching rounded windows.)

From the opposite perspective also, from that of an apparent social and cultural conservatism, Priestley's third England was intolerable. Betjeman's 'Slough' is unavoidable here:

> Come, bombs, and blow to smithereens
> Those air-conditioned, bright canteens,
> Tinned fruit, tinned meat, tinned milk, tinned beans,
>     Tinned minds, tinned breath.
>
> Mess up the mess they call a town –
> A house for ninety-seven down
> And once a week a half-a-crown
>     For twenty years.
>
> (Betjeman 1988: 20)

Valentine Cunningham has sufficiently dwelt on the unpleasantness of this attitude, to the extent of referring to the poem as one of the *bêtes noires* of *British Writers of the Thirties*. The simple snobbishness of it is found also in 'The Outer Suburbs', from the 1931 *Mount Zion* collection, but excluded from the *Collected Poems*:

> And bright within each kitchenette
> The things for morning tea are set,
> A stained-glass window, red and green,
> Shines, hiding what should not be seen
> While wifie knits through hubbie's gloom
> Safe in the Drage-way drawing room.
> Oh how expectant for the bed
> All 'Jacobethan' overhead.
>
> (Betjeman 1931: 44)

The social location of these bumptiously obnoxious poems is not far to seek. It is fifty miles or so to the south-east of Slough, in another part of the suburbs – in fact it's in Croydon:

> In a house like that
>     Your Uncle Dick was born;
> Satchel on back he walked to Whitgift
>     Every weekday morn.

> Boys together in Coulsdon woodlands,
>   Bramble-berried and steep,
> He and his pals would look for spadgers
>   Hidden deep.
>
> (Betjeman 1988: 11)

Here the suburban setting is not a topic for belittling or aggressive humour, but capable of the seriousness of elegy (the last two lines of the poem read 'But your Uncle Dick has left his Croydon / Once for all'). Of course, even this poem is dogged by the danger of falling into a coy whimsy, especially in the use of slang, that fatally undermines its pretensions to seriousness, and indeed I make no particular claims for it as a poem. But the point is that Betjeman's assault on the horrors of suburban England (can you believe it – they eat tinned food and pay for their houses by a *mortgage!*) merely comes from someone who inhabits an older and more established suburb. This is a point well made by Valentine Cunningham when he writes of 'a distinct note of old rentier snootiness towards the small-time mortgagee' (Cunningham 1988: 257).

What of course is disturbing – and widely remarked upon by subsequent writers as they reflected back on the thirties – is that similar attitudes pervade the writers on the Left. I have already adverted to the case of Spender in *Forward from Liberalism*, but the Auden of 'Letter to Lord Byron' is at times unnervingly close to the simple snobbery of Betjeman:

> Turn to the work of Disney or of Strube;
>   There stands our hero in his threadbare seams;
> The bowler hat who strap-hangs in the tube,
>   And kicks the tyrant only in his dreams,
>   Trading on pathos, dreading all extremes;
> The little Mickey with the hidden grudge;
> Which is the better, I leave you to judge.
>
> Begot on Hire Purchase by Insurance,
>   Forms at his christening worshipped and adored;
> A season ticket schooled him in endurance,
>   A tax collector and a waterboard
>   Admonished him. In boyhood he was awed
> By a matric, and complex apparatuses
> Keep his heart conscious of Divine Afflatuses.
>
> (Auden 1974: 52)

It is important to remember that this section of the poem is addressing much the same worry as Priestley, namely the susceptibility of suburban man to Fascism. Is this the sort of man, the poem is asking, who will resist the ogre of Fascism? The answer is that he will not, but whereas Priestley gives a broadly economic and sociological explanation ('Monotonous but easy work and a liberal supply of cheap luxuries might between them create a

set of people entirely without ambition or any real desire to think and act
for themselves, the perfect subject for an iron autocracy'), Auden's account
is more fully psychological and indeed dialectical:

> The ogre knows his man.
> To kill the ogre that would take away
> The fear in which his happy dreams began,
> And with his life he'll guard dreams while he can.
> Those who would really kill his dream's contentment
> He hates with real implacable resentment.
>
> (Auden 1974: 53)

Here suburban man's relationship to authority – comically belittled in the
authority figures of petty-bourgeois life – means that he requires the pleas-
ure of rebellion in fantasy but hates the prospect of being liberated from
that fantasy by real revolution. This is engaging and indeed penetrating, but
not unmarked by that *de haut* haughtiness that is so much more marked in
Betjeman. Francis Hope's comment in the sixties about the thirties retains
at least some of its force: 'the barrister's clerk sneered at the clerk's, and
called it socialism' (Hope 1984: 181).

And of course, we can add to this catalogue the C. Day Lewis of 'Letter
to a Young Revolutionary'. He too is considering the commuters on the
train out of the city:

> Before long the whole crew will be scurrying back to their burrows.
> They will sit in front of football matches, films, radios, novels, inflamed
> hearts watching action they cannot emulate, revelling in situations to
> which they dare not aspire, envying a life they haven't the guts to create.
> A few in their allotments, a barren soil, try to revive their severed roots.
> Is this the best we can do?
> And now, the country at last. Past factories, sports grounds, tame
> rusticity of 'garden cities', bogus Elizabethan villas, petrol stations
> disguised as mosques, chapels like mausoleums and amusement parks like
> death. The country at last.
>
> (Day Lewis 1933: 39–40)

Just to flog the point to death, this of course reproduces not only the snob-
bism of 'Slough' but also the same romantic suspicion of the inauthenticity
of suburban existence. If the inhabitants of Slough do not know the birdsong
from the radio, and drink in 'bogus Tudor bars', the inhabitants of these
more anonymous suburbs of Day Lewis's live in equally bogus Elizabethan
villas and live out a fantasy, compensatory life in front of the forms of new
mass entertainment.

It should be said that this Day Lewis is not the Day Lewis of his poetry,
where the suburbs scarcely figure. There is perhaps a submerged thematics
of the suburban landscape in the largely allegorical landscape of *The Magnetic Mountain*. Thus the 'enemies' of the poem – four figures representing

some kind of modern lust, newspaper proprietors, ultra-rationalists, and escapist Georgian poets – are condemned:

> These drowned the farms to form a pleasure-lake
> In time of drought they drain the reservoir
> Through private pipes for baths and sprinklers.

They live 'At bay in villas from blood-relations'. And the bourgeois, more explicitly, are to be found thus:

> Bent double with lackeying, the joints out of place;
> Behind bluffs and lucky charms hiding to evade
> An overdue audit, anaemic, afraid.
> Trimmers and schemers, pusillanimous dreamers,
> At cinemas, shop-windows and arenas we've found them
> Bearing witness to a life beyond them.
> They're paying for death on the instalment plan
> Who hoped to go higher and failed to be men.
>
> (Day Lewis 1954: 107, 117)

This last extract certainly reproduces the thematics so far elicited – the suburbs as arena of inauthentic lives, coupled with contempt for the failure of suburban man to *be* a man given the absurdity of the problems that beset him. The susceptibility of suburban people to the mass media is another aspect of these same thematics, and links in to it the recurrent critique of the mass media that runs through the thirties and which Day Lewis himself articulated powerfully in 'Newsreel'.

One further point of comparison between 'Slough' and 'Letter to Lord Byron'; both are comic poems, or to use Auden's own term, 'light verse'. I allude to this obvious point because both poems are particular resolutions of the problem of genre that besets writing about the suburbs in the thirties (though of course 'Letter to Lord Byron' is not only or even explicitly about the suburbs). If we glance back to Priestley's account of the matter, we will remember that he complained, as a novelist, of the failure of his third England to supply much material for him – or at least, material that would come strongly marked with its own inherent interest. That is not to say that novelists could not find ways of handling suburban life in the thirties; plainly they could, via modes that included both the ironic and the sympathetic. But I think that poetry had a different problem, or at least poetry which wished to escape the pervasiveness of an ironic attitude. Perhaps I am inventing difficulties here, but I can focus them by recalling a friend of mine at university who used to write quite accomplished poems in a Wordsworthian manner, full of lines like: 'So once again I tread the road to Warlingham . . .' In retrospect I am very uncertain about the absurdity of this, or at least I am suspicious of myself for finding such a line absurd. The point is simply this: was there a poetic genre available in the thirties

115

that might both avoid this absurdity (if it is absurd) and equally avoid the temptations of irony and the mock-heroic? If there was, would the poets have used it?

I use 'genre' here in a broadly Bakhtinian sense, in which it is an inescapable aspect of all utterances, providing the manner in which relations between speaker and listener (or writer and reader) are mediated. It dictates the level of seriousness of the topic, provides characteristic inflections and disposes the participants in any dialogue in determinate mutual relations. At all these points, questions of social class are pressing hard upon the utterance. But a manner of speaking and writing must be *learnt*; genres are not spontaneous. The generic repertoire thus provides an inherited and partly unconscious set of ways of mediating social relations entailing certain relations between writer, reader and topic.

The point of invoking these matters here is that at all these points poetic writing in the thirties was in crisis. In crisis at the level of the relation between writer and reader – for which see the endless debates about the 'difficulty' of contemporary poetry, a question appearing with its particular inflections and urgencies in the debates on the Left about the place of poetry, propaganda, and so on. In crisis too at the level of topic, above all with respect to the handling of the contemporary urban world – we shall come back to this point. And in difficulties, when it comes to writing about the suburbs, about the level of seriousness with which the topic should be treated. This is not to say that there were no appropriate generic models available to these poets, but that these models entailed a set of relations that are in part class relations. Thus Auden's adoption of the mock-heroic, with its roots in Augustan culture, certainly entails a set of relations with his readers that include a shared civility, a consciousness of a set of shared allusions, and an invitation to admire his own bravura performance in the form. I say these things in absolutely no critical spirit – they simply seem to me to be part of the relations of intelligibility which the genre entails.

These matters are discussed by Michael Roberts in his preface to the *New Signatures* anthology, in the following terms:

> It was inevitable that the growth of industrialism should give rise to a 'difficult' poetry. Because our civilisation has hitherto depended directly on agriculture, and because our thoughts have hitherto made use of images taken from a rural life, our urban and industrial society leaves us uncomfortable and nostalgic. Rural poetry in recent years has been, in general, a cowardly escape into the past, whilst urban poetry, the poetry of the machine age, has seemed, even to intelligent and conscientious critics, abrupt, discordant, intellectual. It is hard to find words relating to city life which are such powerful emotive symbols as those which poets have used for centuries, and the reader, not being swept off his feet at once by a poem, reverses the proper order and spends his time puzzling

out the plain sense of a passage (which is seldom as difficult as Donne, never as difficult as Shakespeare), before he allows any scope at all to imagery and sound; he becomes 'too intellectual'.

(Roberts 1934: 8)

This is an interesting case. Implicit in it is an account of the way that readers read, where the difficulty for contemporary poetry is simply the un-familiarity of the characteristic images in it drawn from contemporary urban life. The logic of this is indeed that you have only got to include such images often enough for the right emotional (and not 'intellectual') response to become automatic. But matters are plainly not as simple as that. Roberts is surely right to say that such responses are not simply natural, but are the result of attitudes that have been constructed by particular social histories. But I do not think that he takes this point far enough. It is not simply that people got used to one set of responses because they lived in the country; now they live in cities they will have to get used to another. It is also that both those old genres, and any potential new genres, carry with them a set of social relations, however implicit. It is just the set of social relations – and hence genre – that writers found so difficult to negotiate when writing about the suburbs.

These difficulties are apparent, for example, in MacNeice's 'Birming-ham'. I want to start with the final stanza of the poem:

On shining lines the trams like vast sarcophagi move
Into the sky, plum after sunset, merging to duck's egg, barred with
     mauve
Zeppelin clouds, and Pentecost-like the cars' headlights bud
Out from the sideroads and the traffic-signals, crême-de-menthe or bull's
     blood,
Tell one to stop, the engine gently breathing, or to go on.

Perhaps the first thing to say about these lines is that MacNeice is working very hard in them. This is a very elaborate set of comparisons to be draw-ing; MacNeice is straining to transform the urban landscape. Yet one should add that he is doing so to considerable effect. This is a valiant effort to do – not quite what Roberts was describing in that preface to *New Signatures* – but perhaps its opposite. This is a poetry of redemptive transformation, in which the items of an up-to-the-minute contemporaneity (cars, traffic lights, less so perhaps trams) are defamiliarised and reclaimed by the evident imaginative work performed upon them by the poet. It is important, it seems to me, that the point of view should be from inside the car.

Earlier in the poem, though certainly not separated from these lines by any vast aesthetic gulf, occurs a stanza on the suburbs:

Splayed outwards through the suburbs houses, houses for rest
Seducingly rigged by the builder, half-timbered houses with lips pressed

So tightly and eyes staring at the traffic through bleary haws
And only a six-inch grip of the racing earth in their concrete claws;
In these houses men as in a dream pursue the Platonic Forms
With wirelesses and cairn terriers and gadgets approximating to the fickle
    norms
And endeavour to find God and score one over the neighbour
By climbing tentatively upward on jerry-built beauty and sweated labour.
                                (MacNeice 1979: 17–18)

Here too one can see this same effort of imaginative transformation, especially in the way that the houses have taken on human – or is it animal?
– characteristics. But this seems to me not to work in the same way as the
later section of the poem, if only because this transformation is not redemptive. This is the writing of imaginative documentary, seen in effect from
outside, as the car in which the poet is travelling makes its way through
the suburbs. The implicit social relations in the passage are constituted by
the relationship between poet and reader, the poet providing a report to
the reader on the novel social reality to be viewed from his car window.
In these circumstances the lives on which he reports simply cannot be
imagined as being lived with full seriousness or authenticity.

(Perhaps another footnote here is called for on the perspective created
by the motor car. Most of the accounts that I have given of the suburbs
have been written by writers passing through the suburbs on the way to
other places ('And now, the country at last') – even Priestley, who never
stops in the suburbs, and who indeed completed his English journey in his
car – a chauffeur-driven one. An extreme, futurist-style case might be made
for the car as an agent of sensory transformation, and you could perhaps
quote passages like that final stanza of 'Birmingham' as evidence in such a
case. But it is also true that the car journey through the suburbs becomes
emblematic of the social relations encapsulated in many of these accounts.)

If this is true of 'Birmingham', it is perhaps still more true of sections
of 'Autumn Journal', in particular the section describing the trip to Oxford
for the by-election:

    The next day I drove by night
        Among red and amber and green, spears and candles,
    Corkscrews and slivers of reflected light
        In the mirror of the rainy asphalt
    Along the North Circular and the Great West roads
        Running the gauntlet of impoverished fancy
    Where housewives bolster up their jerry-built abodes
        With *amour propre* and the habit of Hire Purchase.
    The wheels whished in the wet, the flashy strings
        Of neon lights unravelled, the windscreen-wiper
    Kept at its job like a tiger in a cage or a cricket that sings
        All night through for nothing.

Factory, a site for a factory, rubbish dumps,
  Bungalows in lath and plaster, in brick, in concrete,
And shining semi-circles of petrol pumps
  Like intransigent gangs of idols.

(MacNeice 1979: 127)

This repeats some of the characteristic aesthetic gestures of 'Birmingham', written five years earlier. There is the intense interest in the aesthetic sensations produced by driving a car on a wet night ('Corkscrews and slivers of reflected light / In the mirror of the rainy asphalt') and the same effort to find the transforming metaphor or simile. This is in part a question of finding an appropriate genre for writing about the mundane and the ordinary; the North Circular and the Great West roads figure here merely as aspects of the sheer irredeemable presentness of things. But they are also, along with the suburbs that surround them on either side, symbols of what the world has become; it is with this world that the poet must deal, and there is sometimes a sense, in reading MacNeice, of him making the best of a bad job. When it comes to writing about the suburban houses and their inhabitants, there is the characteristic gesture of reading off the lives of the inhabitants from the architecture they inhabit: 'Where housewives bolster up their jerry-built abodes / With *amour propre* and the habit of hire purchase'. The zeugma here is interesting, and can be compared with the zeugmas in 'Birmingham' ('Endeavour to find God and score one over the neighbour'; and 'By climbing tentatively upward on jerry-built beauty and sweated labour'). This typical MacNeicean figure can be read as a generic marker; it is a figure used here as one of reductive comparison, indeed of bathos. While it is one of the strengths of his poetry that it constantly seeks to find satisfactory categories and explanations for what he writes about (and then problematises those explanations), when those explanations or categories emerge from a position solely external to the social landscape he is describing he is liable to adopt a mode which is frankly reductive.

However, my own argument is now in danger of becoming reductive. I don't want to argue that these generic difficulties – how to find a way of writing which treats the lives of the inhabitants of the suburbs with appropriate seriousness – can be easily resolved by writers who inhabit the suburbs rather than by those who only pass through. Stevie Smith's poem 'Suburb', for example, reproduces some of the generic difficulties that I have been describing, though of course in her very own characteristic idiom:

Round about the streets I slink
Suburbs are not so bad I think
When their inhabitants can not be seen,
Even Palmers Green.
Nobody loves the hissing rain as I

> And round about I slink
> And presently
> Turn from the sleek wet pavements to the utter slime
> Where jerrybuilders building against time
> Pursue their storied way,
> Foundations and a pram,
> Four walls and a pot of jam,
> They have their sentries now
> Upon a hundred hillocks . . .
> Do you see that pub between the trees
> Which advertises gin and cyclists' teas?
> Down there I know a lane
> Under the padding rain
> Where leaves are born again
> Every night
> And reach maturity
> In a remote futurity
> Before dawn's light.
> I have never seen
> Anything quite so green
> So close so dark so bright
> As the green leaves at night . . .

(Smith 1978: 57–9)

Does it make a difference here that the point of view of this poem is that of a pedestrian inhabitant of the suburb in question (albeit one who slinks about at night), rather than a motoring correspondent? Well, it doesn't and it does. The poem certainly shares some of those characteristic generic dispositions that we have been discussing – the reading off of inauthentic lives from inauthentic architecture and the trivial paraphernalia of petty-bourgeois lives. Furthermore, it shares with 'Slough' and MacNeice's poems the belief that it is possible to measure that inauthenticity by invoking the forms of the natural world – in this case even the greenery of a suburban wood (actually I think these are very powerfully imagined: 'I have never seen . . . as the green leaves at night'; lines which take their point, following on from Keats, that their particular intensity of greenness is produced as an act of imagination, since of course they can't actually be seen at night). And finally, the poem shares that pervasive comic irony at the suburbs' expense, its tone inviting shared humour at the pub which offers gin and cyclists' teas (the reductive zeugma again).

And yet, this is clearly not the whole story of this poem. The witty and self-mocking misanthropy is aware of no other *social* perspective by which to measure the inhabitants of Palmers Green, so that the ironies of the poem are self-consuming ones. Stevie Smith, in other words, transforms the thematics of thirties suburban poetry in ways that push the poem towards self-destruction or tonal illegibility. This seems to me to be the fate of another of her poems which take the suburbs as its explicit topic rather than simply its assumed landscape: 'The Suburban Classes'.

> There is far too much of the suburban classes
> Spiritually not geographically speaking. They're asses.
> Menacing the greatness of our beloved England, they lie
> Propagating their kind in an eightroomed stye.
> Now I have a plan which I will enfold
> (There's this to be said for them, they do as they're told)
> Then tell them their country's in mortal peril
> [ . . . ]
> 'Your King and Your Country need you Dead'
> You see the idea? Well, let it spread.
> Have a suitable drug under string and label
> Free for every Registered Reader's table.
> For the rest of the gang who are not patriotic
> I've another appeal they'll discover hypnotic:
> Tell them it's smart to be dead and won't hurt
> And they'll gobble up drug as they gobble up dirt.

(p. 27)

The ferocious ironies of this are difficult to disentangle, since it starts as a poem which appears to be going in one direction, and ends by going in the opposite direction – I think. We are certainly in a familiar area in one respect – the susceptibility of the suburban classes to mass suggestion, particularly through the mass media ('If they see it in print it is bound to stick'), and particularly of a patriotic kind. So the poem begins with an irony against a speaking voice – perhaps of a Lord Kitchener-type politician, perhaps of a Lord Rothermere-type newspaper proprietor – who horribly exaggerates his contempt for the suburban classes. But the reader is not allowed to decode this irony too simply against this unpleasant persona, because what it says has a force that grows more forceful as the poem continues. In addition to the suggestion that the suburban classes are susceptible to the power of print, is the suggestion that they are still more in the grip of fashion or of what's 'smart' (though the 'rest of the gang who are not patriotic' might or might not be a section of the suburban classes). The physical repulsion of the last line, in particular, carries the reader quite into the state of mind of the previously ironised speaking voice. Once again, the poem takes up some of the themes that we have seen handled by other poets of the decade, and restates them with a gleeful and disconcerting directness; but like 'Suburb' also, the ironies here are self-consuming and suggest no outside perspective on the topic of the poem, unless it be the complexities of the performance itself.

For the final poem that I wish to discuss, I shall revert to Stephen Spender, rather unfairly represented so far only by a passage from *Forward from Liberalism*. I have discussed the implicit social relations suggested by the

121

poet *travelling through* the suburbs; in 'Landscape near an Aerodrome', of course, the perspective is derived from an air-liner as it 'glides over' the suburbs. Characteristically for Spender in his enthusiasm for machines, he can't write about them without inviting comparison with an organic object; in this case, however, the moth than which the air liner is more beautiful curiously softens and humanises it, so that the impression is the reverse of the hard-edged futurist rhetoric of 'The Express'. The aesthetic problem of the suburb is partially resolved by the device of the airborne perspective, if only because it permits a kind of social mapping to which all landscape is in principle subject. But it is also resolved because Spender permits himself that vulnerable admission of 'love' – 'In the last sweep of love, they pass over fields' – so that even the suburbs are included in the benign perspective. The third stanza provides the fullest account of the suburban landscape:

> Beyond the winking masthead light
> And the landing ground, they observe the outposts
> Of work: chimneys like lank black fingers
> Or figures, frightening and mad; and squat buildings
> With their strange air behind trees, like women's faces
> Shattered by grief. Here where few houses
> Moan with faint light behind their blinds
> They remark the unholy sense of complaint, like a dog
> Shut out, and shivering at the foreign moon.
>
> (Spender 1985: 41)

Of course, this is not quite the Jacobethan landscape that we have been concerned with in this chapter, though it certainly is the third England of Priestley's *English Journey*; this is the landscape round Hendon or Croydon, where in addition to the few houses there is the evidence of light industry which made the prosperity of London between the wars. Spender, like MacNeice, has expended a quantity of aesthetic *work* on this landscape, most visibly in the persistent use of simile – every manmade element of the landscape duly gets its placing comparison. None of them comes off well, and perhaps this is only right for the nondescript and unplanned developments on the fringes of London between the wars. Factories appear threatening, or perhaps mystifying (are those the new factories that 'look like an exhibition hall' which have that 'strange air behind trees'?). The suburban houses, when they do appear, do so in a familiar mode, revealing to the travellers on the air-liner their 'unhomely sense of complaint' – as ever the poet demonstrating a capacity to deduce the inhabitants' spiritual state from the external appearance of their dwellings.

It has often been remarked about this poem that the tone gets out of control at its conclusion: 'Religion stands, the church blocking the sun.'

My interest in the poem, however, focuses on a moment that shortly precedes that overdramatic conclusion:

> In the last sweep of love, they pass over fields
> Behind the aerodrome, where boys play all day
> Hacking dead grass; whose cries, like wild birds,
> Settle upon the nearest roofs,
> But soon are hid under the loud city.
>
> Then, as they land, they hear the tolling bell
> Reaching across the landscape of hysteria . . .

Just whose hysteria is this? Is the suburban landscape itself hysterical, a metonymic extension of the hysteria of its inhabitants? Or does the hysteria spread from the sound of the tolling bell, so that only in that distorted religious perspective does this otherwise benignly perceived landscape appear hysterical? Or, finally, is the poem admitting here its surrealist colouring, the landscape being transformed by unconscious processes? At all events, some process of transference or projection is occurring, giving the relationships in the poem, of poet to social landscape, a particular vividness and intensity. This is a further twist on the generic possibilities that I have attempted to sketch in this essay. When the landscape of suburbia becomes the landscape of hysteria, those generic relationships, implicitly social ones, begin to dissolve into the ambiguities of projection that were always threatening them.

## REFERENCES

**Auden W.H.** 1974 *Collected Longer Poems* (London: Faber & Faber)
**Betjeman J.** 1931 *Mount Zion* (London: James Press)
—— 1988 *Collected Poems* (London: John Murray)
**Cunningham V.** 1988 *British Writers of the Thirties* (Oxford: Oxford University Press)
**Day Lewis C.** 1933 'Letter to a Young Revolutionary', in M. Roberts (ed.) *New Country* (London: Hogarth Press)
—— 1954 *Collected Poems* (London: Hogarth Press)
**Hope F.** 1984 'The Thirties', in R. Carter (ed.) *Thirties Poets: 'The Auden Group'* (London: Macmillan)
**Huxley A.** 1971 *Brave New World* (Harmondsworth: Penguin)
**MacNeice L.** 1979 *Collected Poems* (London: Faber & Faber)
**Priestley J.B.** 1984 *English Journey* (Chicago: University of Chicago Press)
**Roberts M.** 1934 *New Signatures* (London: Hogarth Press)
**Skelton R.** (ed.) 1979 *Poetry of the Thirties* (Harmondsworth: Penguin)
**Smith S.** 1978 *Selected Poems*, James MacGibbon (ed.) (Harmondsworth: Penguin)
**Spender S.** 1937 *Forward from Liberalism* (London: Gollancz, Left Book Club edn)
—— 1985 *Collected Poems 1928–1985* (London: Faber)

# CHAPTER NINE

# Politics and Beauty: the Poetry of Randall Swingler

ANDY CROFT

> 'Regard this sun-haired boy
> easy in the roaring circus
> reading Maxim Gorky on an island
> with buses bulging past,
> preoccupied with beauty.'[1]

'Why do they all write like each other, and, if they must write like each other, why should it be like this?' The *Spectator* was clearly unimpressed by what it called the 'Advance-Guard Actions' of modernism in English poetry in late 1933:

> Does it come naturally to them? One cannot think so. Are they all imitating some admired example? No one writer whose influence would account for it springs to mind. Yet there is something which causes dozens of young writers . . . to produce this sort of work. Under the stress of this prevailing fashion, very few professedly 'modern' poets preserve their integrity. . . . Whatever this influence is, it is in no sense a 'literary' influence.[2]

The four new collections here under review – George Barker's *Thirty Preliminary Poems*, Laura Riding's *Poet: A Lying Word*, John Pudney's *Spring Encounter* and *Difficult Morning* by Randall Swingler – seemed representative enough to require some general observations about contemporary English poetry under the dreadful shadow of the 'modern':

> The ideals that inspire such writers are not aesthetic; they care very little for reading; beauty means little to them, and style less. Their interests are in politics, in progress, in society; in economics, in psychology, in the sciences. They scent an impending social revolution, and they mean to be its brains. But one wonders why they choose to write poetry. Why cannot they be content to behave as if this were the kind of thing they would write if poetry were forced upon them? And if they must write, why do they publish it?

Barker and Riding went on to acquire very considerable critical reputations, while Pudney later enjoyed a popular following during the Second World War as a 'People's Poet'. Randall Swingler, however, is almost entirely forgotten today, except, perhaps, as one of the 'pet literary Alsatians' of the British Communist Party in the late thirties.[3] And yet in December 1933, most reviewers had no doubt which of these four young poets showed the most promise:

> Of all the writers at present before us, Miss Riding and Mr Barker give no indication of possessing any literary ability; only of Mr Pudney and Mr Swingler can it be said that fashion has claimed from them the sacrifice of any poetic gifts. . . . Mr Swingler seems to be altogether much more of a poet, but temperamentally less fitted to withstand the influence of his contemporaries. He can write a beautiful poem . . . and he loves words (a test of a poet, though not commonly admitted nowadays to be one); but he is dreadfully prone to indulge in false verbiage . . . and in the conventional Communist (or is it Nazi?) poetic cant.

Contemporary criticism is of course a notoriously bad guide to literary reputations (although it is also one of the crucial ways in which reputations are made or broken). The *Spectator*'s judgements may seem wrong-headed now, but its apprehension of the 'modern' must seem even odder. It is a warning, perhaps, against exaggerating the presence of modernist ideas in English poetry in the thirties, more particularly against over-estimating the extent to which those ideas were either recognised or understood. These are the lines of Swingler's to which the *Spectator* took particular exception:

> Hardy when friended is the salt north to redeem
> Self that demands whines postures and hoards its time.
> Fatal as turbine possessed with power, so long
> The private will's combustion has churned through
> A miasmal landscape, everywhere superimposing
> Precociously its own synthetic image.[4]

The absence of definite and indefinite articles, the inverted syntax, the stressed feet at the beginning of the lines, the language of machinery set in a mythic Northern landscape – this stanza seems of course now unmistakeably *Audenesque*, an awkward gesture towards a second-hand manner. What these four books demonstrated was nothing more than the apparently irresistible attractions of Auden to younger poets. The fact that the *Spectator* did not recognise this influence for what it was says something about the limits of any literary reputation at the time of its making. It also suggests a rather more limited sense of modernism than is generally assumed in discussions of English poetry in the thirties. First, it simply meant the 'new'; second, the 'modern' was commonly identified with a new, generational poetic which has come to be called the Audenesque; third, the Audenesque seemed to represent forces at best indifferent to poetry, at worse dangerous to its creation, forces above all hostile to 'beauty'. Modernism spoke for other intellectual categories than poetry – progress, science, economics, psychology and politics. And these politics seemed to be identifiably continental, ideological, threatening.

This is not, of course, how we usually consider literary modernism (the assumed association of Communist politics with modernism is particularly striking). And yet it seemed like critical common sense sixty years ago. For the London poetry scene was still dominated by the Georgians, and arguably remained so throughout the thirties. After all, Robert Bridges had only recently published *Testament of Beauty* – *seven years* after the publication of *The Waste Land*. Bridges was appointed Poet Laureate in 1930, the year in which the *Collected Poems* of both Hardy and Blunden were published; Helen Thomas's memoir *World Without End* appeared in 1931, so did Blunden's edition of Wilfred Owen; Houseman did not die until 1936, the year Sassoon's *Sherston's Progress* was first published. Most London literary journals remained resolutely Georgian in sympathy throughout the decade, and the reviewing columns of newspapers were still dominated by writers who had made their reputations before or immediately after the First World War – John Drinkwater, Richard Church, L.P. Hartley, Robert Lynd, Arnold Bennett, David Garnett, Gilbert Frankau, Guy Pocock, Wilfred Gibson, Humbert Wolfe. When the Australian poet Jack Lindsay arrived in London in 1926 to spearhead an attack on English literary culture, it was, as the name of his magazine suggests, aimed at Jack Squire and the *London Mercury*. But Lindsay's *London Aphrodite* was equally vociferous in its attacks on Eliot and the *Criterion*. And neither argument involved importing modernist aesthetics from the Continent.

Of course there were some important modernist bridgeheads – *New Verse*, *Twentieth-Century Verse*, *Contemporary Poetry and Prose*, the *Criterion*. But *Twentieth-Century Verse* only lasted two years, *New Verse* only six, and *Contemporary Poetry and Prose* only eighteen months. The *Criterion* was selling only 200 copies a month. They were none of them serious rivals to the *London Mercury*, and all four journals had folded by the end of the decade. Anyway, Geoffrey Grigson was always rather less interested in promoting modernism in the pages of *New Verse* than he was in promoting Auden. And although Auden's verse-dramas may have imported a kind of second-hand Expressionism on to the London stage, it is hard to describe his poetry after *The Orators* as 'modernist', even if the Audenesque was by then readily identified as the nearest equivalent (Surrealism apart) to the 'modern' in English poetry. If English fiction in the thirties demonstrated any debt to the modernist novel it was to Jules Romains rather than Kafka, Dos Passos rather than Joyce.[5] The great English modernist writers of the twenties (and there were never that many) were either dead (Lawrence), in exile (Aldous Huxley, Richard Aldington, Nancy Cunard), or silent – Edith Sitwell published almost no poetry for a decade after *Gold Coast Customs* (1929). By the early thirties Eliot's anti-semitism had effectively isolated him from second-generation Bloomsbury; Douglas Garman, whose *The Jaded Hero* (1927) had been one of the few successful attempts to follow Eliot's example, was by the middle thirties working full-time for the Communist Party, where he joined other poets and critics from the proto-Modernist *Calendar of Modern Letters* such as Edgell Rickword, A.L. Morton and Jack Lindsay in the intellectual culture of the Popular Front. By the end of the thirties even Virginia Woolf was writing for the *Daily Worker*.

To say that some of the High Modernist literary texts appeared to have outlived their usefulness by the thirties is not to argue that the movement among English letters towards Marxism and the Communist Party involved a repudiation of modernism. The post-Georgian, left-Leavisite 'Anglo-Communism' of that generation of writers who found their way into the Communist Party in the thirties did not reject modernism *per se*. (That came later, as a reaction to the re-invention of modernism in the late forties as the arts establishment of the Cold War.)[6] It was simply that, as the career of Randall Swingler suggests, modernism was not the only way of addressing the issues of modernity. The new and the experimental never lost their appeal for Swingler, but that sense of newness was not restricted to the poetry of Eliot. It was there for him in younger poets – particularly Auden, later Dylan Thomas – as well as older ones like Edward Thomas and Robert Bridges. Most of Swingler's verse in the thirties was written a long way from the intellectual capitals of modernism, firmly rooted in the rural landscapes of the Georgians. The story of Swingler's poetry in these years is the story of a writer living in the Modern world but inhabiting a premodern literary culture. Negotiating the claims of both, Swingler eventually cleared a passage for a distinctive poetry of his own, a body of work that was neither modernist nor anti-modernist, somewhere between Auden and Bridges, politics and beauty.

The reasons why Swingler's work has fallen into neglect lie outside the scope of this chapter, though it is fair to say that his cause has not been helped by the version of literary history shared by both modernist and anti-Communist critical orthodoxies, which assumes that modernism was an unqualified improvement on the Georgians, and that because the Communist writers of the thirties supposedly rejected modernism, they could not move forward except into slogans, bad faith or silence. Such is the Myth of the thirties. There can be few writers who fit so comfortably into the Myth of the thirties as Swingler; there is none whose career invalidates it so completely.[7] In other words, the poetry of a long-forgotten poet like Randall

Swingler may tell us more about the contours of English literary culture in the thirties than the work of writers who are better known today largely because they helped to construct that Myth.

Randall Swingler was born in 1909 into a wealthy and privileged Edwardian household. His father was an Anglican priest, his uncle, Randall Davidson, the Archbishop of Canterbury; one of his grandfathers was a colonel in the Indian Army, the other an Iron Master from Derby. His great-grandmother was a cousin of Sir Walter Scott. After governesses and a preparatory school in Sussex Swingler went to Winchester, then New College, Oxford, where he read Classical Greats, earned a running Blue, rowed for his College, played in the University Orchestra, was secretary of the Mermaids' Society and published his first poems. After Oxford he taught at a preparatory school in London. He married the concert pianist Geraldine Peppin, and they left London to live in the Cotswolds. Desmond Hawkins writes:

> Randall Swingler leaves a particularly strong impression on my mind. Physically he resembled a quieter, unemphatic Auden. A golden straw-thatch of hair and intensely blue eyes gave him a Scandinavian look. When I first knew him, he and his wife Gerry lived at Milton-under-Wychwood. In this Cotswold setting Randall looked every inch a poet in the romantic English tradition. Great things were expected of him. . . . To visit them at Milton was to make a firm connection with a very English cultural continuity. Partly it was the landscape . . . the warm positive affirmation of Cotswold stone, the bright air stirring with the exuberance of downland, the ability to look over and across so much that was quintessentially English. Partly it was the quality of the rural cottage-home, the high endeavour and the gaiety, the dawning parenthood and the exulting ambitions that we shared. Of all my friends they had most conspicuously a steady tranquillity of spirit. I thought of Randall as a man wholly dedicated to the poetic role for which he seemed so well endowed.[8]

Swingler's first collection, *Poems*, was published in April 1932 by the Shakespeare's Head Press in Oxford. Dedicated to 'her, to whom only they belong already', the book consisted of twenty-two love poems for Geraldine, mostly written between April and September 1931:

> As you lay sleeping, out of the extreme
> Serenity of your face arose my dream:
> That we had found the delectable hill which climbs
> Out of all common clangour, where golden limes
> Stoop with solitary gesture, shy and tall
> As if some god had checked them with a cry
> Circling in slow pavan – and there you lay
> Among the grass, and I that ran all day
> Beside you, with no weariness at all
> Could watch you sleeping now interminably.[9]

The Cotswolds, Sherborne and Lulworth – the location of this poetry is a conventionally Georgian landscape:

> Over the down the light softens and pales
> With a fluster of moths: and gulls searching the night
> Like ghosts go misting along their unseen trails
> Or stand in effortless poise at the taut wind's height,
> Moon-coloured arrows caught on the brink of leaping.[10]

The same month, however, John Lehmann published Michael Roberts's *New Signatures*, the anthology which first brought the poetry of Auden, Day Lewis and Spender to a wider audience. Swingler immediately bought a copy, and must have been struck by the very different conception of poetry it proclaimed. Whereas his ideas about poetry had derived from Bridges, Brooke, Thomas and Houseman (and Keats, Shelley and Blake), *New Signatures* rejected what Roberts called 'obsolete technique' and 'sentimental feeling', calling on the contemporary poet instead to be 'abreast of his own times' in order to 'express precisely those subtleties of thought and feeling in which he differs from his predecessors'.[11]

The following summer, Swingler published his second book of poems. The break with the work of *Poems* could not have been more clear. *Reconstruction* contains only six poems from a much longer work about the impact of London – the 'snore of metal' and the 'traffic's shingle-roar', 'sprawling industry's benighted limbs', and the 'rank allotment'. Swingler was reconstructing himself as an urban poet, renouncing the rural landscape of his previous poetry in favour of the 'Tentacular town'. This poetry was a political as well as an emotional response to London. The 'jungle-city' becomes 'perplexed England', her 'self-contained defensive / houses' ruined by 'that power which division squanders, that poor love / that rots in hoarding'. In 'Ode to a Plane Above the City' the plane has the larger vision which recognises that the city – and therefore England – also contains its salvation in the 'common music' heard across the city, in 'the tenement yard / whose washing flags the defiant week'. The easy elision of urban pastoral and rural wasteland, and the apocalyptic glow with which each poem ends, sounds like something from *New Signatures*, or better, Michael Roberts's next anthology, *New Country*:

> Vehement in their fear we saw the middle class withdraw
> To patch up their old house, benignly disregarding
> The landslip near the garage and the empty well
> Discovered under the floor.
>
> Futile they bar their doors against the beleaguering future
> With signification of time's foreshortened values still,
> Like where on glad sands shining bodies laugh,
> The mobled shark moves near the shore.

> Plunging through these unheroic ruins, bugle to lip,
> Coarser we seem than once, uprooting the dunghill,
> Until by barest poverty unthinking we arrive
> At true delight of the sun, the elemental touch.[12]

*Reconstruction* looks now very period, highly derivative, reaching after the manner of early Auden, Spender or Day Lewis. Samuel Hynes has suggested that it is a good example of the way in which, by 1933 the 'thirties generation was its own influence'.[13] Between Georgianism and Communism there was only one available voice – the Audenesque – of which Swingler's writing seems a poor, but typical example. As the *Spectator* noted, *Reconstruction* was the product of a 'habit of mind which, in its preoccupation with certain psycho-sociological problems of today, has become almost *de rigueur* among poets of the post-War generation, and which places Mr Swingler geographically, if not politically, alongside of Mr Auden and Mr Day Lewis':

> Mr Swingler is another of these young men (I suspect) who get
> themselves into trouble in a variety of places for being 'obscure' . . . On
> occasion they come dangerously near to private-code productions and
> one is not always sure, after unravelling the significance of a passage that
> the intellectual effort involved is repaid, poetically, by the result. . . .
> Like Mr Day Lewis he is all for a fresh start, for cutting the cable and
> finding a new Promised Land. The difficulty, as always, is to know
> which way to set the helm. Mr Swingler offers us only hopeful hints, a
> solution in too general terms. Reduced to a crude statement his poems
> are an earnest of a better time coming or, failing on our part the will
> and insight to achieve this, an uncomfortable catastrophe. The burden is
> not new, and in voicing it Mr Swingler is less specific in attack and no
> more positive in recommendation than others of his contemporaries.[14]

But if Randall Swingler sacrificed his 'poetic gifts' for the Audenesque, he also made the mistake of taking the political rhetoric of the Audenesque seriously enough to join the Communist Party. Soon after the publication of *Reconstruction* Swingler gave his inherited wealth to the Party, returned to London and threw himself into day-to-day political activity – speaking at Communist Party and YCL rallies, lecturing at Marx House and addressing Left Book Club meetings. He wrote pamphlets for the Communist Party, propagandist plays for Unity Theatre and political songs for the Workers' Music Association; he edited *Left Review* and the books page of the *Daily Worker*. And he did not publish another collection of poetry for the rest of the decade. It would be hard to find a better example of the myth of the thirties, a young man of Great Possessions who betrayed his inheritance, the faith of his fathers and his career as a poet for a lost cause.[15] Even if he is remembered now only as a footnote to the period, no one apparently illustrates better than Swingler the thesis that politics and poetry (or as the

*Spectator* saw it, the 'modern' and the beautiful) are mutually antagonistic worlds.

There are, however, serious problems with this kind of account, although there is not enough space here to do more than indicate some of the main issues raised by Swingler's relationship with the 'modern' which, taken together, might suggest a different way of considering the history of English poetry in the thirties.

We may consider first the question of the source of the dramatic changes in Swingler's poetry between *Poems* and *Reconstruction*. This is more than simply a matter of identifying the influences on one particular writer since it requires a larger re-evaulation of the origin of the 'modern' whose presence in English poetry so alarmed the *Spectator*. Consider the following poem:

> But the young men are moving together:
> Have felt the reservoirs crack, have seen
> The shadows lurch down from the hills and the meadow green
> Grown lurid beneath the grave thunder-weather.
>
> The young limbs stir from sleep: as yet
> Outward towards the fingers runs
> The swift blood, always out from the heart: will soon
> The marsh be drained, the channels loud in spate.
>
> Look out you walled in wool of night
> That crouch; these are salvation, these
> Hands turn not back, take all that darkness has
> And with strong tension wrestle it into light.[16]

It is from a nine-poem sequence by Swingler entitled 'Revolutionary Poem', invoking the Holy Spirit and calling for the gift of tongues to express a militant crusade on behalf of the 'people of the sun / That have been hid so long away'. The poems run through the generational iconography of the Audenesque – sunlight against shadow and cloud and night, desire against reason, movement against stasis, spring against winter, youth against middle age ('Age is a hooded hawk'), the future against the weight of the past. But it was written in December 1931, like most of the poems in *Reconstruction* – at least *five months* before the publication of Auden's *The Orators*. That winter Swingler was also writing a one-act Passion Play, a verse-drama designed for liturgical rather than dramatic effect. As *Crucifixus* opens, Fear and Waste are preparing the Cross, discussing the folly of the man who will soon die upon it. Fear half admires the way he stood up to 'those ferrety priests' but thinks he 'went too far' ('There might have been a revolution'), while Waste believes he was a 'menace to reasonable society' ('Tell them their dirt is gold and they are happy. / But he is teaching them to look for something better'). Having raised the Cross centre-stage, they are replaced by Pedantry ('some quite original ideas. / But of course he was hopelessly muddled') and Policy ('determination like his might have carried him far / if directed along the proper channels'), a procession of shepherds, plough-men, fishermen, manual labourers, factory-hands and clerks, their eyes upon the figure on the Cross, a counter-procession of usurers, barristers and jailers, eyes averted, and a crowd of soldiers marching blindfold, followed by sui-cides, thieves, harlots, a drunkard, a plutocrat, a priest and a teacher. The crowds combine to become the play's Chorus, a rising lamentation for the defeat of the world's only hope. *Crucifixus* ends with the death of Christ and not with the Resurrection, but it does not doubt Christ's divinity; instead it uses the Easter story to claim a sort of parallel divinity for the resurrection of the common human spirit over adversity, oppression and death. The play certainly uses Christ's teaching as a lever of social criticism – it is more anti-*clerical* than anything else – but it was written from within the Christian tradition, as the introductory poem makes explicit:

> Drinking the blood we celebrate them that live
> Who through their forging feet
> Felt the evolving pulse: who never lost
> And shall never lose the conclusive compact
> Of love's gorgeous arrival.[17]

Swingler was clearly moving towards Communism, and he may already have begun leaving behind elements of his Christian faith, though for the moment he seems to have pitched his tents on the moral and prophetic border between the two. The play was never performed, but parts of it were published in the *Twentieth Century*. This was the journal of the Promethean Society, founded in 1931 as a result of an extraordinary cor-respondence about the 'Revolt of Youth' in the magazine *Everyman*. The Prometheans took their social criticism from Shaw, Lawrence, Huxley and A.S. Neil; their politics from Lenin, Trotsky and Ghandi; their economics from Marx and Major Douglas; and their psychology from Freud and Have-lock Ellis; while in Wells' *The Open Conspiracy* they found a text-book for changing the world. Not surprisingly, these young Prometheans saw them-selves as above ideology ('We want to cut across the field of contemporary party politics, accepting here, rejecting there'). And they saw themselves pitted against the 'Old Men', the representatives of the 'pre-war' who were likely to lead Britain into another war:

> Renouncing every pretentious tyranny within ourselves
> Advance with the wind from a new station of humility
> To extend governorship over that obscure territory.
> Advance with no bugle clamour nor the imposture of banners
> But with ingrained assurance of the trained
> Muscle's immediate contact with good

And of the benediction of selfless labour.
This is our valuable dream
That washes the globe of brain through with brightness
Of the world's harmony and the beautiful
Communities of men. Of broken thraldoms
Of self in the liberation of service.[18]

In other words, Swingler was already turning himself into a 'modern poet' several years before he became a Communist, and a long time before the publication, in 1933, of either Spender's *Poems*, Day Lewis's *Magnetic Mountain* or *New Country*. The fact that he was writing *Crucifixus* at the same time as he was putting together the love lyrics of *Poems* suggests that it was possible to be open to both 'beauty' and the 'modern', that not all English poets were obliged to break with one in order to choose the other. Moreover, in the work of this poet at least, the 'modern' was clearly a native, English phenomenon – an idiosyncratic combination of Anglican notions of community, Wykehamist ideas of service, the Georgian dream of the common people and vague Promethean calls for social revolution. Other writers later followed different routes – via Berlin, Vienna, Spain and the Soviet Union – to similar conclusions. Swingler's poetry in the early thirties was thus arguably part of the constituting moment of 'the Audenesque', and therefore of thirties poetry. It is not that Swingler was consciously imitating his already famous contemporaries, but that reading their work confirmed the direction in which his own verse was moving. Each of these young poets was trying to find a way of writing that seemed adequate to their generation and to the years of social, economic and political crisis in which they came to adulthood. Sharing almost exactly the same upper-middle-class Anglican background, the same public schools and the same university, it is not surprising that their poetry (and later the work of others like Warner, Lehmann, Madge and Todd) should follow a similar trajectory in these years. Why so many gifted, gilded young men from the upper middle classes should have chosen Marxism and Revolution in these years is a wider question than this chapter can address, although Swingler's own slow progress towards Communism may remind us just how serious a commitment it was, and how remarkable a development it represented inside the British ruling classes – a rather more significant development than most accounts of the 'Red Decade' usually allow. Swingler's debt to the Georgians, like his deeply-held Christian faith, may have caused the trajectory of his commitment to curve at first a little less steeply than some of his contemporaries. But it was to last rather longer.

A second consideration is that Swingler's 'modern' verse was not always quite as modernist as some critics believed it to be. Even in *Reconstruction*, Swingler was concerned to reveal the potential of the city for its own kind of beauty, as in 'Sunset Over Camden Town':

> At whom the sun set over tangled rails,
> spidering gantreys and the tall emaciated
> mansions ghosted into a fading past:
> suddenly those wells of excitement of which he tells
> were true in me, hot springs breaking the heart's crust,
> splashing the sky with the huge emotion of kindness,
> clearance of white decks for a new day, endowment
> to a few arms of unsuspected power.[19]

Anyway, by the middle thirties Swingler's verse was located not in the city but in rural England, detailing the loveliness of the natural world with an unaffected simplicity which surely nominates him as the true heir of the Georgians:

> Morning is young, its widening
> Candour surprises mist
> And rabbits sleeping by the road,
> The valleys unroll from bandages,
> Villages blink, and birds with sleepy flight
> Unfold the stiff pleats of the trees.[20]
>
> I see the wood-pecker
> Lurching out of an ash-tree
> And above my head the cuckoo
> Drops absent-minded comment common
> And welcome as the daisies.[21]

This continuing preoccupation with 'beauty' was apparent in Swingler's next, full-length collection, *Difficult Morning*, published at the end of 1933. His poetry had never been so explicit about its political objectives ('the worldstate') or its enemies ('the nightmare of finance') although both were rapidly becoming familiar tropes in contemporary English poetry. Within a decaying de-industrialised landscape ('this moss-grown siding') lies the work of the future ('tunnelled the mountain range') a metaphor held together crucially by exhortation ('the points are changed'). The mixture of imperatives and second-person plurals, false-starts, betrayed springs and long-waited beginnings is now a familiar one. But *Difficult Morning* also shows Swingler beginning to move out from beneath the shadow of the Audenesque and making a qualified return to pastoral writing, entering a kind of post-Georgian England, observed and unidealised, politicised and internalised in poems like 'Paddock Wood', 'Autumn Values', 'August Swallows', 'Before the Sea' and 'Imperial June':

> Imperial June, stretched easily in yellow
> Through leagues of the hot fields,
> You smother with content the wide wounds
> Of our permanent need, ugly to be revealed,
> Still raw, by autumn's scavenging winds.

In white London, where the sun stood in the streets
Till all their ivory faces shone,
I knew that we must wait for the dream to pass,
For life, contracted to a stone,
To sour the no more flowering wilderness.
I knew that green siesta must postpone
Their critical hour, and prayed for the bare frost soon
To make tense their fields in fallow, and complete
The circumference of the spring's incipient change.[22]

Although the poem is alert to the temptations of Pastoral ('the dream' of harmony with which nature and the seasons 'smother with content' the 'critical hour') it relies at the same time on the vocabulary of the seasons to assert its politics, struggling to make a new kind of poetry out of a still-admired but now inadequate poetic vision. *Difficult Morning* feels like a transitional collection (even before the book was published Swingler told George Barker that the poetry it contained was 'dead' for him).[23]

A third consideration is that the presence of the 'modern' voice was always a point of tension in Swingler's verse. Contemporary critics consistently identified the Georgian elements of Swingler's poetry as its most successful and attractive elements. The *Fortnighty Review*, for example, liked the 'sensitiveness' of *Difficult Morning*, its 'delicate descriptive touch', while the *Sunday Referee* admired Swingler's 'real gift for large landscape', offering the opinion that he would make an excellent poet 'when he forgets to be clever'. 'Cleverness' was clearly a synonym here for the 'modern'. The *Times Literary Supplement* disliked the 'ultra-sophisticated' poetry of *Reconstruction* with its 'excessive self-consciousness' and 'morbid sensibility'. The *London Mercury* admired the poems to the extent that they did not seem to rely on contemporary models of poetry:

Mr Swingler's name will be already familiar to those who have kept pace with the development of poetry during the last few years. He is modern in that his primary concern is the problem of living in the world today. But he is not one of the dreary industrialists whose verse sounds like the metallic ticking of a metronome.[24]

For most reviewers the similarity with recent collections by Auden, Spender and Day Lewis was a point of *weakness*. *Difficult Morning* was 'too full of echoes of those contemporaries (such as Mr Day Lewis and Mr Auden) under whose influence he has fallen' for *Time and Tide*, although the paper was confident that when 'these several and quite natural influences have been assimilated or forgotten there is every reason to believe Mr Swingler will stand forth as a poet in his own right'. The *Listener* was irritated by the 'syntatical idiosyncracies' of the poems, which reminded them of Day Lewis; 'Mr Swingler, in particular, lays the greatest possible strain on the reader's enjoyment by the deliberate ommission of articles, pronouns and conjunctions.' The *Scotsman* criticised what it called 'Mr Swingler's struggle with belated Imagism', apparently a reference to the obscurity of some of the poems, while the *New English Weekly* lamented the influence of *Eliot* in the book. Even George Barker – hardly a Georgian – writing in the *Week-end Review*, deplored the influence of Auden, Day Lewis and Spender, but he liked the apprehension of Beauty in some of the poems, particularly 'The Swans':[25]

> Only to those who have climbed the dusky hill
> To watch the simple contortions of the land
> At evening, a beautiful and calm apparel
> For our thought, and the mature light
> Fallen slanting among trees, shaping them
> Palpably, the thought itself the richness
> And the consistence of sensitive life;
>
> Only then at last in the moment ordained
> By cast of beauty, the swans come: silverly skeined
> Above the water's deepened animation,
> Their hard unplaceable distant susurrus of wings
> Mixing most gently with the sun-shifted birches'
> Light behaviour and the childish wind's agility.
>
> Only then caught in the shock of wonder,
> Folding again with easy rings, the surface
> Of contention shows an equal image
> Stealing white in the enclosing river's incredible silk
> At the grey conclusion of flight,
> The locked wings, the calmed heart.[26]

Only Geoffrey Grigson thought the poems were not 'modern' enough. 'Unselectively he employs Hopkins, Mr Eliot, Mr Day Lewis, Mr Spender and Mr Auden, borrowing from them kinds of words, or word arrangement, of imagery and of attitude; but he appears devoid of what Mr Eliot calls "auditory imagination"'; 'Mr Swingler should give up poetry for politics or prose.' Reviewing *Difficult Morning* in the *Criterion*, Grigson scoffed at young poets writing about revolution who twenty years earlier would have written about love:

> Mr Swingler has been reading Mr Auden, taking from him more of an attitude than a manner and not realising that one of the best things of Mr Auden's verse is the quality of being dramatic. Mr Swingler should read his six poems again just to see how he denies them active life by using empty, idle, adjectives.[27]

On the other hand, F.R. Leavis in *Scrutiny* thought the poems in *Difficult Morning* were 'decidedly enough of their time and seriously interested in poetic technique to be read with an attention that one cannot give to Mr Aldington, the Sitwells, Mr Humbert Wolfe'. Humbert Wolfe meanwhile, writing in the *Observer*, observed that Swingler was the victim of the fashionable 'stupid blasphemy' which believed 'awareness of the object is the poet's sole duty' instead of attention to the 'old professional rhythms'.[28]

The critical reception of Swingler's poetry in the early thirties is a good account of some of the problems encountered by the Audenesque at that time, even before it had been given the name (and when it was identified with Day Lewis rather than Auden). It says a good deal about the condition of contemporary poetry reviewing, but it was also a measure of the tensions in Swingler's poetry between the 'old professional rhythms' and the fashionable 'stupid blasphemy' of 'modernism'. He wrote several unpublished collections in these years, including 'Winter Sonnets', 'Winter Soliloquies' and 'Pastorals', each attempting to articulate and resolve this tension, using pastoral conventions in order to examine its external and internal landscapes, the dislocation of England in the middle thirties, and the conflict between his own private happiness and growing public dismay:

> Looking about me I saw a curling country
> Of hills and valleys like a heap of snakes,
> At the edge, beyond their heads, the magnificent mountains
> Like clouds; and at first a comfort like falling water
> And universal delicate sorrow
> Sank out of all my veins.
> I was joined to this hill with roots like a nipple
> To the breast and I thought the plains
> Were flowing with waves of light like eternal lakes
> Where cranes flew up out of the enormous grasses
> Freighted with legends, and the curious grebe
> Darted and elegantly towed their icy reflections
> And sunlight floated warm and rich on the grasses
> Buoying their seeds. And I thought for a time
> I was alone and joined with this delectable
> Land. But I was wrong.
>
> For looking longer that landscape came
> Within a new focus. Not snowy were those mountains
> But rolling trains of smoke; under the hills
> Furnaces glared like lions and the hiss
> Of their running metal was a serpent's laughter.
> Thicker and blacker were those hills forested
> With slums than with cat-like pinewoods, and the rush
> Of people passing in the streets, the crush of their feet
> Denser than any wind over summer grass.
> Not cranes in the air slanted, but planes
> Side-slipped from the hanging clouds
> And ran out, easeful on to the polished grass
> Like ducks on water, leaving their whale-like hangars
> White-bellied behind them. And I knew
> That I was not alone.[29]

The result was a distinctive series of poems in which Swingler sought to create an inclusive, unified vision of England, both urban and rural, shaped by English poetic tradition but sharpened by a sense of modernity, in what might be called Anglo-Communist pastoral:

> Acres of power within me lie,
> Charted fields of wheat and rye
> And behind them, charted too,
> Brooding woods of beech and yew.
> Beyond them stretch, uncharted yet,
> Marsh and mountain, dark and wet,
> Whence sometimes in my dreams and ease
> Strange birds appear among the trees.
>
> The fields of corn are action's fruit,
> Gripping the earth with puny root,
> The surface pattern neatly planned
> Upon the chaos of my land.
> Against the ruminating wood
> They set a fence, but to no good;
> The shadow and the sap of mind
> Still weighs the harvest of my hand.
>
> And the wild marches and the hills
> Shut out by the imposing will
> Yet hurl their livid storms across
> To smash the fence and flood the fosse
> And all his dictates and his laws
> Cannot restrain that surging force,
> For the whole land is my power still,
> Divided, fenced, and no less real.
>
> And one man only mourning goes
> By day through the stiff planted rows
> By night through tangled wood, to gaze
> On the vast savage wilderness.
> The born surveyor, he that would
> Turn the whole acreage to good,
> Subject to one coherent plan
> Dispensing the whole power of man.
>
> But he between the fences dour,
> This organiser of my power,
> By rigid areas is confined
> That sever impulse, hand and mind.
> For he is only paid to see
> That the fields grow obediently
> And that the woods do not encroach
> Nor the trees part to show the marsh.

For if the power that lavish there
Breaks into sterile air,
Were planned and planted, fibre and juice,
And all my earth enlaced with use,
Then evil for his ruler's case
Whom to maintain in idleness
My fields of power are bought and sold
And all their goodness changed for gold.

Thus the land that is my life
Divided, ruled, and held in fief,
All the power it could produce
He cannot sell, but I could use.
And my surveyor, grim and harsh,
In secret now reclaims the marsh
That cultivated acres there
May bear a fruit for all to share.[30]

The return to metre, rhyme and stanza was entirely consistent with the sub-ject of this poetry – the aspiration to *control* and unify all aspects of living, to break down the barriers within the individual ('impulse, hand and mind'), between the individual and society ('Divided, fenced') and between the social classes ('Divided, ruled, and held in fief'). The obvious debts to Blake, Sassoon and Edward Thomas here helped to Anglicise the revolutionary con-tent of the poem by invoking a deepened sense of belonging to an older, native, radical tradition. But it was as much a Freudian landscape as it was a Marxist one, a transformed pastoral vision, moving from contemplation to action, from wonder to understanding, solitude to collectivity, seed-time to harvest.

A fourth consideration, which concerns Swingler's relationship to the critical establishment, is that once he had learned to negotiate the influ-ences of his contemporaries (and few poets in the thirties did not have to struggle to do that) his Communism was far less of an obstacle to critical success than his 'modernism' had ever been. This is evident in the critical reaction to his first novel, *No Escape*, published by Chatto & Windus in January 1937. It was the semi-autobiographical story of a young man grow-ing into maturity, love and politics in a small English village before the First World War:

In the late May evening, the sun swarmed wonderfully over the cottages squatted along the one straight green-sleeved street of the village. Here and there a chestnut tree with its full white plumes stood up crisp and glowing against the tingling blue of the sky. The swallows raced at their games around the eaves and darted just above the the heads of the cyclists, who wheeled back and forth along the idle canal of the street. On the rising ground, black in the melting blaze of the sun and skirted with fan-branched beech trees, the church stood over one row of houses.

A flight of sagging stone steps, divided by an iron hand-rail down which the children slid as they returned from school through the churchyard, led up to it, between the grocer's shop and the parish hall. At their foot on the broad paving stood the old stone cross, the recognised leaning-post for the young men who had nothing to do but wallow in the sunshine, and call like gulls to those who cruised by on bicycles, but had little to say to each other. The sun-bathed walls smiled warmly and the young leaves of the creepers stirred sleepily like a hide upon the little houses. . . .[31]

The first review to appear was by L.P. Hartley in the *Observer*:

Mr Randall Swingler is a poet, with a poet's gift of making articulate and vivid those niceties of thought and feeling which, though experienced, may remain unlocked and inaccessible in our memories unless released by a delicate and complex key. He excels, too, in description of natural scenery; he responds to landscape not only with his eye but with his whole mood; all his sensory perceptions are alert and contribute to his feeling for beauty.[32]

A few days later the Georgian poet Wilfred Gibson reviewed *No Escape* in the *Manchester Guardian*:

the first novel of a young writer who has hitherto been known as a modernistic poet and journalist with left-wing affinities. Rather surprisingly, it is not at all revolutionary in its technique. . . . The distinction of the writing, though a little youthfully overprecious in places, is such that the novel is not merely a work of remarkable promise but one of considerable achievement. The truly poetic precision of the descriptive passages and the felicity of phrasing have tempted even a harassed reviewer to dally in delightful appreciation.[33]

'His sense of words and his sensitiveness to beauty give his novel a lovely quality of its own', said *Time and Tide*; the *London Mercury* liked 'Mr Swingler's beautiful and sensitive prose, his power of evoking the scents and sounds of the countryside, and his delicate handling of adolescence . . . one looks forward to his next book with considerable interest.' 'A first novel by a not undistinguished young poet', announced the *Times Literary Supplement (TLS)*, 'essentially, both in thought and expression, a poet's novel'. Writing in *Life and Letters Today*, Arthur Calder-Marshall said it was 'a book worth reading, if only for individual scenes and passages of beauty'. John Brophy in the *Daily Telegraph* thought the novel was distinguished 'by a highly cultivated sensitiveness, a quivering response to the natural scene, to implications of speech and mood, to every sort of emotional refinement. . . . Mr Randall Swingler is a poet, and unlike so many poets of the last few years he has an authentic and sustained interest in that out-moded quality, beauty.' 'An excellent picture of village life and character', said *John O'London's Weekly*; the *Daily Herald* called it a 'serious, pacifist novel, written as only a poet who is not lost in dreams can write'; while Vikki Darragh in the *Daily Worker*, though less inclined than most reviewers to overlook the structural problems of the novel, had to admire the prose, which showed, she felt, 'a poet's mastery of words'.[34]

The frequent invocation here to 'poetry', the 'poetic' and 'sensitivity' was manifestly a kind of shorthand for a premodern literary sensibility, which permitted the novel to transcend the limitations of its avowedly Communist politics (the novel ends with Rolf distributing the *Communist Manifesto* in the trenches shortly before he is sent to his death). 'He has a lyrical imagination and a real power of shaping images in words', observed William Plomer in the *Spectator*; 'he is a poet and may be described, I think, as an Anglo-Communist.'[35] Although the *TLS* recognised that the novel was about 'the inequalities of class, fear and ignorance, sex obscurantism and the futility of war' this was not an obstacle to the paper's general approval:

> Many a far more tendentious book has escaped the imputation of 'propaganda'; Mr Swingler is not a pamphleteer. Yet the propagandist element must be mentioned if the book is to be described at all. Like other young poets of many ages, and particularly the younger poets of today, his politic – now often vaguely labelled 'Communism' – is keenly felt rather than logically argued: unlike many, he is content to recognise it as such. It is his particular merit that he is an artist first and the other, not indeed nowhere, but a bad second.[36]

All this brings us to a fifth issue, which is that Swingler did not recognise or see as problems the conflicting interests inherent in his poetry. In *New Writing* he argued that the supposed antagonisms between art and politics, the 'modern' and the beautiful, the private and the public were false:

> The quarrel between those who say that poetry can only deal with the most refined of human feelings and the most rarified consciousness, and those who say it must always appeal directly to the mass, is a false quarrel . . . we want poetry that we can read at home, that will enrich our friendship, articulate our sensibility to environment, clarify our knowledge and control of ourselves. We also want poetry that can be cried in the streets, from platforms, in theatres; that will be sung in concert-halls and in pubs and in market places, in the country and the town. We do not want either the one or the other, we want both.[37]

It was a false argument for Swingler because the intimate poetry of the Georgians enjoyed enormous popularity, while the public poetry of modernism was read only by the initiated. For him, the key question for poets in the thirties was not technique (what he called the knack of 'producing cheap goods of intricate design to look expensive') but *audience*. And few poets of his generation wrote so successfully for both the 'circle of friends' and the 'crowd'.

A sixth and final issue which concerns us here is that although Swingler may not have published another collection of poems in the thirties, it is hard to describe these years as unproductive. In fact the years following *Difficult Morning* were Swingler's most prolific and successful. He published two novels, *No Escape* and *To Town* (1938). His short stories were published in the *Bookman*, *Life and Letters Today*, *New Stories*, *Under Thirty*. His poetry was published in a wider range of magazines than that of many of his contemporaries – the *Adelphi*, *The Bookman*, *Caravel*, *Left Review*, *Life and Letters Today*, *The Listener*, the *Literary Review*, the *London Mercury*, the *Modern Scot*, the *New Oxford Outlook*, *New Verse*, *New Writing*, *Poetry*, *Poetry and the People*, *Purpose*, *The Scottish Bookman*, the *Spectator*, *Twentieth Century*, *Twentieth-Century Verse*, the *Week-end Review*. He was reviewing regularly for the *Daily Worker*, *Life and Letters* and *New English Weekly*. His work was represented in a number of anthologies: *Recent Poetry 1923–33*, *The Year's Poetry 1935*, *The Best Poems of 1936*, *Poems of Tomorrow* and Nancy Cunard's series, *Les Poetes du monde defend le peuple Espagnol*. In 1936 he wrote a version of *Peer Gynt* for Rupert Doone and the Group Theatre, and a long declamatory poem 'Spain' for Unity Theatre, performed by Unity groups all over Britain to raise money for the Republican Government. He was involved in Labour Stage, an evening school for amateur actors, and taught at weekend and summer schools for the Left Book Club and Unity Theatre. He co-authored two plays for London Unity: 'Crisis' in 1938 (about Munich) and 'Sandbag Follies' in 1939. His poetry was set to music by John Ireland, Alan Bush, Alan Rawsthorne and Benjamin Britten, and he and Bush wrote many songs for the Workers' Music Association. In 1937 Swingler wrote the text for Bush's First Piano Concerto, and 'Peace and Prosperity' for the London Choral Union. With Bush he edited *The Left Song Book* for the Left Book Club in 1938; that year too they adapted Handel's oratorio *Belshazzar's Feast* as a three-act opera for the combined choirs of the London Co-operative Societies. As editor of *Left Review* from July 1937 to May 1938, Swingler published Nancy Cunard's famous questionnaire, *Authors Take Sides on the Spanish War*. After the closure of *Left Review* he established his own publishing company, Fore Publications. He was active in 'For Intellectual Liberty', the Communist Party's 'Ralph Fox (Writers') Group', the Left Book Club Writers' and Readers' Group and the LBC Poets' Group, where he launched the magazine *Poetry and the People*. In 1939 he wrote a Marxist historical pageant for the 'Music and the People' festival, performed in the Albert Hall and set to music by – among others – Vaughan Williams, Elizabeth Lutyens, Edmund Rubbra, Elizabeth Maconchy and Alan Rawsthorne. The festival also included the premiere of Benjamin Britten's *Ballad of Heroes*, performed by the London Symphony Orchestra at the Queen's Hall in April 1939 to mark the return of the last British volunteers from Spain. The libretto was written by Auden and Swingler. It opens with Swingler's simple 'Funeral March':

> To you who stand at doors, wiping hands on aprons,
> You who lean at the corner saying: 'We have done our best,'
> You who shrug your shoulders and you who smile
> To conceal your life's despair and its evil taste,
> To you we speak, you numberless Englishmen,
> To remind you of the greatness still among you
> Created by these men who go from our towns
> To fight for peace, for liberty, and for you.[38]

This was followed by part of Auden's 'It's Farewell to the Drawing-room's Civilised Cry':

> So goodbye to the house with its wallpaper red,
> Goodbye to the sheets on the warm double bed,
> Goodbye to the beautiful birds on the wall,
> It's goodbye, dear heart, goodbye to you all.[39]

It is clear that Auden and Britten were both saying farewell not only to England but to the political commitments of the thirties. But *Ballad of Heroes* was only partly a valediction. It is certainly full of elegy, hollowed by a sense of defeat. But in Swingler's text at least, there was an avowal to avenge the defeat in Spain and to disentangle the contradictions elided by the political rhetoric of 'fighting for peace':

> They were men who hated death and loved life,
> Who were afraid, and fought against their fear!
> Men who wished to create and not to destroy,
> But knew the time must come to destroy the destroyer.
> For they have restored your power and pride,
> Your life is yours, for which they died.[40]

By the time Auden and Britten returned from the United States to England, Corporal Swingler was in the Eighth Army, in which he served for five years – in Palestine and North Africa, and up through the mud of Italy (where he was awarded the Military Medal) to the Yugoslav border. There in 1945 he was wounded; temporarily out of action, he wrote to Geraldine, excited by the approach of the Red Army, the imminent end of the fighting and the prospect of returning home:

Two mornings ago I had rather an extraordinary experience; it had been a pretty deadly and hectic night, and as these things so often do for some unfathomable reason, everything quieted down to utter silence just before dawn. And the dawn began to spread, very timidly, like a maltreated child coming into a room, pale green and faint rose with sharp slashes of flame colour under dark fingers of cloud, over the dead flat and sodden grey fenland. And then as the sun grew stranger and there were sharp golden sparks in the air as well as the flat background of light, suddenly, and apparently from miles away, there drifted over the whole battlefield like an unreal mist, the sound of millions of birds singing. But it was quite real, not a mirage or mystical at all, only the sound must have come for miles. And I thought of that funny little fragment of a poem by Edward Thomas about Adelstrop. . . . I remember at Salerno, and again later at Anzio when everything was very sticky, how wonderful it was to see the morning come and just remind yourself that you were still alive and that out there was still the same world, wide and brimming with light and lovely and quite new every day and somewhere holding the very heart of desire – just as I did think this time – the first thing I pictured was you walking knee-deep in daffodils in the* orchard, pensive and wild and lovely and part of April itself, all April to me.[41]

The reference to Edward Thomas here is not coincidental; this was a vision of a radical English Georgianism, a poetry which survived the deaths of Thomas and Brooke and the impact of T.S. Eliot, made new again in the conditions of another, terrible, modern war. It is a voice and a sensibility to which literary histories of the thirties have rarely attended, since it clearly disappoints the expectations of both modernist and anti-Communist critical orthodoxies, and the version of English poetry in the thirties – the Myth of the thirties – to which they subscribe. Randall Swingler's poetry simply offers another, less limited sense of that history. It might also therefore represent the starting point for the long overdue re-evaluation of those orthodoxies.

## NOTES

I am grateful to Ian Patterson and Arnold Rattenbury for their comments on an earlier draft of this chapter. I also wish to thank Judy Williams for permission to quote from her father's papers and unpublished poems.

1. 'Ode to a Plain above the City', *Reconstruction* (Oxford: Shakespeare Head Press, 1933).
2. *Spectator*, 15 December 1933; the reviewer was John Sparrow.
3. David Caute, *The Fellow Travellers* (London: Weidenfeld & Nicolson, 1973; Quartet, 1977), p. 118; at least Caute got Swingler's name right – he appears as *Raymond* Swingler in both Neal Wood, *Communism and British Intellectuals* (London: Gollancz, 1959) and in Eric Ambler, *Here Lies* (London: Weidenfeld & Nicolson, 1985), while he turns up as *Randolph* Swingler in Michael Kenny, *The First New Left* (London: Lawrence & Wishart, 1995); Swingler's long poem 'Spain' is not included in Valentine Cunningham's *Penguin Book of Spanish Civil War Verse* (Harmondsworth: Penguin, 1980); the only poems of his that are in print are the three included in Robin Skelton's *Poetry of the Thirties* (Harmondsworth: Penguin, 1964), though Swingler was already so thoroughly

forgotten by the time this was published that the reviewer in the *TLS* referred to the 'late Randall Swingler', prompting Swingler to write the following week announcing his continued existence.

4. 'Difficult Morning' in *Difficult Morning* (London: Methuen, 1933), p. 1.
5. See Andy Croft, *Red Letter Days: British Fiction in the 1930s* (London: Lawrence & Wishart, 1990).
6. See Andy Croft, 'Authors Take Sides: Writers and the Communist Party, 1920–1956' in Kevin Morgan, Nina Fishman and Geoff Andrews (eds), *Opening the Books: New Perspectives in the History of British Communism* (London: Pluto Press, 1995).
7. For Swingler and the Myth of the thirties see Arnold Rattenbury, 'Total Attainder and the Helots', in John Lucas (ed.), *The 1930s: A Challenge to Orthodoxy* (Brighton: Harvester Press, 1978).
8. Desmond Hawkins, *When I Was: A Memoir of The Years Between the Wars* (London: Macmillan, 1989), p. 151.
9. 'As You Lay Sleeping', *Poems* (Oxford: Shakespeare Head Press, 1932), p. 22.
10. 'Lulworth', *Poems*, p. 6.
11. Michael Roberts, Preface to *New Signatures* (London: Hogarth Press, 1932).
12. 'Prelude to Revolution', *Reconstruction* (Oxford: Shakespeare Head Press, 1933), p. 16; this poem was originally called 'Diary of a Revolutionary'.
13. Samuel Hynes, *The Auden Generation* (London: Faber & Faber, 1976), p. 110; while it is undoubtedly true that writers of this generation influenced each other, this happened in more complex ways than Hynes suggests (Auden and Day Lewis were both admirers of Swingler's work, for example); unfortunately Hynes attributes 'If now the curtain dropped', the poem with which he supports his thesis, to *Reconstruction*, when it was in fact published in *Difficult Morning*, by which time Swingler was beginning to outgrow the influence of his contemporaries.
14. *Spectator*, 18 August 1933.
15. 'The change in the tone of his letters was disturbing', recalls Desmond Hawkins, talking darkly of Swingler trying to lose himself in the 'anonymity of the Party – almost as if something monastic in his nature had found its personal solution', *When I Was*, p. 152.
16. 'Revolutionary Poem'; part of this poem was later used in 'Sunset Over Camden Town' in *Reconstruction*.
17. *Crucifixus* was published by the Temple Bar Publishing Company, 30 St Martin's Court, London; the play was later rejected by T.S. Eliot on the grounds that 'versification alone cannot take the place of dramatic interest'! (letter to Randall Swingler, 11 May 1935).
18. *Twentieth Century*, October 1932; for the Promethean Society see Geoffrey Trease, *A Whiff of Burnt Boats* (London: Macmillan, 1971) and Desmond Hawkins, *When I Was*.
19. 'Sunset Over Camden Town', *Reconstruction*, p. 9.
20. 'Pastoral V', in 'Pastorals' (unpublished MS).
21. 'Pastoral VI', ibid.
22. 'Imperial June', *Difficult Morning*, p. 16.
23. Letter from George Barker to Randall Swingler, 10 December 1933.
24. *Fortnightly Review*, January 1934; *Sunday Referee*, 26 November 1933; *TLS*, 7 December 1933; *London Mercury*, March 1934.
25. *Time and Tide*, 16 May 1934; *The Listener*, 13 December 1934; *The Scotsman*,

4 December 1933; *New English Weekly*, 4 January 1934; *Week-end Review*, 9 December 1933.

26. 'The Swans', *Difficult Morning*, p. 6.
27. *New Verse*, February 1934; *Criterion*, April 1934.
28. *Scrutiny*, June 1934; *Observer*, 11 March 1934.
29. 'The Entrance to the City' (unpublished MS).
30. 'Acres of Power', *New Writing*, spring 1938; by 'pastoral' I mean the creation of an illusion of social harmony by reference to the order and beauty of the natural world; for a contemporary account of the convention see William Empson, *Some Versions of Pastoral* (London: Chatto & Windus, 1935).
31. *No Escape* (London: Chatto & Windus, 1937), p. 46.
32. *Observer*, 31 January 1937.
33. *Manchester Guardian*, 2 February 1937.
34. *Time and Tide*, 13 February 1937; *London Mercury*, March 1937; *TLS*, 6 February 1937; *Life and Letters Today*, March 1936; *Daily Telegraph*, 2 February 1937; *John O'London's Weekly*, 12 February 1937; *Spectator*, 12 February 1937; *Daily Herald*, 28 January 1937; *Daily Worker*, 24 February 1937.
35. *Spectator*, 12 February 1937.
36. *TLS*, 6 February 1937.
37. 'History and the Poet', *New Writing*, Christmas 1939.
38. 'Funeral March' from *Ballad of Heroes*.
39. 'Scherzo (Dance of Death)', *Ballad of Heroes*; for discussion of the valedictory qualities of *Ballad of Heroes* see Donald Mitchell, *Britten and Auden in the Thirties* (London: Faber & Faber, 1981) and Valentine Cunningham, *British Writers of the Thirties* (Oxford: Oxford University Press, 1988).
40. 'Funeral March'. This collaboration has had an unhappy critical history; musicologists have variously argued that Britten's music was 'hampered' by Auden and Swingler's libretto (Anthony Milner in Christopher Palmer (ed.), *The Britten Companion* (London: Faber & Faber, 1984)), or that Britten's music was a 'too glib response to the even more glib text' of his librettists (Michael Kennedy in *Benjamin Britten* (London: Dent, 1981)); on the other hand, Charles Osborne in *W.H. Auden: the Life of a Poet* (London: Eyre Methuen, 1979) argues that Auden's text was embarrassed by its association with 'the mediocre propaganda poem by a communist poet', an odd assertion, since it is not clear whether the recitative sung by the tenor solo was written by Auden or Swingler, or both men together.
41. Randall Swingler to Geraldine Swingler, 16 April 1945.

# CHAPTER TEN

# 'Irritating Tricks': Aesthetic Experimentation and Political Theatre

STEVE NICHOLSON

> Man:  Tonight we present a play about YOU (*points to the audience*), all
> of you sitting there, watching and watching . . . yourselves.[1]

Both the content and the forms which dominated the mainstream of British theatrical practice through the twenties and thirties looked backwards rather than forwards. These perspectives were challenged by a left-wing movement comprised of overlapping but distinct strands. The Workers' Theatre Movement, Unity Theatre, Left Theatre, Group Theatre and Theatre of Action introduced a range of new techniques and forms which included agit-prop, cartoon plays, living newspapers, mass declamations, poetic dramas, political pantomimes and political pageants. Yet the principal strength attributed to left-wing theatre – somewhat patronisingly acknowledged even by those not sympathetic towards its politics – has usually been the conviction of its performers. Actors were not merely reciting a playwright's lines to earn a living, but expressing personal beliefs: 'There was no shamming . . . all of us believed passionately in what we were doing and what we were saying.'[2]

Discussions of political theatre in the thirties have tended to imply that such passionate convictions resulted in a single-minded determination to communicate narrow and unambiguous messages, and were the driving force behind any experiments with form. According to this interpretation, debate centred almost entirely on whether agit-prop or naturalism would be more effective in promoting revolution. In this chapter I want to suggest that the supposed abandonment of artistic concerns for political didacticism has been exaggerated, and that the two imperatives cannot be so easily separated. Within the theatre, the relationship between art and politics was constantly being renegotiated, and I shall focus on particular areas of artistic innovation and specific texts to demonstrate this, referring in detail to the British productions of Irwin Shaw's *Bury the Dead*, and Francois Porché's *Tsar Lénine*.

It is not hard to see why it has been possible to define the political theatre of the thirties within a narrow frame. Denying itself any contact with the professional theatre, the Workers' Theatre Movement identified its task as 'the conduct of mass working-class propaganda and agitation through the particular method of dramatic representation'.[3] For the WTM, performance did indeed become a weapon in the revolutionary struggle rather than an Art, as capitalism, escapism and aesthetics were tarred with the same brush. Even Ewan MacColl, surely betraying the complexity and creativity which were fundamental to the work of Theatre of Action, later insisted: 'I don't believe that any of us regarded ourselves as artists or, indeed, as being in any way involved with art. We saw ourselves us guerrillas using the theatre as a weapon . . . to hell with art, let's get on with the job.'[4]

In 1933, the distinguished critic and playwright St John Ervine warned that theatre was 'foundering between Marx and Hitler', and was in danger of being reduced to a 'machine for party propaganda'.[5] He was responding not just to the aggressive and agitational use of street theatre as a weapon, but also to a growing theoretical analysis of how power maintained itself and to a proposed disruption of cultural control through performance. Three years earlier, in a book entitled *The Workers' Theatre*, Ness Edwards had insisted that cultural agitators should cease devoting their energies to making 'High Art' accessible to the masses since this could only have the effect of educating the working class into ruling-class values. For Edwards, even Shakespeare was ultimately a propagandist who 'dramatises the class distinctions of his age, not to whip the classes, but rather to keep them satisfied with "their appointed places"'.[6] Edwards does acknowledge the official Communist Party line on culture by prefacing his first chapter with a quotation from Bogdanov which asserts the need for workers to 'master the artistic treasures created in the past and assimilate all that is great and beautiful in them, without submitting to the spirit of bourgeois and feudal society reflected in them'.[7] But Edwards's main demand was for a theatre which would dramatise the problems of the workers, focusing on 'injustices . . . oppressions . . . miseries of society'. Furthermore, it must not only expose and reflect an injustice but 'work for its removal . . . indicate upon the stage the solution to the problems . . . give a lead to the working class movement . . . providing an object lesson in working class tactics.'[8]

For Edwards, it was the content of a play which was significant, and to change other elements was to be guilty of introducing 'reforms for the bourgeois theatre'. If a play showed a failed revolt then it must still be sure to end 'with a note of optimism' and to emphasise the fact that the defeat had been a 'necessary experience to achieve ultimate victory'. Accuracy was less important than the task of influencing audiences, so in depicting the working class all 'points of degradation should be subordinated' and writers must concentrate on 'idealising the rank and file' and 'bringing forth the wonderful potentialities of the workers'. Looking at mainstream or even marginalised playwrights associated with broadly left-wing views, Edwards found none of them measuring up to his demands. George Bernard Shaw was 'the John the Baptist of the Workers' Drama, but the times demand a Christ'. Toller was of limited use because of his failure to offer solutions and because he had 'not saturated himself with a truly working class spirit'. Edwards offered only one text as an appropriate model for writers to imitate; this was *R.U.R.*, in which the robots rebel against their masters, but even production of this was advisable only 'provided its mistakes are avoided and its deficiences impaired'.[9]

By contrast, Ervine concentrated much of his attack on the politicisation of performance which he identified as having taken place over recent decades. He blamed a politically fashionable obsession with democracy, his very language inviting us to apply what he says about the theatre to a broader social context:

> Acting, until the founding of the Little Theatres, was the business of great individualities who reduced other actors to small proportions. . . . Time has not proved that this system was wrong, but in the Little Theatre it was regarded with dislike and even contempt. Here, team-work, as it is called, was considered to be more important. . . . Aristocracy was abolished . . . democracy prevailed . . . a host of Higher Grade Civil Servants, but not one Dictator . . . a crowd of good 'supports', but no genius for them to support.

The writing of plays which created great roles and star-performers had been gradually eroded, says Ervine, by a misplaced desire for collectivity and equality.

> The authors, either because they were themselves infected with this idea of democracy or were compelled to pay heed to it, began to write plays in which no one 'took the centre of the stage', and, eventually, to write plays about unheroic characters. The nadir of this neo-democracy was reached, in England, in John Galsworthy's dramas of depressing people.[10]

Ervine was right to identify a deliberate downgrading of the importance of the individual in the Left's approach to characterisation. In the mid-thirties, the playwright Montagu Slater agonised in *Left Review* over the depressing popularity of Korda's film dramatising the life of Henry VIII, which had foregrounded personal and human details to create what Slater called 'exploitable mythology'. How, he wondered, could a socialist artist create inspirational propaganda without precipitating an ideologically unsound cult of the individual as hero:

Exploitation of 'our ancestors' is the stalest fascist trick . . . *Henry VIII*
. . . involves just that simple-minded sense of history which produces
patriotism and jingoism if necessary. It's not debunking. It's humanizing.
. . . What's the opposite of *Henry VIII* is what I keep asking myself?
What is our left to its right? . . . Fables insist on such a ridiculous spot-
lighting of the leading man. What is to be done about it? Can we
permit the spot-lighting?[11]

In 1931 Terence Gray had planned a production of Sergei Tretiakov's
*Roar China* in Cambridge.[12] Though the production never took place because the Lord Chamberlain refused to license for public performance such
'anti-Western civilisation propaganda', Barbara Nixon argues in the introduction to her published translation that Tretiakov's play breaks fresh ground
in making the mass its central character and hero. She tries to pre-empt criticism of the crudity of the characterisation by stressing that the Chinese
are intended to be 'types rather than personalities' and that the Western
capitalists have been deliberately created as symbols of imperialism rather than
as individuals: 'The author has intentionally refused to create the "brilliant
thumb-nail sketches" which too often are the only means of saving our
society dramas from complete banality.' Nixon argues that the political and
artistic elements of Tretiakov's play are absolutely indivisible:

> The Russian artist does not make his film or play, and then add the
> propaganda. . . . The propagandist idea forms not only the background to,
> but the essential structure of, his work. In the West we have grown
> accustomed to artists racking their brains to find a new way of saying the
> same old things – but in Russia . . . there is everything to say; and this
> abundance of matter has quite naturally evolved a new method of
> expression.[13]

Indeed, the de-centring of the individual can be seen as a direct reflection of the play's political and revolutionary thrust, for Tretiakov's message
is that society can be changed if the oppressed learn to act with and for
each other rather than as individuals. Power lies with the collective strength
of the mass, once they realise they have no need of individuals or outsiders
to liberate them:

| 1st Boatman: | (*raging*) When – when will they come? |
|---|---|
| Stoker: | Who? |
| 1st Boatman: | They over there who drove out their masters. |
| Stoker: | They are here. |
| 1st Boatman: | Show me one of them. |
| Stoker: | (*pointing to the boatmen*) He is one – and he is another and you are one. We don't need to wait for others. We must fight ourselves, gun in hand.[14] |

150

*Roar China* also disallowed another artistic convention which cloaked an ideological assumption. Tretiakov's introduction insisted that the titillating orientalism which had been cultivated in the West should be scrupulously avoided, and in particular that 'the stage must not be decorated with pretentious curved roofs, screens, dragons or lanterns'.[15] Instead, he demands an accurate reproduction of the details of working life around the harbour. To the mainstream theatre – producers, censors, critics and presumably audiences – the main justification for foreign plays and settings was the attraction of the exotic. The very presence of foreign plays within British theatre was itself a contentious issue which led to some of the most heated confrontations between theatre managers and the Lord Chamberlain, since one of the more difficult elements for the Establishment to control was foreign work which had not been created with the restrictions of the Lord Chamberlain in mind.[16] Such plays were often transgressive of British norms in form and content, and were inevitably resisted and condemned. The writings of Toller, for example, were dismissed with particular contempt by the Lord Chamberlain's office:

> It is a mixture of obscenity and raving, and had it not been written by an over-rated German no one would dream of producing it here. . . . Why women want to translate and force on the stage the works of this German author, whose only claims to merit are sadistic views and language, I fail to appreciate . . . it is an hysterical and unpleasant affair and would have no chance of being produced here if it had been written by an Englishman. To some *soi-disant* 'intellectuals' anything foreign is good.[17]

An arrogant and politically charged desire to protect the British theatre from unpleasant and disturbing material was turned into an issue of nationalistic pride, and the so-called infatuation of 'highbrow' British intellectuals with subversive foreign drama was seen as a betrayal of national identity. The astonishing attack in 1932 by the editor of *Plays and Players* on foreign plays, and more especially on those directors and managers who would import them, invokes the unpleasantly jingoistic spirit which was growing within Europe:

> The country that mixes up its art is a decadent country; its red blood is leaving it; its muscles becoming flabby, its mental faculties pining to atrophy. For a score of years the British drama lived. It survived the attack of the Norwegian microbe, and the insidious Teutonic virus. . . . I have no use for these intellectual (so-called) mediums. I like neither the Bosche [*sic*] nor his works. The Middle Europe crowd is loathsome; its literature concerns itself, mainly with the dregs of humanity.[18]

Terence Gray, who ran the Festival Theatre in Cambridge, was one of a handful of managers committed to piercing the insularity of British culture through the introduction of foreign texts and practices. Gray complained that the British theatre was effectively 'prohibited from presenting the master-pieces of today', and his insistence that theatre was neither a business nor an entertainment but rather an Art immediately placed him in opposition to Establishment codes. He argued that a willingness to innovate is crucially linked to political freedom, since experimentation becomes impossible when-ever 'art comes under the sway of commerce'. In a chapter of his book entitled *The Degradation of Drama*, Gray had argued that the very success of Establishment theatres was the major obstacle in the way of creative ori-ginality, and that 'the sentries who guard the highways' along which drama must travel 'demand a passport'. Sometimes full houses are more depressing than empty ones: 'The fundamental cause of the present state of dramatic art, the basic factor in the inhibition which hinders its development and full expression is the popularity of the theatre as a means of public diversion, relaxation and digestion.'[19]

Montagu Slater, the editor of *Left Review* and a prolific writer, similarly insisted that to create art was in itself a political act which challenged the basis of society's ethics. Under capitalism, says Slater, 'Art has lost its subject matter', and only Communism will restore it: 'Literature concerns human relationships. Capitalism destroyed these . . . substituting money or com-modity relationships. . . . The cultural legacy of capitalism has been almost exclusively scientific in form.'[20] By contrast, Ervine attacked the intellectual tendencies within recent theatre for having 'taken away the drama's blood'. He maintained that it was actually 'the earnest student of the drama' who had destroyed it: 'People went to repertory theatres as some Dissenters had formerly gone to chapel, woebegonely and as if they had come to atone for lamentable sins. . . . A night in a repertory theatre was almost as cheerful as a night in a morgue.'[21]

One area in which left-wing theatre challenged the naturalist/realist conventions of the Establishment concerned the relationship between stage and audience. Still reacting against melodrama, most mainstream theatre constituted its audience as the Stanislavskian fourth wall. Left-wing per-formances were much more inclined to address and involve them directly. Plants in the auditorium were a regular device, being crucial, for example, to the celebrated climax of Unity's *Waiting for Lefty* in which audiences were persuaded to stand on their chairs and chant revolutionary slogans. Montagu Slater's *Stay Down Miner* cast and re-cast the audience in a vari-ety of roles – not all of them positive. At one point they are abused and counted as blacklegs, supposedly imported to the village to steal the jobs of striking miners:

> Gwevril: ( *facing the audience*) You, you, you, marching on our mine, invaders. You're not even Welshmen. You've got English faces.

*Bronwen*: Twelve, fourteen, sixteen, eighteen, twenty . . .
*Gwevril*: (*facing the audience*) You look mean as if you've been robbing the poor box. . . . You're robbing our jobs. D'you hear? You're robbing our jobs.
*Bronwen*: Twenty-two, twenty-four, twenty-six, twenty-eight, thirty.

At the climax, however, they become jurors in the Court – fellow-workers entrusted with an important and not necessarily fictitious duty to fulfil:

*Bronwen* (*to the audience*):   You people of Cwmllynfach –
*Magistrate*:   No more speeches, please.
*Bronwen* (*with great emphasis*):   Tell the world.
*Magistrate*:   Please.
*Bronwen*:   Tell England and Scotland.
*Magistrate*:   I said no speeches.
*Bronwen*:   Tell them to join Wales.[22]

Although Brecht's theoretical writings were hardly known in Britain during the thirties, his perception of how the naturalistic form leads inevitably to a confirmation rather than a questioning of the way society is constructed is relevant to the Establishment's insistence on the naturalness of naturalism and the tendency to dismiss work which challenged this assumption.[23] Expressionism was a particular *bête-noir* for the Establishment, though the term was rarely defined and became a catchphrase used as a shorthand to indicate anything which did not fit the dominant mode of superficial naturalism. Ervine criticised the 'vogue of Expressionism' precisely for its refusal to concentrate on psychology and great individuals, claiming it produced 'dreary works on people who had neither character nor purpose, not even names. They were called Mr X or Miss Z'. He satirises a supposedly typical Expressionist piece in which a bank clerk is driven mad by his job and his family and turns to theft, a prostitute and suicide. Ervine's complaint insists that plays must imitate the surface of everyday life: 'I found myself unable to respond sympathetically to this drama. The bank clerks that I met in my few visits to banks appeared to be unusually cheerful men, and were not, as far as I could see, nagged by their wives.'[24]

The Lord Chamberlain's report had described Slater's *Stay Down Miner* as 'formless and at times obscure', and condescendingly suggested this was due to 'want of experience on the part of the author'. Predictably, the style was dismissed as 'more or less expressionist', and its experiments as merely 'the usual irritating tricks, actors among the audience, and efforts to bring the audience into the action and so on'.[25] In the same playwright's *Easter 1916*, the gap between stage and audit-orium is blurred still further, as actors planted in the audience emerge on to the stage to take part in the performance. The play starts with the Chorus informing the audience, 'Tonight we present a play about YOU (*points to the audience*), all of you sitting there.' This is more than a formal gimmick. Even though it relies on a fictionalisation, an ideological point is registered about whose lives and history the theatre should dramatise, and who should be doing the staging:

> *Man*:     We want a few of you to come on the stage to act. Now –
> don't get shy. We don't want people who've been trained in the
> Royal Academy of Dramatic Art. . . .
> *Woman*:   We want a tram-driver and a conductor. Come now. All you
> need know is how to drive a tram. (*Two men get up in the
> audience*.)[26]

The play focuses on the Dublin uprising of 1916, and at one point the audience becomes a Dublin theatre audience watching a pantomime. They are interrupted by an IRA man who comes on stage to announce that the revolution has begun. Houselights are turned on, guns are fired from the stalls and rebels apparently fight their way out of the theatre, as Slater's audience becomes implicated as actual participants in the rebellion. The performers in *Cinderella* then lead the audience of *Easter 1916* in singing *The Wearing of the Green*, while IRA men urge them to remain in their seats, and volunteers crowd on to the stage from different parts of the auditorium. The scene was a powerful theatrical moment, but it was more than that. *Easter 1916* begins and ends with the Chorus accusing the audience of complicity with the forces of British oppression; for much of the rest of the play they witness events from an Irish perspective; at this moment they are included in the struggle for freedom.[27]

One of the most remarkable though since neglected plays to be performed in London during the thirties was *Tsar Lénine* by the French playwright François Porché.[28] Porché's script offered a vision of Lenin and the Revolution which was both theatrically and ideologically complex. The performance required the simultaneous use of two stages, and in the first Act those who appear on the central stage are individuals, and the events which occur do so in real time and space. On a stage surrounding this, Porché places characters who symbolise different sections of Russian society – an aristocrat, a Bolshevik workman, a poor peasant, a monk, and a General – who are outside time and space, observing and discussing the action. They function partly as a chorus, though as Porché himself indicates, by contrast with Greek theatre his chorus is composed of people with conflicting perspectives and identities. At the end of the first Act these figures become giant chess pieces which Lenin sweeps from the board as he counters their arguments and temptations. The second Act is also built on metaphor as Porché uses a stylised and choreographed sequence to trace the Bolsheviks' rise to power through a continuous and uninterrupted 'danse macabre'. The Act is presided over by the figure of Death and accompanied by a nightmarish orchestra playing distorted music, while a valet in funeral dress hands out glasses of champagne to the symbolic characters. Porché describes the act as 'la peinture stylisée d'une grande période historique', and explains in a stage direction that the grotesque visual image is specifically derived from the paintings of Holbein and Dürer. The pre-revolutionary government is represented by wax mannequins, and at the end of the second Act Lenin stands directly in front of Death to proclaim the inauguration of the Socialist order and to institute the Terror. As the peasants salute their new leader, Death makes a gesture to signal the start of a frenetic dance by the prisoners.

Porché's play ends with the figure of Death saluting Lenin on his death-bed as an equal or superior: 'You have served me superbly! I salute you, Tsar Lenine, peerless gravemaker.'[29] This was hardly pro-Soviet propaganda, and it is somewhat ironic that the original British production was cancelled because the Lord Chamberlain felt obliged to censor a scene in which Lenin expressed doubts about his successor: 'If the play is licensed I suppose this Stalin part should be omitted as he is a kind of reigning potentate. Whether or not Lenin's memory should be protected by leaving out the final scene is another matter: I think not.'[30] When it was eventually performed four years later in 1937, most critics responded negatively to the unconvention-ality of the form and the theatrical devices. They wrote as though the play could sometimes have existed independent of these, as though content and form were easily divisible. In fact, the two were inseparable. It is no empty or merely aesthetic sign, for example, to represent the Tsarist government with a set of wax mannequins, or Kerensky's taking of power by the sub-stitution of an identical set. Porché even convincingly justifies his use of stereotypes defined by class and social identity and excluding individuality on the grounds that this reflects Lenin's own way of framing people. But the play was routinely dismissed as expressionist, as 'tiresome and pretentious' and as likely to be of interest only to 'those who have shown no great aptitude for growing up'. One critic patronisingly suggested that Porché 'would really have liked to write a sensible play, but he kept reminding himself that sense is out of fashion, that he ought to be modern, and so every now and again he pulled himself up with a jerk and dragged in some of the really old-fashioned "Expressionistic" ballyhoo'.

In its review of Tsar Lénine, The Times found itself 'inclined to remem-ber how much better the same thing has been done by Russian films', and another critic framed his comments within an even more pejorative com-parison of the two media:

> Film-minded people would call this play by a cumbrous title very dear
> to them, 'a documentary'. Certainly M. Porché has taken the easy line of
> the very modern dramatist who, unable to build a scene, does not try to

do so, but simply bombards his audience with a volley of bits and pieces and knows that his audience, being used to films, will not notice his slackness or incompetence.[31]

To most of the theatrical Establishment cinema was an inferior form and, because of its attraction to audiences, a threat. For Ervine it was 'written by the half-educated for the half-witted'. Perhaps inevitably, given the literary background and assumptions of most theatre critics, the potential for cinema to be transmuted into art was seen to be dependent on its use of the spoken word: 'When the moving-picture can be associated, as the drama can, with names so potent . . . as those of Aeschylus, Euripides and Sophocles, Shakespeare, Moliere, Sheridan, Goethe, Ibsen and Bernard Shaw its power to prevail over the play may be evident.'[32]

British theatre had been predictably resistant to the use of cinematic vocabulary or, indeed, to the use of actual film within stage performance. In 1929 Gray's intention to project film during his production of Toller's *Hoppla!* was prevented by a ruling of the British Board of Film Censors: 'Many of the scenes in this film show soldiers firing *on* the unarmed populace, including women and girls, who are seen falling, and afterwards lying dead. We regard such scenes as unsuitable for exhibition in this country.'[33]

In the same year, a Soviet play entitled *Rasputin* was performed in London; two years earlier in Berlin, Piscator had used the script as the basis for an innovative theatrical and cinematic montage focused on the revolution. By contrast, the London production was a faithful and tedious translation of the original text, performed in a pedestrian style.[34] Again in London in 1929, Hubert Griffith's episodic *Red Sunday* charted Russian history between 1906 and 1920.[35] The staging required nine different settings, cutting rapidly between them, but the production was unable to escape the demand that each scene be presented in the kind of 'naturalistic' frame which necessitated regular and lengthy waits by the audience. Perhaps Griffith was unconsciously straining towards a more fluid theatrical form than was currently available: 'It was almost immediately obvious that what Mr Griffith had assembled was the scenario of a film. And how much better, we reflected, it would all have been as a film!'[36]

*Tsar Lénine* consciously drew on several elements of film vocabulary, and in his introduction to the published text, the author explores at length the relationship between cinema and theatre. In showing the events between December 1916 and October 1917 as one continuous and uninterrupted action, Porché cites the influence of nature films which compress time to show the germination of a plant or the metamorphosis of a chrysalis into a butterfly. Such compression, argues Porché, *reveals* rather than *alters* reality, and is closer to the selective way in which our own memories and perceptions work. Yet he felt it necessary to justify his use of cinematic language and insisted on the fundamentally theatrical conception of *Tsar Lénine*: 'Tous ces moyens . . . sont du theatre pur, rien que du theatre' (*All these devices . . . are absolutely theatrical, belong only to the theatre*). Porché maintained that while theatre must discover the essence of theatricality and not seek to compete on cinema's terms, the two media could borrow ideas from each other. Crucially, however, 'il devra les transposer sur son terrain propre, les adapter a son usage'[37] (*It must translate them to its own terrain, adapt them for its own uses*).

The Left was fully aware of how cinema could be used as opium to take people's minds away from social issues. But to reject the manipulations of Hollywood did not necessarily mean rejecting all the lessons which cinema could teach theatre. The influence of film is probably most apparent in some of the aggressively anti-establishment American plays staged by Unity Theatre in the second half of the thirties. Unity's first major success was Clifford Odets' *Waiting for Lefty*, the publicity for which claimed that it introduced 'a new cinematic technique to the stage'.[38] The play combines a single, realistic set with several other settings, as a strike meeting forms the constant background to a series of domestic and work-place scenes of oppression and exploitation. Cutting rapidly between the meeting and these other scenes, Odets' play collided the conventional theatrical form of the period with the cinematic. Rather than becoming an unfortunate compromise, this clash becomes fundamental to the play's power, enabling it to communicate in ways not available either to cinema or the naturalistic stage. The small scenes are played in spotlights within the space of the strike meeting, as the stage direction specifies: 'The lights fade out and a white spot picks out the play-ing space within the space of seated men. The seated men are very dimly visible in the outer dark.'[39] Odets himself described the function of the character Fatt, who in strictly realistic terms is only present at the meeting:

> Fatt, of course, represents the capitalist system throughout the play. The audience should constantly be kept aware of him, the ugly menace which hangs over the lives of all the people who act out their own dramas. Perhaps he puffs smoke into the spotted playing space; perhaps during the action of a playlet he might insolently walk in and around the unseeing players. It is possible that some highly gratifying results can be achieved by the imaginative use of this character.[40]

For its production of Irwin Shaw's *Bury the Dead*, Unity created a pro-gramme consisting of an overlapping montage of wartime images, and the performance itself extended the relationship between theatre and cinema in several ways.[41] An anti-war drama set during 'the second year of the war that is to begin tomorrow night', *Bury the Dead* is constructed around the striking image of a group of corpses who refuse to allow themselves to be buried. Despite all attempts to persuade them to lie down they remain standing in their graves until the final moments of the play, when they climb out and walk offstage past a General who is vainly pumping machine-gun bullets at them. But the play's social attack is not simply on war itself, which is shown as an extreme but logical example of the exploitation of one class by another. The point is made by the wife of one of the corpses, expressing anger with her husband for having left his protest so late: 'What took you so long then? Why not a month ago, a year ago, ten years ago? There's plenty for live men to stand up for! . . . Tell 'em all to stand up!'[42] Crucially, at the end of the play the living soldiers who have been detailed to bury their dead colleagues ignore the orders of their commanding officers and follow the corpses offstage.

Terence Gray had defined the lessons he thought theatre could learn from cinema in relation to a play he had staged in Cambridge which depended on 'a swift panoramic view of events, revealed in a rapid series of scenes, each of which stands on its own dramatic merit. The scenes, impressionistically painted, are loosely knit together by the story.'[43] *Bury the Dead* follows this in making extensive use of short scenes, often cutting swiftly from one to the other. Yet as in Odets' play, it was central to both the emotional and the political impact of the performance that the audience sees even those confrontations which would in realistic terms occur elsewhere against the permanent background of the corpses standing in their graves. Even if they are not specifically lit, the audience is always aware of the corpses since, according to a stage-direction, they are on a platform raised seven feet above the main stage. As with the strike meeting in *Lefty*, the trench scene's physical intrusion into the theatrical space has metaphorical undertones. At times the image is almost reminiscent of a split-screen effect, and elsewhere we are presented with another classic film shot as we see the backs of the heads of the corpses and the faces of those talking to them.

Like Odets and Porché, Shaw does not so much abandon theatrical tradition as add to it. Though short scenes and swift cutting are crucial to the style, there are also some painfully long and slow-moving word-based sections of inaction which would have been less likely to be accepted within a film. The play's heart lies in a series of lengthy dialogues between the corpses and their wives, mothers, sisters and girlfriends. By contrast, the climax creates a fragmented montage out of fleeting images and unseen voices, some of them momentary flashbacks echoing earlier scenes and images. The use of lighting also mixes cinematic and theatrical languages. Shaw's stage-directions frequently demand extremely tight frames of focus which isolate particular characters in close-up and mean that little movement is needed by the actors within the frame. Again, the audience sometimes arrives in the middle of a scene, and even the language of the lighting directions shows that the spotlights – and especially the follow-spot – are conceived of almost as cameras:

Fade-out. The spotlight is turned on to the lower stage . . .

The light fades from the Generals. It follows the Captain as he walks across stage . . .

The light is thrown on the burial scene, where the Doctor is seen examining the corpses. . . . The doctor is talking as he passes from the first man. . . .

Spotlight on a radio-loudspeaker. A Voice, mellow and beautiful, comes out of it. . . .

The spotlight follows Katherine Driscoll as she makes her way from Corpse to Corpse. . . .

The next set of characters walks through a stationary spotlight. . . .

A bolt of light comes down to a machine-gun set to the left of the grave. . . . The Generals are clustered around it.

But Shaw also uses lighting in other ways, most notably in the moment when Dean, the youngest of the corpses who has had his face blown away, is reluctantly persuaded to look at his mother:

He turns his face to her. The audience can't see his face, but immediately a spotlight, white and sharp, shoots down from directly above and hits Dean's head. Mrs Dean leans forward, staring. Another spotlight shoots down immediately after from the extreme right, then one more from the left, then two more, from above. They hit with the impact of blows and Mrs Dean shudders a little as they come, as though she were watching her son being beaten.[44]

Where film would have used close-ups and make-up, Shaw relied on the audience's capacity to imagine what Dean would have looked like, aided by a stylised and choreographed effect and the offstage sound of a continuing scream. The image was censored by the Lord Chamberlain as 'too horribly brutal and wholly unnecessary'.[45]

Writing in *Left Review* in 1935, Slater suggested that 'our Mayakowsky may be nearer than we suppose' and predicted the arrival of a great political play in the near future. It might require an individual genius, but it would appear not in isolation but out of a broader culture: 'It comes, like the Shakespeare play, in the midst of a crowd of inferiors, jostling its way among them, climbing their shoulders, swallowing them whole.'[46]

We let the Establishment off too lightly if we fail to recognise the power it exerted to control what the theatre was able to say and how it should say it. By focusing on specific examples, I have argued that we do a dis-service to the theatrical developments and experiments of the thirties if we allow the myth to be perpetrated that aesthetics were always enslaved by the message, and that the conviction of the performers represents the only quality worth celebrating. Perhaps nostalgia for a time when naïve beliefs could be passionately held and crudely expressed has tended to prevent us from paying due regard to some of the artistic inventions which were also part of political performance in the thirties. Such inventions need not be viewed either as marking a retreat into formalism, or as mere devices to disguise an otherwise unpalatable didacticism. Rather they contributed to a continuing debate and struggle over the relationship between aesthetics and ideology. As some practitioners were well aware, the foregrounding of aesthetics necessarily embodied a challenge to dominant capitalist structures. Political and aesthetic challenges to the status quo were not separate issues, but part of the same battle.

## NOTES

1. Montagu Slater, *Easter: 1916* (London: Lawrence & Wishart, 1936), p. 9. The script won a playwriting competition organised through *Left Review*, and the production was toured by Left Theatre.
2. Ewan MacColl, in the introduction to Howard Goorney and Ewan MacColl (eds), *Agit-Prop to Theatre Workshop* (Manchester: Manchester University Press, 1986), p. xxvii.
3. Tom Thomas, quoted at length in Raphael Samuel, Ewan MacColl and Stuart Cosgrove, *Theatres of the Left 1880–1935* (London: Routledge & Kegan Paul, 1985), pp. 33–4. Thomas was one of the most important figures in the early days of the Workers' Theatre Movement.
4. *Agit-Prop to Theatre Workshop*, p. xxvi.
5. St John Ervine, *The Theatre in My Time* (London: Rich & Cowan, 1933), pp. 131, 135.
6. Ness Edwards, *The Workers' Theatre* (Cardiff: Cymric Federation Press, 1930), p. 26.
7. Ibid., p. 1. The quotation is attributed to Bogdanov.
8. Ibid., p. 70.
9. First staged in Prague in 1920, *R.U.R.*, by the Capek brothers, coined the word 'robots'. They are created to take the place of the working class and are then used in wars against each other. Lacking national distinctions, however, they unite against their oppressors in a successful revolution. According to Edwards, there is no doubt that the robots represent the workers, but his interpretation could be seen as slightly problematic. The first British production was by Nigel Playfair at St Martin's Theatre in 1923, using Paul Selver's translation of the same year.
10. Ervine, *The Theatre in My Time*, pp. 157–9.
11. Montagu Slater, *Left Review*, I (4), January 1935: 144.
12. Gray opened the Festival Theatre in Cambridge in 1926, and ran it until he abandoned all theatre and went to grow vines in France in 1933. His commitment to artistic innovations and foreign work led to frequent confrontations with sections of the Establishment, including the Lord Chamberlain.

    For discussion of this see Steve Nicholson, ' "Nobody Was Ready For That": The Gross Impertinence of Terence Gray and the Degradation Of

Drama', *Theatre Research International*, 21 (2), Summer 1996. *Roar China,* by Sergei Tretiakov, the Russian translator of Brecht, was an attack on W imperialist practice in China, and was based on an actual incident involving a British ship. The Admiralty insisted the play be banned, commenting: 'We consider it especially undesirable that young and inexperienced undergraduates should be subjected at their age to this kind of malicious anti-British propaganda.' For discussion of this play in relation to censorship, see Steve Nicholson, 'Censoring Revolution: The Lord Chamberlain and the Soviet Union', *New Theatre Quarterly*, VIII (32), November 1992.

13. Barbara Nixon, 'Introduction' to Sergei Tretiakov, *Roar China* (London: Martin Lawrence, 1931), p. 3.

14. Tretiakov, *Roar China*, ibid., p. 78.

15. Tretiakov, ibid., 'Author's Note'.

16. For discussion of this see Steve Nicholson, ' "Unnecessary Plays". European Drama and the British Censor in the 1920s', *Theatre Research International*, 20 (1), spring 1995.

17. From the Reader's Report on Toller's *Mass-Man* by G.S. Street, 6 May 1924. See the Lord Chamberlain's Correspondence Files.

18. *Plays and Players*, II (15), November 1932: 3.

19. Terence Gray, *Dance-Drama: Experiments in the Art of the Theatre* (Cambridge: W. Heffer, 1926), p. 7.

20. *Left Review*, I (4), January 1935: 126–7.

21. Ervine, *The Theatre in My Time*, p. 160.

22. Montagu Slater, *New Way Wins* (London: Lawrence & Wishart, 1937), pp. 31, 70. The play was also performed by Left Theatre as *Stay Down Miner*.

23. One article by Brecht, 'The German Drama: Pre-Hitler' was published in *Left Review* (July 1936, II (10): 504–8), and in 1938 Unity Theatre gave the first British production of *Señora Carrar's Rifles*. However, Brecht's writing was not widely known in Britain till the second half of the fifties. Writing in 1984, John Allen, one of Unity's principal directors, recalled that Stanislavsky had been the main inspiration, rather than Brecht 'of whose theories we really knew nothing'. See John Allen's 'Introduction' to *Busmen/One-Third of a Nation* (Nottingham: Nottingham Drama Texts, 1984), p. 1.

24. Ervine, *The Theatre in My Time*, pp. 159–60.

25. From the Reader's Report by H.C. Game on *Stay Down Miner*, 7 September 1936. See the Lord Chamberlain's Correspondence Files.

26. Montagu Slater, *Easter: 1916*, p. 9.

27. For a detailed discussion of Slater's dramatic work during the thirties see Steve Nicholson, 'Montagu Slater and Theater of the Thirties' in Patrick Quinn (ed.), *Recharting the Thirties* (London: Associated University Presses, 1996).

28. *Tsar Lénine* was written in 1930 and produced in Paris by Charles Dullin. Its first actual production in Britain was in 1937 at the Westminster Theatre.

29. From the unpublished translation of the script, p. 69, made by Roy Newlands, submitted to the Lord Chamberlain by the Festival Theatre in 1933 and currently housed in the Lord Chamberlain's Collection of Unlicensed Plays in the British Library.

30. From the Reader's Report on *Tsar Lénine* by G.S. Street, 23 January 1933. See the Lord Chamberlain's Correspondence Files.

31. See *The Times*, 28 June 1937 and the *Observer*, 4 July 1937.

32. Ervine, *The Theatre in My Time*, p. 247.

33. From the 'Minute of Exception' issued by the British Board of Film Censors, 21 February 1929, to the Lord Chamberlain in response to his request they should ajudicate on the proposed film. See the Lord Chamberlain's Correspondence Files. The production by Gray went ahead without the film, but he subsequently described the performance as having been 'mutilated'.

34. *Rasputin*, by A.N. Tolstoy and P.E. Shchegoleff, was adapted from the Russian by Clifford Bax and produced for the Stage Society in April 1929. The *Stage* found it 'alternately dull and crudely realistic' (25 April 1929) and St John Ervine, fair-minded as ever, described it as 'like most Russian conversation: too long and in places too trivial' (*Observer*, 28 April 1929).

35. Griffith's *Red Sunday* was directed by Komisarjevsky and performed at the Arts Theatre in June 1929 with John Gielgud as Trotsky and Robert Farquharson as Lenin. These were private performances. A licence for public performance was refused after interventions by exiled Russian aristocracy and ministers and by Buckingham Palace.

36. James Agate writing in the *Sunday Times*, 30 June 1929.

37. Francois Porché, 'Introduction' to published text, *Tsar Lénine* (Paris: Flammarion, 1932), pp. 25–8.

38. *Waiting for Lefty* was first performed in America in 1935 and in England by the Rebel Players in the same year. It was performed over 300 times by Unity Theatre in the next few years, and following discussion in parliament was banned from performance on the BBC. John Allen had no hesitation in calling it 'The Greatest Left-Wing play of them all' (*Left Review*, III (7), August, 1937: 419).

39. Clifford Odets, *Waiting for Lefty* (London: Gollancz, 1938), p. 10.

40. Ibid., 'Notes for Production', p. 47.

41. *Bury the Dead* was another of Unity's major successes in the second half of the thirties. It was derived from Chlumberg's *Miracle at Verdun*. At the first performance of Irwin Shaw's play by Merseyside Unity Theatre some members of the audience had to be treated for shock.

42. Irwin Shaw, *Bury the Dead*, published in *Famous Plays of 1936* (London: Gollancz, 1936), p. 382.

43. Gray was discussing the production of *Happy and Glorious* by Wilf Walter. See *The Festival Theatre Review*, 124, 29 April 1933: 1.

44. All quotations from Irwin Shaw, *Bury the Dead*.

45. Note by Lord Cromer, 22 April 1938, in the Lord Chamberlain's Correspondence Files.

46. Montagu Slater, *Left Review*, I (9), June 1935: 364.

## CHAPTER ELEVEN

# Post/Modern Documentary: Orwell, Agee and the New Reportage

KEITH WILLIAMS

Documentary, one of the thirties' most characteristic and international practices, underwent its own peculiar crisis of transition from modernity to incipient postmodernism during the period. This was reached in the British context through Orwell's 'new reportage' such as *The Road to Wigan Pier* and, ultimately, in *Homage to Catalonia*'s self-conscious engagement with propaganda, the mediation of fact and the fabrication of history. However, although there are many scattered insights and hints in his writings, Orwell, temperamentally resistant to systematic theorisation, never mustered a fully-articulated critique of his own discourse's representational techniques. This was arguably achieved in the American context by James Agee's deconstruction of the documentary aesthetic of the New Deal in *Let Us Now Praise Famous Men*.

David Peck argues that the defining moment of thirties culture in both Britain and America was 1936. In February and March, Orwell was travelling around the industrial North of England gathering material for *The Road to Wigan Pier*; in July and August Agee was in Alabama with the photographer Walker Evans recording the life of three tenant families for *Let Us Now Praise Famous Men*: 'In these few months an ocean apart, three journalists were thus creating essential images of thirties life, at the same time that they were helping to shape a documentary genre.'[1] These writers' careers also follow a model 'thirties trajectory'. In this decade of *Proletcult*, neither Agee nor Orwell were working-class, but had privileged backgrounds against which they struggled to re-imagine themselves in their work. Most crucially, both aspired to be serious novelists, under a kind of Bloomian 'anxiety of influence' from Joyce,[2] but 'succeeded, in their own lifetimes at least, at something much more perishable' (in Agee's case even his major reportage did not achieve critical acclaim until reprinted in the sixties). Both were radical, if not cussed, non-conformists. Although by the end of the thirties they had made leftist commitments, these were, paradoxically, inseparable from 'serious suspicions of the orthodox Marxism of their day' (although literary-political culture in neither country was monolithic like the hoary myth of the 'Red Decade' suggests, orthodoxy of a more complex kind did become, arguably, more widespread in the States). Both died before fulfilling their potential (Orwell in 1950, Agee in 1955), were posthumously rediscovered and are, above all, 'still the subject of intense debate over the meaning and value of their work'.[3]

Parallels between the history and style of their major reportage texts are striking. Their genesis was in commissions quickly transgressed, with similarly controversial results. *Fortune* magazine refused to publish the articles Agee was assigned for its 'Life and Circumstances' series, so that he had to reshape them into the book finally published by Houghton Mifflin in 1941. Similarly, although *Wigan Pier* became one of the Left Book Club's contemporary best-sellers (at over 40,000 copies), this was at the price of Victor Gollancz's disclaiming foreword and the withdrawal of Part Two in the second edition. They are also analogous in structure as apparent political and aesthetic 'failures'. Orwell's is notoriously broken-backed, split between telling observation of poverty in the first part and hackle-raising autobiographical 'digression' on class in the second. Though, as we shall see, there are strategic justifications for the disintegrated structure of Agee's, with its 'circular, almost labyrinthine movement', it was considered 'unreadable'. The problem facing both writers was also the same, 'to describe the conditions under which people in the worst of the Depression were living and working' from the inside of the experience – to which they found similar solutions – conversion of 'hard facts of observation into imaginative literature'. Their method was also analogous – a 'particular combination of voice and language' that, paradoxically, went against the grain of the dominant discourse of thirties documentarism, while simultaneously working within its tradition.[4]

Thus Peck makes a convincing case for re-examining these key texts of British and American reportage as crucial to any reconfiguration of the matrix of thirties cultural politics and, especially, their ambivalent relations with modernism. If documentary (virtually the Jakobsonian 'dominant' of thirties culture, since even perhaps the bulk of thirties fictional literature was magnetised toward it)[5] is the impulse towards a factual art, film was the modern medium which epitomised it, but reportage was its written equivalent. That which I term 'new' was an innovative tendency (it never really became a coherent programme in Anglophone writing as such) between the wars which tried to absorb modernism's lessons for politically accountable ends. The new reportage was an extremely flexible literary form, porous to many avant-garde influences and particularly intertextual with the technological mass-media. John Reed's *Ten Days that Shook the World* (1919) gave it early and special resonance for American writers, because the October Revolution and Soviet 'literature of fact', particularly in the work of the Left Front in the Arts (LEF) on Reed's model, reinflected the possibilities of home-grown traditions. These were re-exported to the United States, as well as disseminated across Europe in the twenties, notably via Weimar Germany, with a rehoned political edge as well as a modernised form. In *Ten Days that Shook the World*, Reed's dialogic between I-witness reporting and intertextual documentary montage problematised the conventional boundary between literature and history.[6] The new reportage following on from it was, symptomatically, a reaction against modernism's imploding preoccupation with self-analysis and experiment, but without merely regressing to nineteenth-century Naturalism's unproblematised mimesis. It eventually became an important position in the debate about the nature of the real, and the question of the most effective form for representing it, central to thirties culture in both Britain and America. This acknowledgement that modernism's linguistic self-consciousness, together with new media technology, had transformed categories of realistic representation irrevocably, wasn't only aesthetic, but political. As modernism had shown, by becoming 'naturalised' and 'transparent' such categories could turn repressive, blurring discourse into the real itself, confusing the sign with its referent. The solution sought was paradoxical: an 'objective' art reproducing reality as soberly and authentically as possible, while at the same time 'baring its own devices' in an anti-illusionistic manner. This is not to suggest all documentary writing in thirties Britain and America reflected such concerns. Most of it was naïvely empirical, or relatively uninformed by aesthetic issues. The whole field, moreover, is much too massive and diverse to give a map of it here. What I want to trace is how this crucially symptomatic, avant-garde influence I have termed the 'new reportage' acts on Orwell and Agee's texts, beginning with the British scene.

Early Soviet avant-garde film-makers such as Dziga Vertov edited their factual footage to make significant connections through non-discursive montage 'shocks' and reveal the socio-economic syntax behind the automatised surface of everyday reality. The British documentary film movement spearheaded by John Grierson assimilated Vertov's 'cinema-eye' techniques, but if Soviet documentary eventually fell victim to direct state censorship under Stalinism (anxious to enforce an official, anti-modernist discourse of the real) the radical possibilities of Grierson's project at the Empire Marketing Board and, later, General Post Office, Film Unit were curtailed by the indirect censorship of capitalist sponsors. Grierson's own comments on *Drifters* (1929), his film about the Scottish herring fisheries, show how he originally intended to demystify and render visible the economic and social structure behind a prosaic commodity. Dramatically telescoping spatial and social distances between labour and consumption, its imagery was intended to shuttle between life-and-death ocean drama and hustling fish-market, to underline the process by which labour is converted into exchange value – 'said agonies are sold at ten shillings a thousand . . . for an unwitting world'.[7] *Drifters* was to have traced what Sergei Tretiakov called the hidden 'biography of things'. Grierson himself defined documentary as the 'creative interpretation of actuality', and montage became its 'shorthand method' of relating mundane objects to the interconnecting processes of 'corporate life'.[8] By emulating the method of documentary film in his new reportage *The Road to Wigan Pier* (1937), Orwell would similarly demystify the value of labour in coal-mining to an extent that became increasingly impossible in the medium of British documentary film.

This intertextuality between the media of contemporary factual art in Britain was theorised most extensively by Storm Jameson in the journal *FACT*. Her article 'Documents' was much closer to the thinking of LEF than to Socialist Realism, the orthodox cultural policy of Stalinism, which she regarded as a prescriptive formalising of what genuinely socialist writing might be.[9] Jameson had been a delegate at the 1935 Paris Writers' Congress which featured one of the prime movers of Central European new reportage, Egon Erwin Kisch. The following year, the Congress of the International Association of Writers for the Defence of Culture was devoted to the French delegation's proposal for an international encyclopaedism with revolutionary humanist aims like those of late-eighteenth-century France.[10] This intellectual offensive seems to have influenced Victor Gollancz's Left Book Club, also founded in 1936, which would publish *The Road to Wigan Pier* as its monthly choice the following March. Similarly, Jameson and her colleagues at *FACT* believed that reporting 'the facts' could stimulate necessary changes in social consciousness to produce a new culture that would both safeguard society from Fascism and facilitate Socialist transformation. The writer's task was to find an imaginative, shorthand method that would subvert the subject's imaginary relations to their real conditions of existence (to apply Althusser's formula) propagated by capitalist culture. Where Jameson differed from LEF and Kisch was in limiting reportage to the *instrumental* function of laying the factual basis for future writing, rather than allowing it literary status in its own right. She did not advocate the complete 'funeral of fict-iveness', as LEF had wanted, just its temporary suspension. But she agreed with them that every factual particle of society carried a kind of 'genetic code' of its underlying processes. It did not matter where the cross-section was incised 'if you know what you are looking for'.[11]

Jameson considered it absurd for bourgeois writers, in particular, to adopt hypothetically 'proletarian' forms without first gathering necessary information about the lives of working people as objectively as they could. She demanded they become 'participant observers' (to use the contemporary sociological term) without feeling heroic, adventurous, or even 'curious about their own spiritual reactions'. However, in her view, objectivity applied to the stage of fact-gathering: representing them was a matter of finding the right aesthetic and political strategy. She was astute about the role of cinematic technique for revealing the 'stirring' or symptomatic in mundane realities without intervening authorial commentary.[12] Deploring the dry-as-dust language of a *Times* report on the Durham coalfields, she suggested instead that 'As the photographer does, so must the writer keep himself out of the picture while working ceaselessly to present the *fact* from a striking (poignant, ironic, penetrating, significant) angle.' Her ideal reporter was not only a camera-eyed witness but an editor as well, 'coldly and industriously presenting, arranging, selecting, discarding from the mass of his material to get the significant detail, which leaves no more to be said, and implies everything'. While exhorting fellow writers to become 'field workers in a field no smaller than England, our critical values implied in the angle from which we take our pictures', she also confronted 'the extreme difficulty of finding phrases . . . compressed and highly selective' that would lay bare 'in such a way that they are at once seen to be intimately connected, the relations between things (men, acts) widely separated in space or in the social complex'. Her theory that reportage might provide a more accurate way of re-imagining our relations to the real conditions of existence that would undercut the merely imaginary ones of ideology, extended logically into textual emulation of documentary film montage. It would radically defamiliarise social life, relating classes to commodities and means of production, but avoid the extreme disruption of mimetic plausibility associated with modernism's more anarchic tendencies, such as Surrealism.[13]

A current example of literary use of cinematic devices which Jameson had in mind, was the first half of Orwell's *The Road to Wigan Pier*, though the second also prompted her tirade against 'self-analysis' incarcerating the bourgeois writer 'inside his own small ego at the moment when what is individual to each man is less real, less actual, than that which he shares with every other man'. She had already castigated Orwell for reporting poverty 'subjectively', in contrast to National Unemployed Workers' Movement leader Wal Hannington's *Unemployed Struggles*.[14] In thirties British documentarism, the collier acquired the same iconic status as the Southern tenant farmer of New Deal culture in America. The industrial politics of the time centred around what we might call the battle for 'hearts and mines' which would eventually lead to postwar Nationalisation. Orwell had almost certainly been influenced himself by the small avalanche of documentaries on coal released in the mid-thirties. Though undoubtedly raising some kind of public consciousness, most of them fitted the established Griersonian pattern of official/commercial sponsorship, which played down or begged questions about the conditions of the industry. The GPO's *Coalface* (1935) subjected mining to the same 'poetic' treatment as *Night Mail* did postal work, with material shot by Humphrey Jennings and Basil Wright, and including a score by Benjamin Britten, and verses by Auden and Montagu Slater. Other films were showcases for the Coal Utilisation Council or the Safety in Mines Research Board. Exceptional in its radicalism was *Today We Live* (1937) (collier-writer Lewis Jones possibly saluted it in the title of his second *Cwmardy* novel) on the work of the National Council of Social Services. This confronted the devastating impact of unemployment in South Wales and even contained an interview with an unemployed miner demanding a real job, not the Council's palliatives. Ralph Bond directed and scripted the Rhondda Valley sequence in co-operation with the miners themselves, and Donald Alexander's footage of unemployed men gleaning slag-heaps closely resembles *Wigan Pier* words and images of 'coal-scrambling'.[15]

Orwell employed literary montage to bridge physical and conceptual distances between the use (as opposed to exchange) value of coal-mining and other activities. The 'biography of things' was central to his cross-sectioning of the socio-economic structure. The 'thing' is coal, and, as Gustav H. Klaus and Jürgen Enkemann put it, unlike many documentary film-makers Orwell refused 'to consider the labour process in isolation as "intrinsically interesting"'. As Kisch and other new reporters had done with other industries, he pursued it 'right up to its end product, coal fuel . . . to reveal the character and form of a commodity'.[16] Jameson proposed borrowing film's radical potential for showing hidden causal connections. Similarly, the leitmotif of *Wigan Pier* demonstrates how the economic basis of a complex society is easily mystified by increasing distances between production and consumption:

> Our civilisation, *pace* Chesterton, is founded on coal, more completely than one realises until one stops to think about it. The machines that keep us alive, and the machines that make the machines, are all directly or indirectly dependent upon coal. In the metabolism of the Western world the coal-miner is second in importance only to the man who ploughs the soil. He is a sort of grimy caryatid upon whose shoulders nearly everything that is not grimy is supported.[17]

Orwell's 'grimy caryatid' plays on the connotations of 'founded' and the miners' appearance (later they are monumental 'hammered iron statues under the smooth coat of coal dust' (*Wigan Pier*, p. 20)). It becomes a symbol whose 'imaginative rationality' builds up persuasively through context.[18] As Marina Warner shows, architectural allegory has always had ideological implications. The Greeks named pillars carved in female form after the enslaved Caryae, but, in so doing, also monumentalised their civilisation's *dependence* on the labour of inferior 'others'. (I discuss Orwell's controversial masculinisation of this allegory elsewhere, but his principal motive was to invert social hierarchy by focusing on the vital importance of its economic supports.)[19]

*Wigan Pier* telescopes distances between different sections of society on the basis of real economic relationships, not their mystified refractions:

> Watching coal-miners at work, you realise momentarily what different universes people inhabit. Down there where coal is dug it is a sort of world apart which one can quite easily go through life without ever hearing about. Probably a majority of people would even prefer not to hear about it. Yet it is the absolutely necessary counterpart to the world above.
>
> (p. 29)

Consequently, Orwell revealed the concrete, if ordinarily invisible, links to social strata out of immediate contact with physical modes of production by 'colliding' remote images:

> Practically everything we do, from eating an ice to crossing the Atlantic, and from baking a loaf to writing a novel, involves the use of coal, directly or indirectly. For all the arts of peace coal is needed: if war breaks out it is needed all the more. In time of revolution the miner must go on working or the revolution must stop, for revolution as much as reaction needs coal. Whatever may be happening on the surface, the hacking and the shovelling have got to continue. . . . In order that Hitler may march the goose-step, that the Pope may denounce Bolshevism, that the cricket crowds may assemble at Lords, that the Nancy poets may scratch one another's backs, coal has got to be forthcoming.
>
> (p. 29)

The miner's fundamental use-value is revealed by juxtaposing these immensely divergent, even contradictory, superstructural activities all supported by his work. Moreover, it is not difficult to envisage Orwell's images constellated around the Promethean figure of a 'grimy caryatid' in the dynamic forms of either film- or photo-montage. In effect, *Wigan Pier*'s strategy is a dialectical marriage between industrial underworld and privileged sphere above, between Wigan and Kensington, as it were, which renders all the more unjust the tragic facts of mass unemployment and deprivation in the traditional mining areas by emphasising the indebtedness of the southern middle classes who have the wealth and political influence to change things.[20] Coal, like so many other commodities, seems an inert, history-less fossil: 'black stuff that arrives mysteriously from nowhere in particular, like manna except you have to pay for it' (p. 30). Since capitalist ideology depends on erasing all traces of alienated labour from the products we consume, the miner's work was (to borrow Agee's notable phrase) 'a portion of unimagined existence':

> It is so with all types of manual work: it keeps us alive and we are
> oblivious of its existence. More than anyone else, perhaps, the miner can
> stand as the type of the manual worker, not only because his work is so
> exaggeratedly awful, but also because it is so vitally necessary and yet so
> remote from our experience, as it were that we are capable of forgetting
> it as we forget the blood in our veins.
>
> (p. 30)

Orwell's reportage demystified part of the economic system by showing
consciousness of it to be as automatised as that of our bodily functions, but
also just as vital. This was implicit in the use of 'metabolism' in the quotation above (p. 18) which personified the social whole to suggest an intimate
connection between privileged consciousness and 'low' physical labour.[21]
However, the manual labour of most of Britain's thirties proletariat was
'unimagined' or invisible not because they were underground, but in a far-
away Empire. *Wigan Pier* aimed to further the Left Book Club's objective
of a Popular Front between all classes against Fascism and economic abuses
on the basis of encyclopaedic knowledge of the facts. Orwell, having seen
colonial repression at close quarters, stressed elsewhere that his political
journey to Wigan Pier began in Mandalay and that Imperial products had
concealed histories too. The dividend-drawer's contact with the exploited
was even more dissociated and, all the more conveniently, allowed him/
her to feel morally uncontaminated. Consequently, in 'The Lion and the
Unicorn' (1941), Orwell extended *Wigan Pier*'s strategy to telescope geo-
graphic and economic distances.[22]

The extent to which film and photography became formal models for
topical thirties writing was shown by its saturation with their terminology
and emulation of their devices, and the active involvement of many writers
in film-scripting and film-making. Isherwood typified this enthusiasm, and
almost certainly knew Vertov's work (whether he got his camera-eye via
Dos Passos or not). But he was also typical of writers' growing suspicions
about the privileged objectivity of documentary filmic discourse. His own
selective 'fixings' of fact in *Goodbye to Berlin* (1939) implicitly acknowledge
that the subjectivity of the camera-eyed witness is always present in the
reality reported, whether explicit or displaced.[23]

The most scrupulously honest literary documentarists employed their own
editing to maximise the poetic and political potential of 'raw' factual footage.
For example, another iconic image in *Wigan Pier* – the woman futilely
poking a stick up a blocked drainpipe (pp. 14–15) – differs from its original
context, dated 15 February 1936 in 'The Road to Wigan Pier Diary', while
exploring the backstreets of Wigan on foot with some National Unemployed
Workers' Movement guides.[24] This documentary 'snapshot', which defamil-
iarises middle-class prejudices – that the masses are anaesthetised to misery,

because 'they don't know any better' – was recontextualised and elaborated in the published reportage. Crudely, Orwell transcribed the authentic fact in the Diary and distorted it in *Wigan Pier*, though if the Diary had not survived this rare insight into his 'creative interpretation of actuality' would have been undetectable.

The image's relocation gave it more intense poetic connotations. Placing it at the end of Orwell's 'participant observation' of Wigan life made it representative of the experience. There was a new emphasis on the anonymous woman's typicality – 'the usual exhausted face of the slum girl who is twenty-five and looks forty'. Close-up details – 'her sacking apron, her clumsy clogs, her arms reddened by the cold' – summarised the characteristic impressions of deprivation. In effect, she became the *genius loci* (or, perhaps, extending the filmic analogy, *genius foci*) of Wigan's anti-pastoral landscape. Perhaps Orwell had another, more personal, perhaps unconscious, motive for the changes: the 'lower-upper-middle-class' reporter (as he called himself on p. 113) apparently takes this startling snapshot from a train window – a transparency framing the woman exactly like a lens, but also a barrier to closer contact. Orwell had a return ticket from the underworld, leaving this proletarian Eurydice to her destiny. It was an implicit admission that intertextual, camera-eyed witnessing of facts was not in itself enough to dismantle class-barriers – indeed the suggestion is they were inscribed within its very discourse – unless that prompted nationwide political change.

As already mentioned, Orwell never mustered a fully articulated critique of his own reportage's representational techniques, although his practice reached its crisis in *Homage to Catalonia* (1938). Within the context of Spanish Republican sectarian in-fighting, Orwell's encounter with Stalinist *Realpolitik* propaganda and the documentary fabrication of history anticipates postmodern theories about the simulating power of media 'hyper-reality' and 'performativity'.[25] However, though Orwell cautioned the reader about his own subjective bias in opposing the truth of official accounts with first-person empirical testimony, he did not directly objectify the poesis so crucial (as we have seen in *Wigan Pier*) to the persuasiveness of his own deployment of the facts.

Though the radical potentials of film documentary were diluted by the requirements of official/commercial sponsorship, the Left Book Club, along with periodicals like *FACT* and the Mass-Observation movement, did stimulate a great volume of documentary writing. However, with a government more concerned with concealing facts about social conditions than disseminating them, British reportage remained oppositional until the Second World War, when the Ministry of Information recruited thirties documentary culture for producing the morale-raising social-democratic reconstruction propaganda vital to galvanise resistance. The case was significantly different in the United States, however, where documentary discourses had been gradually assimilated into the official cultural politics of the New Deal from the mid-thirties onwards.

American documentarism, though it also began as an oppositional movement under the auspices of radical magazines such as *New Masses* in the twenties (its 'counter-factual' status was re-emphasised in speeches about the new reportage at the American Writers' Congress of 1935),[26] received a special boost shortly after the election of President Roosevelt in 1932. The belief rapidly spread that to find out 'the facts' about conditions in the Depression would enable the Federal Government programme to deal with them, and this sponsored a climate in which the radical and the semi-official became somewhat merged. The thirties in America were, therefore, the decade of *The March of Time* newsreel, Pare Lorentz's film *The River* (1937), photo-reportage such as *An American Exodus* (1937) by Dorothea Lange and Paul Taylor, Steinbeck's pamphlet on migrant workers in California, *Their Blood is Strong* (1938), transformed into his epic documentary novel *The Grapes of Wrath* (1939), of John L. Spivak's blistering exposé journalism and of Martha Gellhorn's 'downhome' dispatches (material from which featured regularly in Roosevelt's radio broadcasts). Much 'worcorr' and bourgeois reportage on social conditions was also published in liberal American journals like *The Nation* and *The New Republic*. It was also the era of the Federal Writers' Project (under director Henry Alsberg, it produced the American Guides, a kind of documentary road map of 'unknown' America) and of Roy Stryker's Farm Securities Administration photographic unit (for which Walker Evans developed his distinctive style of close portraiture of the rural poor). New Deal documentarism grew into an exercise in mass-communications equivalent in scale to, and partly modelled on, bureaucratisation of the Russian arts by Stalinism and predating the wartime mobilisation of British documentarism. Its net ideological effect was the 'redreaming of America' as Hallie Flanagan put it,[27] and the assimilation of the documentary impulse into mainstream cultural politics. However, the embarrassing riches of sponsored fact-gathering were, arguably, not only designed to enable Federal reforms, but carefully managed to convince the nation they were paying off. Though mostly sincerely assigned and undertaken, documentarism was increasingly hedged by considerations not to question or upset the thrust of Federal policy. Its social-democratic tendency became mortgaged to a specifically American cultural conservatism, desirous of ameliorating, not radically disturbing, the system, by reinventing its image.

This is the context of Agee and Evans's 'participant observation' of the lives of Alabaman tenant farmers. Their close collaboration had no exact equivalent in Britain (photographs in *Wigan Pier*, for example, were assembled illustratively from diverse sources by Gollancz, although Orwell's literary shapshots were probably influenced by the camera of Bill Brandt).[28] Despite relative obscurity during Agee's lifetime, William Stott argues that *Let Us Now Praise Famous Men* was the culminating text of New Deal documentarism, because Agee felt duty-bound to bite the semi-official hand that fed him and deliberately scandalise the proprieties of a discourse which had become a cultural norm by the end of the decade.[29] As his preface cautioned:

> Since it is intended . . . as a swindle, an insult, and a corrective the reader will be wise to bear the nominal subject, and his expectation of its proper treatment, steadily in mind. . . . If complications arise, that is because they [the authors] are trying to deal with it not as journalists, sociologists, politicians, entertainers, humanitarians, priests or artists, but seriously.[30]

His reportage deconstructed the factual art of the New Deal through its critique of its own representational processes, thus marking the transition from the ambivalent assimilation of and/or resistance to modernism in American documentary to the beginning of full-blown postmodernism. The disturbing flock of questions about reality, truth, subjectivity and language raised by modernist writing, which the interwar cult of 'objective' factuality failed to settle, swarm back towards, and are even welcomed into, Agee's text. For Agee, thirties documentarism had intensified them by attempting to make them disappear into the transparency of an official, multi-media discourse of the American real. The debate about realism was for Agee *par excellence* the point at which politics and poetics became indivisible.

The one and a half million semi-destitute farmers of the Southern cotton belt sometimes found New Deal reforms a raw deal.[31] Moreover, Agee came to believe publicisation of the abuses of the tenantry system declined in ratio to the economy's gearing up for the wartime boom: 'Now that we are busy buttering ourselves as the last stronghold of democracy, interest in such embarrassments has tactfully slackened off' (*Famous Men*, p. 208, note). The cultural politics of the situation were, perhaps, more negotiated and dialectical than he allowed (Roosevelt's limited reforms were, after all, fiercely opposed at every step by the Right and its media), but Agee's outrage stemmed from loss of patience with the New Deal's crusading 'exposure' of poverty in the worst sense. This made 'honest journalism' a contradiction in terms, because 'unbias . . . when skillfully enough qualified' was, ironically, 'exchangeable at any bank for money (and in politics, for votes, job patronage, abelincolnism, etc.)' (p. 7).

Agee's bile was directed particularly at Erskine Calder and Margaret Bourke-White's 1937 photo-reportage *You Have Seen Their Faces*.[32] In contrast to such texts, Agee short-circuited any appearance of 'transparent' or straightforward representation of complex facts precisely by directing attention at the politico-aesthetic configuration promoting documentary and, he argued, corrupting its ethical impulse. Some Northern journalists of the American Scene were 'belated virgilians'. By testifying reassuringly that the myth of log-cabin-to-White-House democracy was still sound at its pastoral roots, they assisted in the creation of an operable national reality through fabricated cultural consensus (pp. 340–1). Documentary's critical function, both counter-factual *and* anti-illusionist, as exemplified by the New Reportage tendency, was being neutralised, as it had been in the Soviet Union, by transformation from agitation- to integration-propaganda: 'Official acceptance is the one unmistakable symptom that salvation is beaten again' (p. 15).

Beginning as a modest photo-journalistic assignment for *Fortune* magazine, eventually rejected for its blatant lack of fit with the ethos of the New Deal, Agee's project swelled to the epic proportions he felt were necessary to do justice to its theme. It owed much to the native encyclopaedism of Melville, and to Dos Passos's 'camera-eye', but also Faulkner's modernist novels and, especially, Joycean maximalism. In a very *Ulyssean* manner Agee went into microscopic detail about a quotidian situation, but stubbornly insisting on its macrocosmic implications: 'Actually the effort is to recognize the stature of a portion of unimagined existence, and to contrive techniques proper to its recording, communication, analysis, and defense. More essentially, this is an independent inquiry into certain normal predicaments of human divinity' (p. xiv). Agee rejected the reductive notion of documentary as simply 'fiction's opposite'[33] and demonstrated that their discourses were more properly adjacent and overlapping. Writing the real was more challenging, demanded more creative ingenuity than the invented, because it added the difficulty of representing what existed quite independently of discourse, so that 'all of consciousness is shifted from the imagined, the revisive, to the effort to perceive simply the cruel radiance of what is' (p. 11).

*Let Us Now Praise Famous Men* objectified and probed the very crux of the new reportage which *Wigan Pier* only gestured towards. Agee and Evans's words and images aspired to present 'things in themselves' with more than naturalistic authenticity, but only by simultaneously acknowledging the ultimate impossibility of their own project, the failure, not just of the dominant documentary discourse, but of language itself to be adequate to the complexity of lived experience. Despite Storm Jameson's strictures about confessionalism, Orwell's text never approached the same degree of self-consciousness. Even though both could be seen as the culmination of the forging of their respective autobiographical personae as I-witnesses, Agee's is more overtly and self-reflexively about the subject observing its own production of, and in, language.[34] On the one hand, conveying the facts of the tenants' existence demanded the most immediate and tangible terms:

'If I could do it, I'd do no writing at all here. It would be photographs: the rest would be fragments of cloth, bits of cotton, lumps of earth, records of speech, pieces of wood and iron, phials of odors, plates of food and of excrement' (p. 13). On the other, the mirage of unmediated common-sense' realism had to be denounced. Paradoxically, *Let Us Now Praise Famous Men* flaunts its descent from modernist techniques such as collage and the *objét trouvé* all the more, the more concretely objective it becomes (even utilitarian objects are also metonymic figures for the absent individuals who use them). Unlike Swift's Lagadans in *Gulliver's Travels*, who, distrusting words, lugged around everything they wished to signify, Agee recognised that if a literal, all-inclusive discourse of the actual were possible it would be at once 'the most beautiful and powerful' and 'about the heaviest of all languages'. Like the informationally super-saturated discourse of Joyce's 'Ithaca', it would, ironically, suffocate 'the deftness, keenness, immediacy, speed and subtlety of the "reality" it tries to reproduce'. Conversely, though, for photography 'much of this is solved from the start'. Agee considered it solved with a deceptive ease that, paradoxically, 'becomes the greatest danger against the good use of the camera', as we shall see below (p. 236).

Agee's critique of his own text's poesis led him to a very Jakobsonian conclusion:[35] the necessity of 'the cleansing and rectification of language, the breakdown of the identification of word and object'. Consequently a theory of self-advertising artifice underpins his transitional documentary aesthetic. Though he shared the 'naturalist's regard for the "real"', it was on a plane which brought it 'level in value at least to music and poetry'. So it was vital 'representation of "reality" does not sag into, or become one with, naturalism', lest that fall short 'even of the relative truth you have perceived and intended'. *Let Us Now Praise Famous Men*'s position about what Barthes would call the 'responsibility of form',[36] was to make the best of 'the most dangerous and impossible of bargains' and, thus, get both 'nearer the truth and farther from it' (pp. 237–8). This was balanced by robust denial that reality itself is either totally relativistic, or a mere effect of discursive 'performativity'. It was not simply 'up for grabs', as claimed by certain tendencies in nineties postmodernism.[37] Agee's text even hypothesised a future documentarism comprehensively aware of both its human subjects and the parameters of its medium, of which it was 'merely portent and fragment, experiment, dissonant prologue'. Thus he foregrounded the notion that *Famous Men*'s objective was necessarily postponed or 'elsewhere', beyond itself. (See *Famous Men*, pp. xv and 245, note.)

Agee's reportage is an explicitly intertextual collage of camera-eyed witnessing, documents and literary modes. He suggested this intricately layered and provisional, 'exploded' form be read dynamically 'as music is listened to or a film watched' (p. xv). Since the reader's role was to be co-operative in this 'effort in human actuality', its structure was, therefore, also chronologically 'shuffled' in the best modernist tradition, functioning by evocation and motific cross-referencing (pp. 243–4).

His and Evans's post/modern scepticism emerges most strongly in their attitude to photographic 'objectivity'. Though Agee wrote 'the camera seems to me, next to unassisted and weaponless consciousness, the central instrument of our time', he regarded its privileged access to the actual as duplicitous (p. 11). More explicitly than Isherwood, Agee and Evans made no pretence the camera-eye was neutral in itself or a standard of detachment for literary documentarism to emulate. They insisted the observer was, self-reflexively, 'one of the centers of the subject' (p. xiv). As mentioned, their disquiet about the camera's 'corruption of sight' concentrated on Bourke White. This ex-commercial photographer, who had latched on to the visual rhetoric of Soviet modernism, admitted 'bribing, cajoling and sometimes browbeating her way' into tenants' houses (p. 451). For Agee and Evans, her work epitomised the invasive opportunism of New Deal documentarism. Her 'candid' technique of catching subjects unawares and manipulating the desired effect from angling and other devices was dehumanising and exploitative. It is certainly arguable that Bourke White constructed her subjects on unequal terms, as objects of sensational curiosity for middle-class consumers (for example the Preacher, College Grove Tennessee, captioned 'We've got a first-class God') or of passive misery, for relieving *de haute en bas* by Federal Government (the close-up of a tenant farmer's face from Locket, Georgia, captioned 'It ain't hardly worth the trouble to go on living.')[38] In reaction to this, *Let Us Now Praise Famous Men* foregrounded the contingency of facts under the camera's interventions, as in a shot of a church: 'this light upon it was strengthening still further its imposal and embrace, and in about a quarter of an hour would have trained itself ready, and there would be a triple convergence in the keen historic spasm of the shutter. . . . I watched what would be trapped, possessed, fertilized' (pp. 38–9). Their initially underhand snapping of share-cropper Fred Ricketts was quickly repented of – 'Walker under the smoke screen of our talking made a dozen pictures of you using the angle finder', after they noticed 'how much slower white people are to catch on than negroes, who understand the meaning of a camera, a weapon, a stealer of images and souls, a gun, an evil eye'. Rickett's wife Sadie impressed them with the same understandable photophobia: 'as if you and your children and your husband and these others were stood there naked in front of the cold absorption of the camera in all your shame and pitiableness to be pried into and laughed at' (pp. 362–4). From then on the families were always given time to wash their faces and present themselves on their own terms, often gazing steadily back at the lens (compare Orwell's camera-eye contact with his Wiganite Eurydice – merely momentary and eventually deleted from the final version) as other subjectivities to be respected, not violated. Negotiation and consent were vital, precisely because of mechanical reproduction's power to falsify or annihilate the individual's Benjaminesque 'aura'.[39]

If middle-class documentarists couldn't avoid patronage and voyeurism altogether, argued Agee, they could reduce them by sensitivity and trust. Cosmic uniqueness and complexity had to be preserved from documentary's potentially reductive typology. As Agee put it, 'how am I to speak of you as "tenant farmers" as "representatives" of your "class", as social integers in a criminal economy, or as individuals, fathers, wives, sons, daughters, and as my friends and as I "know" you?' (pp. 100–1). From this viewpoint, unlike Orwell's tendency to alternate between bourgeois disgust and proletarian-pastoral, criticised by Jameson, *Let Us Now Praise Famous Men* confronted the 'picturesque' implications of poverty without ignoring or sentimentalising them. The decor of sharecropper shacks contained 'classicisms . . . created of economic need, of local availability, and of local-primitive tradition' which were aestheticised only by the documentary form of the photographs which recorded them. Consequently, 'To those who own it . . . this "beauty" is . . . irrelevant and undiscernible.' Most importantly, this discrepant consciousness of the beautiful was a function of the economic inequality of the positions of observed and observers, who 'have only a shameful and a thief's right to it . . . in proportion that they recognize the ugliness and disgrace implicit in their privilege of perception' (p. 203 and p. 313). In this way, Agee acknowledged the ideological impasse in which his own discourse was caught: its very subjects were disabled from fully understanding his self-conscious analysis of their predicament by the facts of that predicament itself as they were lived. This contradiction, confronted head on rather than by the subliminal means we saw in Orwell's 'snapshot' of the Wiganite Eurydice, could only begin to be resolved by genuinely reforming conditions. *Let Us Now Praise Famous Men* may not have succeeded in negotiating all the disjunctions in consciousness between the creators, subjects and audiences of thirties documentary discourse, but its transitional post/modern form strove to objectify them more fully than perhaps any other reportage, American or British, of the period.

NOTES

1. See David Peck '"The Morning is Yours": American and British Literary Culture in the Thirties' in Massa and Stead 1994: 214–31, especially p. 214.

2. It is of course striking that the pervasive influence of Joyce should be a common link between the two most representative figures of British and American reportage. This connection is too broad and complex to cover here. I dealt with it in a paper given to the 1996 Conference of the British Association of American Studies: ' "The Unpaid Agitator": Joyce's Influence on the Anti-Naturalistic Fiction and Documentary of James Agee'.

3. Peck in Massa and Stead 1994: 214–15, 224.

4. Ibid., pp. 215–16.

5. See Roman Jakobson 'The Dominant' in Matejka and Pomorska 1971: 82–7, especially p. 82.

6. For a fuller account of the origins and dissemination of the 'new reportage', see my unpublished 1991 thesis. Also 'The Will to Objectivity: Egon Erwin Kisch's *Der rasende Reporter*' (*Modern Language Review*, January 1990: 92–106). For Reed's role in particular, see ' "History As I Saw It": Inter-War New Reportage' (*Literature and History*, Autumn 1992: 39–54).

7. John Grierson (1946) 1966: 135, 138. See also Winston 1995: 36–7.

8. Sergei Tretiakov quoted in Willett (1978) 1982: 107. Also Grierson 'The Documentary Producer' *Cinema Quarterly*, 1933: 7–9, especially p. 8; and Grierson (1946) 1966: 193–4.

9. Storm Jameson 'Documents', *FACT*, July 1937: 1–18.

10. Kisch's speech was 'Reportage als Kunstform und Kampfform'. For a detailed account of the influence and coverage of these events on the British Left, see Croft 1990: 52–3.

11. See Jameson, July 1937: 13, 9–10, respectively. Louis Althusser's definition can be found in his 'Ideology and Ideological State Apparatuses' (see Althusser 1971: 153). The 'funeral of fictiveness' was coined by Nikolai Chuzhak (see Lawton and Eagle 1988: 274). Chuzhak also edited the 1929 LEF anthology *Literatura Fakta*. For an account of LEF's theory of 'The Literature of Fact', as developed from the beginning of its second journal, *Novy Lef* (January 1927), see Williams 1991: 86–93, and, more extensively, Stephan 1981: 59–60, 71 and 165–6.

12. Jameson, July 1937: 10.

13. Ibid., pp. 15–16, and pp. 17–18.

14. Ibid., p. 12. See also her 'Socialists Born and Made' *FACT*, 2, May 1937: 87.

15. See George Orwell (1937) 1989: 93–6 and plates.

16. For Sergei Tretiakov's theory that documentary should focus on the 'biography of things', see Willett (1978) 1982: 107. Also Klaus 1985: 154–5.

17. Orwell (1937) 1989: 18. Henceforth, all page references to *Wigan Pier* will be given in brackets in the text.

18. For the argument about metaphor/metonymy as 'Imaginative rationality', see Lakoff and Johnson 1980: 193–4. A simile deployed by Orwell later suggests how miners' bodies support the social cross-section above like pit-props holding up geological strata: 'hundreds of yards of solid rock, bones of extinct beasts, subsoil, flints, roots of growing things, green grass and cows grazing on it – all this is suspended over your head and held back only by wooden props as *thick as the calf of your leg*' [italics mine] ((1937) 1989: 21).

19. See Warner (1985) 1987: 35–6. Also Williams 1991: 338–41.

20. Orwell may have taken his cue here from J.B. Priestley's *English Journey* which suggested that 'If there had been several working collieries in London itself, modern English history would have been quite different.' Priestley then went

on to fantasise a labour conscription scheme from Kensington to bring home the facts of conditions in the mining industry to the prejudiced. (See Priestley (1934) 1987: 302–3, and 310–11.)

21. Frank Kermode has compared Orwell's heroicisation of the miner's physique with proletarian Lewis Jones's depiction of an underground encounter with the coal-owner's son in his novel *Cwmardy*, to show that, even at its most positive, the reportage of bourgeois observers still inscribes an ambiguous rhetorical inversion, rather than deconstruction, of class difference. For Jones's miners, the Oxbridge undergraduate's ' "magnificent body" stands for what they cannot have: he is taller, healthier than men who are enfeebled by their abnormal labour and the coal dust they continually breathe . . . [Orwell's] way of knowing the world of the miners derives from the other world: and this despite his extraordinary efforts to familiarise himself with theirs'. (See Kermode (1988) 1989: 90–2. Also Jones 1937: 111–13.)

22. 'Once check that stream of dividends that flows from the bodies of Indian coolies to the banking accounts of old ladies in Cheltenham, and the whole sahib–native nexus . . . can come to an end' (Orwell (1968) 1970: Vol. II, 123). For Orwell's views on the invisibility of the imperial proletariat, see 'Marrakech' and 'Not Counting Niggers', Vol. I, 426–33, and 434–8.

23. For an extended discussion of Isherwood and Vertov, see Williams 1996: 124 and 147–8.

24. See Orwell (1968) 1970: Vol. I, 203. Orwell's 'snapshot' may have been influenced by Bill Brandt's 'Young Housewife: Bethnal Green', from his *The English at Home* (1936). (See Cunningham 1988: 240.) In turn, Brandt admitted following Orwell's writing to photograph the 'other country' of both that collection and his subsequent one, *A Night in London* (1938). (See Mellor 1985: 93.)

25. For prefigurings of Jean Baudrillard and Jean-François Lyotard's concepts of 'hyper-reality' and 'performativity' in Orwell's writings on Spain, see Williams 1996: 1–4.

26. See Williams Autumn 1992: 42–3, and North 1935: 'Reportage' pp. 120–3. Also Peck 1985: 'Joseph North and the Proletarian Reportage of the 1930s' pp. 210–20.

27. Flanagan quoted in de Rohan 1973: viii.

28. See note 24 above.

29. See Stott (1973) 1986: especially p. x and pp. 261–6.

30. James Agee (1941) 1988: xv. Henceforth, all page references to *Famous Men* will be given in brackets in the text. Agee's 'Alabama Record', submitted for a Guggenheim fellowship, shows how far his intentions had already evolved by 1937 (see Agee 1972: 133–4).

31. For the mixed findings of other reporters such as Lorena Hickok, Martha Gellhorn and Harry Hopkins about the effectiveness of New Deal reforms in the Cotton Belt, see the chapter 'The South: A Saga of Despair and Hope' in Bauman and Coode 1988: 140–74.

32. May Cameron's *New York Post* article 'Margaret Bourke-White Finds Plenty of Time to Enjoy Life Along With Her Camera Work' seemed to confirm documentary's modishly bankable status. It had all the cringing tone of a glam interview and discussed Bourke-White's clothes, ambition and earnings all before her experience among the Southern tenants was mentioned (see Agee (1941) 1988: 450–4).

33. Stott's term (1986: x–xi).
34. For comments on the inadequacy of his language, see Orwell (1937) 1989: 52–4 and 75–6.
35. Cf. for example 'The function of poetry is to point out that the sign is not identical with its referent . . . since without it the connection between the sign and its object becomes automatized and the perception of reality withers away' (Roman Jakobson quoted in Erlich 1955: 181).
36. See Roland Barthes 1986: 94.
37. See note 25 above.
38. For reproductions of these photographs from Caldwell and Bourke-White (1937), see Puckett 1984: 41, 44.
39. For Walter Benjamin's concept of the erosion of the authenticity of personal and aesthetic 'aura', see his 'The Work of Art in the Age of Mechanical Reproduction' in Benjamin 1969: 221–32.

## REFERENCES

**Agee J.** 1972 *Collected Short Prose of James Agee*, ed. Robert Fitzgerald (London: Calder & Boyars)
—— (with photographs by W. Evans) (1941) 1988 *Let Us Now Praise Famous Men* (New York: Houghton Mifflin; repr. London: Pan)
**Althusser L.** 1971 'Ideology and Ideological State Apparatuses', in *Lenin and Philosophy and Other Essays*, trans. Ben Brewster (London: New Left Editions)
**Barthes R.** 1991 *The Responsibility of Forms: Critical Essays on Music, Art and Representation*, trans. Richard Howard (Oxford: Basil Blackwell 1986)
**Bauman J.F., Coode T.H.** 1988 *In the Eye of the Great Depression: New Deal Reporters and the Agony of the American People* (Illinois: Northern Illinois University Press)
**Benjamin W.** 1969 *Illuminations*, ed. Hannah Arendt (New York: Schocken)
**Brandt B.** 1936 *The English at Home: Sixty-Three Photographs* (London: Batsford)
—— 1938 *A Night in London: Story of a London Night in Sixty-Four Photographs* (London: Country Life)
**Caldwell E., Bourke-White M.** 1937 *You Have Seen Their Faces* (New York: Modern Age Books)
**Chuzhak N.** (ed.) (1929) 1972 *Literatura Fakta* (Moscow: Federatsiia; repr. München: Wilhelm Fink Verlag)
**Croft A.** 1990 *Red Letter Days: British Fiction in the 1930s* (London: Lawrence & Wishart)
**Cunningham V.** 1988 *British Writers of the Thirties* (Oxford: Oxford University Press)
**de Rohan P.** 1973 *Federal Theatre Plays* (New York: Da Capo)
**Erlich V.** 1955 *Russian Formalism: History – Doctrine* (London: Mouton)
**Grierson J.** 1933 'The Documentary Producer', in *Cinema Quarterly*, II (1)
—— 1946 (repr. 1966) *Grierson on Documentary*, ed. Forsyth Hardy (London: Faber)
**Jakobson R.** 1971 'The Dominant', in Ladislav Matejka and Krystyna Pomorska (eds) *Readings in Russian Poetics: Formalist and Structuralist Views* (Cambridge Mass.: MIT Press)

**Jameson S.** May 1937 'Socialists Born and Made', *FACT*, 2
—— July 1937 'Documents', in *FACT*, 4
**Jones L.** 1937 *Cwmardy: The Story of a Welsh Mining Valley* (London: Lawrence & Wishart)
**Kermode F.** (1988) 1989 *History and Value: The Clarendon Lectures and the Northcliffe Lectures 1987* (Oxford: Clarendon Press)
**Klaus G.H.** 1985 (in collaboration with J. Enkemann on Chapter 7) *The Literature of Labour: 200 Years of Working-Class Writing* (Brighton: Harvester Press)
**Lakoff G., Johnson M.** 1980 *Metaphors We Live By* (Chicago and London: Chicago University Press)
**Lawton A.** and **Eagle H.** (eds) 1988 *Russian Futurism Through Its Manifestos 1912– 1928* (Ithaca: Cornell University Press)
**Massa A.** and **Stead A.** (eds) *Forked Tongues? Comparing Twentieth-Century British and American Literature* (Harlow: Longman)
**Matejka L.** and **Pormorska K.** (eds) *Readings in Russian Poetics: Formalist and Structuralist Views* (Cambridge, Mass.: MIT Press)
**Mellor D.** 1985 'Brandt's Phantoms', in *Bill Brandt Behind the Camera: Photographs 1928–1983* (New York: Aperture)
**North J.** 1935 'Reportage', in Henry Hart (ed.), *American Writers Congress* (London: Martin Lawrence)
**Orwell G.** (1937) 1989 *The Road to Wigan Pier* (London: Gollancz; repr. Harmondsworth: Penguin)
—— (1968) 1970 *Collected Essays, Journalism and Letters of George Orwell*, ed. Sonia Orwell and Ian Angus (London Secker & Warburg; repr. Harmondsworth: Penguin)
**Peck D.** 1985 'Joseph North and the Proletarian Reportage of the 1930s', in *Zeitschrift für Anglistik und Amerikanistik*, 33 (3)
—— 1994 '"The Morning is Yours": American and British Literary Culture in the Thirties', in Anna Massa and Alistair Stead (eds) *Forked Tongues? Comparing Twentieth-Century British and American Literature* (Harlow: Longman)
**Priestley J.B.** (1934) 1987 *English Journey* (London: Heinemann; repr. Harmondsworth: Penguin)
**Puckett J.R.** 1984 *Five Photo-Textual Documentaries from the Great Depression* (Ann Arbor, Michigan: UMI Research Press)
**Stephan H.** 1981 *'LEF' and the Left Front of the Arts* (Munich: Verlag/Otto Sagner)
**Stott W.** (1973) 1986 *Documentary Expression and Thirties America* (New York: Oxford University Press; repr. Chicago and London: Chicago University Press)
**Warner M.** (1985) 1987 *Monuments and Maidens: The Female Allegory in Art* (London: Weidenfeld & Nicolson; repr. Pan)
**Willett J.** 1978 (repr. 1982) *The New Sobriety: Art and Politics in the Weimar Period 1917–33* (London: Thames & Hudson)
**Williams K.** January 1990 'The Will to Objectivity: Egon Erwin Kisch's *Der rasende Reporter*', *Modern Language Review* 85 (1)
—— 1991 *Reportage in the Thirties* (University of Oxford; thesis)
—— Autumn 1992 '"History As I Saw It": Inter-War New Reportage', *Literature and History*, 3rd series, 1 (2)
—— 1996 *British Writers and the Media 1930–45* (London: Macmillan)
**Winston B.** 1995 *Claiming the Real: The Documentary Film Revisited* (London: British Film Institute)

# CHAPTER TWELVE

# Modernism and the People: the View from the Cinema Stalls

JEFFREY RICHARDS

The thirties – a decade of modernism or postmodernism? From the perspective of popular culture it is best seen as a decade of premodernism. There is no denying the importance for *high* culture of the modernist aesthetic. But modernism and all it stood for – secularism, individualism, experimentation and innovation, 'art for art's sake', above all a rejection of the artistic rules and social conventions of the Victorian world – isolated the artist from society in a way that was unimaginable in the nineteenth century.

In the nineteenth century there had been a cross-class national culture and a uniformity of taste that began to be eroded after the First World War. David Vincent has shown how that common culture was rooted in the key texts of popular Protestantism – the Bible, Milton, Bunyan, Foxe.[1] Dave Russell has demonstrated that a cross-class musical taste had been securely established by the end of that century, characterised by its love of melody and sentiment, patriotism and sacred music.[2] Patrick Joyce has persuasively argued for an all-pervasive populism which transcended class and party.[3]

Accessibility was axiomatic, and paintings, music and plays were as much designed to be 'read' as poems and novels. Novels, poems, plays, music and paintings overlapped and interpenetrated to an extraordinary degree.[4] Artistic figures were major national celebrities – Dickens, Tennyson, Sullivan, Millais. Underlying all art was a common belief, a Ruskinian belief, in the role of art to uplift, enlighten, ennoble, educate, to reflect the dominant spiritual values of the age. As Sir Henry Irving, the leading actor of his age, suggested: 'to merely reproduce things vile and squalid and mean is a debasement of Art'.[5] For him Truth was only an element of Beauty and Beauty was his ultimate objective.[6] In the late nineteenth century Irving and Tree brought this organic, uplifting, accessible, integrated culture to a peak, taking it as far as it could go within the bounds of the theatre. The next stage was the cinema and the vision of Irving and Tree was taken over by D.W.

Griffith and Cecil B. De Mille. To maximise its appeal and in consequence its profits, popular cinema aimed at consensus, reassurance, familiarity and saw this to lie in an appeal to the common culture.

The old organic culture was to fragment under the impact of modernism and painting, music, sculpture and drama split between on the one hand the popular/traditional/middle-brow/accessible/representational and on the other hand the avant garde/high-brow/experimental/abstract/arcane/inaccessible, and the two have never matched up since. The cinema was firmly located in the former camp, much high culture in the latter, rendering itself irrelevant to any consideration of the mind-set of the age. As Suzi Gablik points out:

> To the public at large, modern art has always implied a loss of craft, a fall from grace, a fraud or a hoax. We may accept with good grace not understanding a foreign language or algebra, but in the case of art it is more likely, as Roger Fry once pointed out, that people will think, when confronted with a work they do not like or cannot understand, that it is done especially to insult them. It remains one of the more disturbing facts about modernism that a sense of fraudulence has, from the start, hung around its neck like an albatross.[7]

Indeed it might be argued, as John Carey has claimed, that modernism, with its insistence that art and literature should be 'difficult', represented a deliberate attempt on the part of the intelligentsia, whose reaction to mass culture was frequently one of fear and loathing, to exclude the masses.[8] Yet the cinema was one of the characterising features of the modern world. When the Commission on Educational and Cultural Films declared in 1932: 'The cinema has become the staple entertainment of the average family', it was enunciating a truth universally recognised by contemporary commentators and confirmed by subsequent historians.[9] It has been estimated, for instance, that five-eighths of the total expenditure on entertainment in Britain in 1937–38 went on the cinema.[10] The number of cinemas and average attendance at them rose steadily throughout the thirties. The bulk of the mass audience was drawn from the working classes.

Cinema-going was particularly important to women, children and the unemployed. The cinema became a place where unaccompanied women could go without fear of misinterpretation, unlike the public house, where lone women were often assumed to be in search of sex. Women both married and single became devotees of the cinema. The Wartime Social Survey (1943) analysed cinema enthusiasts, those who went at least once a week, and defined them as young, working-class, urban and more often female than male. This analysis applied equally to the thirties.

There was a marked increase in middle-class cinema patronage in the thirties as Oscar Deutsch spread his new Odeon cinemas across the nation, bringing luxury cinema-going to the suburbs and aiming to put one of his upmarket picture palaces on the high street of every big town and city.[11]

Why did people go to the cinema? It was cheap. But more important, when questioned, cinema-goers would invariably talk about the cinema supplying entertainment, escapism, dreams. 'Films take you out of yourself', they would say.[12]

Several in-depth analyses have been made of film-making and cinema-going in thirties Britain on the national level. But there has not yet been much investigation of whether there were significant regional variations in film-goers' tastes. Lancashire is a good place to start. For Simon Rowson's 1934 survey of cinema attendance revealed that Lancashire along with Scotland was top of the league in the proportion of available cinema seats, one for every nine people in the area.[13]

Before the nineteenth century, Lancashire as a whole was a sparsely populated, remote, forested and backward region, the poorest in Britain. The Industrial Revolution changed all that. The North, and especially Lancashire, decisively came into its own. It became 'the workshop of the world', the source of Britain's global pre-eminence.

A strong Northern culture developed, both in Lancashire and Yorkshire, with a flourishing local press, vigorous party political organisations, a rich dialect literature, a distinct musical tradition centred on brass bands and choirs, and a growing interest in regional history and archaeology. Given the inevitable existence of sub-groups and sub-cultures – in Lancashire immigration produced a substantial Irish Catholic minority which was never entirely integrated – and given the fact that there was always strong loyalty to individual towns, the county was nevertheless remarkably cohesive. Its heart was Cotton Lancashire, a society characterised by the premier historian of the county, John K. Walton, as a stable, tightly knit, conservative society, which, despite a significant minority of badly-off people and the problems of pollution, disease and overcrowding, generated a uniquely prosperous high-income working-class culture.[14] It was bound together by shared employment experience, traditions of good neighbourliness and mutual assistance. Its communality was enhanced by participation in the commercialised leisure industries that emerged in Victorian Britain and centred on the music hall, seaside holidays, football and the pub. This population took easily and rapidly to the cinema.

Culturally and geographically this was an urban, industrial, working-class world, which came into existence in the early years of the nineteenth century and remained in place until the 1960s. J.B. Priestley observed it when he toured England in 1933 for his classic work, *English Journey*. He discovered three Englands coexisting. There was 'Olde Worlde' England, 'the country of the cathedrals and minsters, and manor houses and inns, of

Parson and Squire; guide book and quaint highways and byways England' and there was postwar England, of cinemas, dance halls, Woolworths and motor coaches, a democratic, accessible, cheap, mass-produced England. In between came the second England, 'the nineteenth-century England, the industrial England of coal, iron, steel, cotton, wool, railways', the England of railway stations, chapels, mills and factories, back-to-back houses and slag heaps.[15]

This was the world of the North. Life in this world was, according to Richard Hoggart, 'dense and concrete', a life whose main stress was on the intimate, the sensory, the detailed, the personal, where conversations centred on people, relationships, sex, work and sport, and not on theories or ideas. It was a world of hierarchies, traditions, rituals and routines, bound together by shared beliefs in patriotism, luck, fate and clear definitions of manliness and womanliness.[16] It was to this world and to this mind-set that the cinema needed to appeal and with its eye always on box-office receipts, the film industry did take account of audience preference in stars, stories, themes and values. The people seemed to like what they were getting. The number of cinemas increased. In Manchester and Salford the number rose from 137 in 1930 to 156 in 1939. In Bolton, the number increased from eighteen in 1919 to twenty-six in 1939, in Blackburn from five to seventeen, in Oldham from six to seventeen, in Preston from eight to twenty-one, in Stockport from four to twenty-five. Eleven new Odeons appeared in Lancashire between 1934 and 1939 at Blackpool, Burnley, Chorley, Clevelys, Lancaster, Morecambe, Bolton, Bury, Ashton-under-Lyne, Oldham and Radcliffe. Reminiscences and oral histories of working-class life in the North-west from the turn of the century to the Second World War testify to the centrality of the cinema to popular leisure, particularly to the leisure of the young.[17]

What precisely did cinema-goers in Lancashire go to see? Here we are fortunate to possess some hard evidence. In 1937 a group of earnest, young, middle-class intellectuals descended upon the cotton town of Bolton, intent upon studying the patterns of Lancashire life for a new organisation called Mass-Observation. They christened Bolton 'Worktown', and set out to place it under the microscope like anthropologists studying a native tribe. One of their interests was cinema. 'From the beginning film was of the highest interest to us. We were film-minded', said their co-founder Tom Harrisson.[18] Cinema-going was in Bolton, as everywhere, a prime leisure activity. Film lexicographer and lifetime cineaste Leslie Halliwell grew up in Bolton during these years, and his affectionate autobiographical account of his childhood, *Seats in All Parts*, vividly recalls cinema-going in thirties Bolton: 'For a film fanatic, Bolton was almost like Mecca. At one time there lay within easy reach no fewer than forty-seven cinemas of varying size, quality and character. None was more than five miles from Bolton's Town Hall, and twenty eight were within the boundaries of the borough.'[19]

Harrisson and his team produced an outline of proposed research, and, as part of the information-gathering, Mass-Observation devised a competition, seeking information from the patrons of three Bolton cinemas on their cinema-going habits. There were 559 replies received,[20] and this gives us a virtually unique insight into the cinema-going preferences of a single urban community in 1938. We know what the top box-office films of the thirties were nationally, but I know of no other local survey with such depth and density of information about the reasons for and nature of individual audience preference.

The three cinemas seem to have been chosen to represent three different levels of cinema operation. The Odeon, Ashburner Street, opened amid great ceremony in 1937, was one of Oscar Deutsch's city-centre, art-deco showplaces, an up-market cinema, seating 2,534 people, at prices ranging from 6d to 1s 6d. It had a weekly change of programme, continuous shows from Monday to Friday and three separate houses on Saturday. There was a staff of forty-one, including page boys, girls selling chocolates, usherettes and doormen. There was an organ and a resident organist (Hubert Selby) and a cinema café, though Halliwell recalls that it was 'notorious for serving the toughest buttered crumpets for miles around'.[21] The respondents' addresses and the greater literary fluency of the Odeon replies suggest a higher proportion of middle-class and upper-working-class patrons at this cinema than at the other two.

The Crompton, Crompton Way, was a middle-range cinema, of the 'mixed family audience' kind, with seating for 1,200, twice-weekly programme changes, daily matinées and continuous evening performances. There was a special children's matinée on Saturday. Seat prices ranged from 3d to 1s 3d.

The Palladium, Higher Bridge Street, was a down-market cinema, frankly a 'fleapit'. It had seating capacity for 1,238, twice-weekly programme changes, afternoon matinées, continuous evening performances and Saturday matinées for children. There was a staff of twelve. Seat prices ranged from 4d to a shilling. The Palladium's audience came in the main from the working-class city-centre area around the cinema.

The cinema questionnaire offered two prizes of a pound for the two most comprehensive answers, and six double complimentary tickets for the next six in order of merit. It asked for name, address and age, though an original plan to include occupation was regrettably not followed up. It asked seven questions: (1) Do you go to the cinema regularly? (2) How many times a month do you go? (3) Do you go regularly on the same day, if so which day? (4) Do you think you see people on the screen who live like yourself?

(5) Which are the best films, British or American? (6) What type of film do you like best: crime, westerns, war, spying, historical, cartoons, nature and reality, travel and adventure, musical romance, drama and tragedy, slapstick comedies, love stories, society comedies? (7) Which of the following would you like to see more of in films: more humour, more religion, more politics, more action, more killing, more knowledge and educational subjects, more beautiful things, more beautiful people, more people like you and I, more royalty and aristocrats? A space was also left for the respondents to write any comments they liked about films.

Of the 559 respondents, 304 were men and 255 women. Of these 409 said they went regularly to the cinema on the same day, which emphasised the ritual nature of cinema–going. Frequency of attendance varied from once a month to twenty-four times a month. Nine respondents went twenty times or more a month. Sixty-two per cent of respondents were aged thirty or under.

Asked if they saw people like themselves on the screen, 363 said 'no', including two women who said forcefully 'No, thank goodness' and 'No and I don't expect to', and 196 said 'yes'. On the question of preference, 63 per cent preferred American films, 18 per cent British films, 19 per cent thought they were about the same. There was a slightly higher female preference for British films.

When it came to the choice of film types, the first choice of categories break down as follows:

| | | |
|---|---|---|
| (1) | Musical romance | 171 |
| (2) | Drama and tragedy | 99 |
| (3) | History | 60 |
| (4) | Crime | 60 |
| (5) | Nature and reality | 39 |
| (6) | Travel and adventure | 35 |
| (7) | Love stories | 23 |
| (8) | Society comedies | 21 |
| (9) | Spying | 16 |
| (10) | Westerns | 16 |
| (11) | War | 10 |
| (12) | Slapstick comedies | 5 |
| (13) | Cartoons | 2 |

There is some variation in choice between the sexes. Women give a higher priority to history and to love stories than men, and men give a higher priority to crime than do women. But both sexes give musical romance and drama as their first choice, with war, slapstick comedies and cartoons amongst the least preferred.

There are instructive variations in the choice within individual cinemas. A most interesting feature is the prominence of crime the further down the scale you go. It is the first choice of Palladium men, narrowly misses being the first choice of Crompton men, but as fourth choice comes a long way after musical romance and drama with Odeon men. It is furthermore noticeable that the overwhelming majority of Palladium men preferring crime films come from the fifteen–twenty age group. Conversely, society comedies rank lower the lower down the scale you go. In general, women's choices in all three groups tend to be closer to each other than to the men's.

Asked what they wanted to see more of in films, the respondents placed the categories in the following order:

(1)   More humour
(2)   More beautiful things
(3)   More action
(4)   More people like you and I
(5)   More knowledge and education
(6)   More beautiful people
(7)   More royalty and aristocrats
(8)   More religion
(9)   More politics
(10)  More killing.

Men give a higher priority to action than women. Women give a higher priority to beautiful things than men. But both are agreed about wanting more humour as top priority, and neither wanted more royalty and aristocrats, religion, politics or killing.

The general profile is on the whole repeated at individual cinemas with some interesting and perhaps characteristic variations. Almost all groups want more humour and are least interested in killing, politics, religion, royalty and aristocrats, though Palladium men give a higher priority to more killing than any other group and a lower priority to more people like you and I than the rest.

Fifty-one respondents chose to write about why they went to the cinema and the reasons they gave were all variations on entertainment, amusement, relaxation, to be taken out of themselves, to escape the cares of the world and everyday life. A further twenty-six mentioned that they valued films as a source of education, inspiration and knowledge. Fifteen more mentioned that they liked to see films with a good moral.

However, the greatest majority (eighty-six) chose to write about why they preferred American films to British films. The overwhelming complaint was that there was not enough action in British films. They were dull and lifeless. The settings were restricted and poverty-stricken. The acting was stiff and artificial. By contrast, American films were slick, polished, fast-moving and often spectacular, and American actors were natural and life-like. Only thirteen respondents declared that they wanted to see more British films. Ten respondents thought British films were improving. Five mentioned a dislike of 'Oxford accents' in British films. But eighteen mentioned a dislike of American accents and American slang. Twenty-eight respondents called for greater realism in characters, settings and stories which reflects the comparatively high priority given to seeing more people like you and I. But the overwhelming impression gained is that the reasons for preferring American films to British are aesthetic rather than political or social: an important conclusion in view of the fact that it is frequently stated that American films were preferred because they were more democratic and egalitarian than British films.

There is no doubt that British films were on the whole less popular than American. Henry Kendall, star of many British B pictures, gave tickets to his charlady and her husband to see one of his films in the West End; when he asked her if she had enjoyed it, she replied: 'Oh sir, it was wonderful, only we couldn't quite hear what you said on account of the booing.' Kendall thought that there was some reason to believe that big American companies employed claques to barrack British films.[22] But I doubt if they did so in Bolton, and British films were no more popular there than in London.

Many respondents chose to name and talk about their favourite films, and it is possible to construct a list of Bolton's ten most popular films according to this group of cinema regulars. They are:

(1)  *Victoria the Great* 38 (21 female, 17 male)
(2)  *Stella Dallas* 26 (19 female, 7 male)
(3)  *A Star is Born* 25 (16 female, 9 male)
(4)  *Mutiny on the Bounty* 19 (4 female, 15 male)
(5)  *Charge of the Light Brigade* 18 (7 female, 11 male)
(6)  *Maytime* 18 (9 female, 9 male)
(7)  *Lost Horizon* 14 (10 female, 4 male)
(8)  *Action for Slander* 11 (6 female, 5 male)
(9)  *San Francisco* 10 (6 female, 4 male)
(10) *The Lives of a Bengal Lancer* 9 (all male)

The films cover the period 1936–38 and all of them except for *Action for Slander* were hits nationally, the top three most recently, the last longest ago. This clearly indicates the emergence of a national cinematic taste. There were 131 other films also mentioned, mainly by one or two people. Of these, thirty-seven were British, the rest American. Of the top ten, only two (*Victoria the Great* and *Action for Slander*) are British, the rest American.

But only three of the ten (*Stella Dallas*, *A Star is Born* and *San Francisco*) have American settings.

This list of films accords almost exactly with Leslie Halliwell's memoir of his childhood cinema-going in Bolton, and he was drawing on memory rather than the archives of Mass-Observation. He recalls the popularity of *Lost Horizon*, Frank Capra's inspiring vision of a world of peace, plenty, serenity and good neighbourliness ('The Theatre Royal was packed and had queues stretching both ways'). It is significant that the preferred Utopia should be James Hilton's liberal humanist vision with its donnish élite in a Himalayan equivalent of All Souls College preserving the 'frail elegances' of civilisation rather than H.G. Wells's Fabian socialist utopia in *Things to Come*. Halliwell also singles out the imperial saga *Lives of a Bengal Lancer* ('The whole town turned out to see this oddly-titled Indian adventure'), the historical epics *Mutiny on the Bounty* and *San Francisco*, any films with Nelson Eddy and Jeanette Macdonald, the stars of *Maytime* ('A queue of Boltonians would form at the mere mention of their name') and *Victoria the Great* ('most popular of them all').[23] The popularity of *Victoria the Great* might seem to contradict the low priority given to seeing more royalty and aristocrats. But cinema-goers' reservations probably extended principally to more aristocrats, given the high proportion of them appearing as characters particularly in British films. This dislike of aristocratic characters would then be the converse of the desire to see more people like you and I. The popularity of films about the monarchy – *Victoria the Great* was only one of several – confirms the view that the monarchy had moved out of and above the class system, to function as a symbol of the nation and national feeling. But only one of the films (*Stella Dallas*) has anything like a working-class setting and characters. Half the films have historical settings.

What is striking about the list of Boltonian favourites is not so much the penchant for films which gave you a 'good cry' (*Stella Dallas*, *A Star is Born*, *Maytime*) and a 'good tune' (*Maytime*, *San Francisco*) but the strong patriotic note about the titles, the way the list conforms with the popular preference for musical romance, drama, tragedy and history, and the gender differentiation of the choices. Some films are equally or almost equally popular with both sexes (*Victoria the Great*, *Maytime*, *Action for Slander*, *San Francisco*), but others have a much greater appeal either to men or to women. In general, the women seem to have been drawn to films about sensitive, long-suffering, self-sacrificing women, often tied to ungrateful or unworthy husbands or children, and the men to films about tough, macho he-men, who are good in a fight, stand up for what is right and love their country. There is revolt against the system in some of the films but it is invariably punished or defused. These choices tell us something about the self-image of men and women in thirties Bolton. It is an image which is in all its essentials Victorian.

The fondness for the essentially old-fashioned operettas of Nelson Eddy and Jeanette Macdonald, many of them based on pre-First World War works, rather than the sophisticated musical comedies of Astaire and Rogers and the modern urban musicals of Busby Berkeley, plus the penchant for historical recreations of a heroic and romanticised British past, suggest a fundamental conservatism of outlook. This is reflected on the national level in the thirties by the election and re-election of a largely Conservative National Government, and on the local level by Bolton's voting record in parliamentary and council elections. In voting terms both Bolton in particular and Lancashire in general were almost solidly Conservative throughout the thirties. In his magisterial social history of Lancashire, John Walton says that in thirties Lancashire the majority of the Lancashire working class remained 'stolidly politically apathetic and conservative in all senses of the word'.[24] Paul Harris, in his meticulous study of Bolton's social leadership, points to 'the lingering deference of the working class voter for the "natural" leadership of the capitalist parties'.[25]

I would take issue with the use of the term 'apathetic'. The fact that the working classes were not on the whole spending their spare time plotting the overthrow of capitalism is not apathy. It is because, as both Dave Russell and Ross McKibbin have pointed out, they have got better things to do, different priorities: choral singing, brass-banding, flower-growing, pigeon-fancying, whippet-racing, reading, tending the allotment, going to church, fishing, evening classes, rambling, making love or going to the cinema – fulfilling and rewarding activities which allowed the participants to confirm an image of themselves and their standing in the world.[26]

Between 600 and 750 new films were released annually in Britain between 1930 and 1939. Given the number of films and the number of cinemas, it was possible to go every day to the cinema and still not see everything. So there is active and positive choice being made from the alternatives on offer. As J. Hutchison noted in his 1937 handbook for managers: 'Regular kinema-goers frequently have a better knowledge of films and particularly of film stars than the manager himself. Their views must be treated with respect.'[27] If the commercial cinema did not appeal, there was a whole alternative radical political film culture available. But its support was infinitesimal compared with commercial cinema. The evidence suggests it attracted only the already committed rather than the mass audience which preferred to see Gracie Fields from the comfortable stalls of the local Odeon rather than a piece of modernist radical agitprop from wooden benches in a draughty hall.[28]

The fact that the choice of Bolton cinema-goers confirms the national picture lends strong support to the argument advanced by D.L. Le Mahieu for the emergence in the thirties of a common culture which flourished within the pre-existing boundaries of class, gender and region.[29] It transcended those boundaries, he argues, without eliminating or lessening their social significance. He concedes that the common culture might be experienced differently by a wide variety of groups, yet retain its value as a mutually acknowledged frame of reference. It had its roots in the nineteenth century, but technological change made it all the more pervasive. It centred on the commercial cinema, the BBC, the national newspapers, all of which became more accessible during the decade. The themes binding this culture together, were, just as in the nineteenth century, patriotism and sportsmanship, a belief in monarchy and empire, law and order, Christianity and parliamentary democracy, a profound sentimentality and traditional gender images, continually endorsed and reinforced by these mass media, and further isolating the high culture which rejected most of these values.

Popular culture gives us a profound insight into the nature, aspirations and preoccupations of its participants. The idea that the cinema, like its predecessors, theatre and music hall, is a complete fantasy world or a drug used to stupify the working classes (an idea advanced in the thirties by such left-wing commentators as Ralph Bond and Allen Hutt, and revived in recent years by Gareth Stedman Jones as the 'culture of consolation') is a gross oversimplification of the role of cinema in society.[30] There is a two-way process operating between the producers and consumers of cinema. The consumers by what they buy tell the producers what they want, the producers, aiming to maximise profit, to avoid controversy and thereby censorial interference, seek for the most part to dramatise what they perceive to be the majority view of society. Popular cinema is undeniably selective in what it chooses to show. It provides images of society, constructed of selected elements and aspects of real life, organised into a coherent pattern governed by a set of underlying presuppositions. The process of selection confers status on issues, institutions and individuals which regularly appear in a favourable light. It legitimises, romanticises and glamorises particular attitudes and mind-sets. There is of course an element of escapism in cinema-going. But films did much more than provide escape. They provided role models and gender images. They reinforced ideals and standards of conduct. They validated certain attitudes and viewpoints while discouraging and discrediting others. They resolved 'magically and allegorically' problems and ambiguities in life and the wider world.

In the case of gender images, Bolton's choice of films confirms the sociological studies of the period. That women define themselves in terms of marriage and the family, and men in terms of toughness and group loyalty are ideas that emerge, for instance, from Marie Jahoda's 1940 study of female factory workers and from Jack Common's 1938 study of the culture of the streets.[31]

So what was there of modernism in films? The main site of modernist expression was probably the British documentary film movement. But the movement was itself divided between Soviet-style socialist realism, the tradition of the didactic illustrated lecture and avant-garde aesthetic experimentation; and, more significantly, documentaries were not on the whole seen by the mass movie-going public. As Mr T.H. Fligelstone, president of the Cinematograph Exhibitors Association (CEA) told the Moyne Committee in 1936, the public would not accept documentaries: 'The public come to our cinemas to be amused, not educated.'[32]

What of the mainstream studio-produced fiction films which were the main staple of cinema-goers? In his excellent book *Designing Dreams* Donald Albrecht demonstrates how Hollywood absorbed and transformed the modernist style and helped to condition the response to it of the mass movie-going public.[33] The cinema has always been creatively eclectic in its traditions of set design, and it embraced modernism as a visual synonym for the kind of go-ahead, outward-looking optimism with which it sought to uplift its audiences.

It was in the Hollywood of the thirties that modernism achieved its greatest success. Three studios in particular, MGM, RKO and Paramount, set out to create distinct architectural house-styles for their output of high-society comedies, madcap musicals and wish-fulfillment dramas. Albrecht persuasively argues that these design styles mirrored the themes, enhanced the mood and helped dictate the visual shape of the films. Paramount became a Californian outpost of the Bauhaus school of design, the elegant simplicity and horizontality and all-white decor of its sets providing the airy locales for Ernst Lubitsch's sophisticated romantic comedies like *Trouble in Paradise* (1932). At RKO, the high contrast black-and-white blend of modern architecture and streamlined Art Deco achieved its apotheosis in the entrancing series of Astaire–Rogers musicals. At MGM, it was glittering geometric design and innovative spatial organisation that became the hallmark of the early Greta Garbo talkies like *Grand Hotel* (1932).

Not only could average movie-goers see modernist styles on the screen, they could also experience them at first hand in their local picture-house. Oscar Deutsch's cinema circuit put an Odeon in every town in England. The Odeon, with its streamlined curves, clean lines, fin towers and floodlights was the quintessence of modernism. With symbolic appropriateness, the lamasery in *Lost Horizon* (1937), that haven of spiritual peace to which Ronald Colman and his companions escaped from the rat-race of the outside world, looked exactly like a modernist cinema building.

But at the same time as Hollywood made modernist styles familiar and even palatable, it neutralised the radical intentions of modernism's creators. Modernism was viewed by its proponents as progressive, egalitarian and liberating. But the cinema, which valued the style more for its modish chic than its ideological underpinning, transformed it into a symbol of wealth and privilege. For the locations most often given the modernist treatment were nightclubs, penthouse suites, ocean-liners and grand hotels, the playgrounds of the rich and leisured in a fantasy world of unattainable luxury.

There was also a darker side to modernism, fuelled by fears about technology. Streamlined modernist offices and factories in films like *The Crowd* and *A nous la liberté* were often seen as depersonalising and soul-destroying. While on the one hand, the gleaming, many-towered city of the future in H.G. Wells's optimistic *Things to Come* (1936) psychologically and aesthetically prepared the English people for the brand new blocks of flats that enlightened municipal authorities were erecting in place of Victorian slums, on the other hand Fritz Lang's *Metropolis* (1927) warned of the tyranny of the machine and showed the skyscrapered future-world built on the slavery of the toiling masses. So modernism attained glamour and exposure on the cinema screen at the price of the reinforcement of popular fears about its exclusivity and inhumanity. In the movies then the modernist style came to be associated with an essentially heartless and undesirable Utopianism. It took the architects and planners forty years to catch on to what the moviemakers and movie audiences had realised before the Second World War.

If modernism influenced the 'look' of films up to a point, what about 'the sound' of films. This remained securely rooted in Victorian culture. The musical scores for films were the products of late European Romanticism, with which emigré European composers imbued the Hollywood films on which they worked. By common consent, the dean of US cinema composers was Erich Wolfgang Korngold, erstwhile Vienna child prodigy and proclaimed as the heir of Richard Strauss. His scores for such memorable Hollywood films as *Captain Blood*, *The Adventures of Robin Hood*, *The Private Lives of Elizabeth and Essex*, *Escape Me Never*, *Devotion* and *Deception* are squarely in the European symphonic and operatic tradition, and made Hollywood the last bastion of High Romanticism. At Korngold's shoulder stood such luminaries as Max Steiner, Miklos Rosza, Dimitri Tiomkin, Franz Waxman and Alfred Newman, all working in the same tradition.

What of the content of mainstream popular cinema films? It is instructive to examine who were the most popular authors for cinematic adaptation in the decade – a decade of which A.J.P. Taylor has written: 'The bestsellers of the Thirties were predominantly realistic in tone. Priestley, Cronin, Louis Golding, offered chunks of ordinary life, usually in drab surroundings.' But if the literary thirties were the age of Priestley and Cronin, the cinematic thirties were pre-eminently the age of Edgar Wallace and Ben Travers. During the thirties there were thirty-three films based on the plays and stories of Edgar Wallace and eighteen based on the plays and original scenarios of

Ben Travers. Both were masters of their craft and had brought to perfection the genres within which they worked – respectively the thriller and the farce. Each consisted of tightly constructed mechanisms within which a range of recognised and established plot conventions and stereotyped characters were expertly manipulated. It is very revealing of audience tastes and preferences that in the golden age of the detective story, it was not the clever intellectual puzzles of Dorothy L. Sayers or Agatha Christie that dominated the screen – only one Sayers film and four Christie films appeared in the entire decade – but the less demanding thriller, full of chases, fights and mayhem. Similarly, although sophisticated stage comedies like those of Noel Coward were transferred to the screen, farce was more popular with the mass audience.

Of the characteristic 'social realist' writers listed by Taylor, A.J. Cronin was represented on the British screen only by *The Citadel* (1938) and *The Stars Look Down* (1939) (though several others were produced in Hollywood), Louis Golding only by *Cotton Queen* (1937) and Priestley by *The Good Companions* (1932) and *Laburnum Grove* (1936), though he also provided scripts for two of Gracie Fields' best films, *Sing As We Go* (1934) and *Look Up and Laugh* (1935). To these titles might be added Winifred Holtby's *South Riding*, filmed in 1938. Significantly, proposals to film Walter Greenwood's best-selling novel and hit play, *Love on the Dole*, were regularly rejected by the censors on the grounds that there was 'too much of the tragic and sordid side of poverty' and scenes of the police fighting with hunger marchers.[34] Greenwood was recruited by the cinema, however, to provide a screen story for George Formby – *No Limit* (1935).

The role of the censors in determining what could be seen on the screen is undoubtedly important. But the industry itself, with an eye on maximum profit, tended to fight shy of the avant-garde and to turn to established literary classics which had instant name recognition, track records in terms of sales and the kind of narrative structure that lent itself to straightforward screen adaptation. This meant nineteenth-century novels, many of which had the added advantage of being out of copyright and therefore cheap to adapt.

Between them in the thirties, Britain and Hollywood produced four Shakespeare adaptations (*As You Like It, The Taming of the Shrew, Romeo and Juliet, A Midsummer Night's Dream*), nine Dickens adaptations (*Dombey and Son, A Tale of Two Cities, Oliver Twist, Great Expectations, David Copperfield, The Mystery of Edwin Drood, The Old Curiosity Shop, Scrooge, A Christmas Carol*), five Kiplings (*Elephant Boy, Gunga Din, Captains Courageous, The Light That Failed, Wee Willie Winkie*), two Brontës (*Jane Eyre, Wuthering Heights*), a Thackeray (*Becky Sharp*) and a Wilkie Collins (*The Moonstone*). Particularly popular were the late nineteenth century's Counter-Decadents:

Robert Louis Stevenson (*Treasure Island, Dr Jekyll and Mr Hyde, Kidnapped, Trouble for Two, Ebb Tide*), H. Rider Haggard (*King Solomon's Mines, She*), A.E.W. Mason (*The Four Feathers, Fire Over England, The Drum*), Anthony Hope (*The Prisoner of Zenda*), Stanley J. Weyman (*Under the Red Robe*) and Arthur Conan Doyle (*The Hound of The Baskervilles* and many other Sherlock Holmes stories).

European literary classics were represented by adaptations of Tolstoy (*Anna Karenina, Resurrection* (filmed as *We Live Again*)), Dostoyevsky (*Crime and Punishment*), Victor Hugo (*Les Miserables, The Hunchback of Notre Dame*) and Alexandre Dumas (*The Three Musketeers, The Count of Monte Cristo, The Man in the Iron Mask*).

Hollywood's record of dramatising Britain's literary heritage reminds us that we should not overrate the distinction between British and American cinema. Another link between the cultures is the common code of chivalry that continued to underpin them as it had in the nineteenth century. Revived and promoted by key figures of the age to counteract the effects of materialism, philistinism and untrammelled individualism, it entered the cultural mainstream and remained there until the sixties. John Fraser in his important book *America and the Patterns of Chivalry* points out:

> The family of chivalric heroes has been by far the largest and most popular one in twentieth-century American culture, and its members, in whole or in part, have entered into virtually everyone's consciousness. They include Robin Hood . . . and Zorro, and the Scarlet Pimpernel, and gentlemen buccaneers, like Rafael Sabatini's Captain Peter Blood. . . . They include the officers and gentlemen of *Lives of a Bengal Lancer*, and the gentlemen rankers of *Beau Geste*, and the First World War aviators of *The Dawn Patrol*, and clean-cut American fly-boys like Steve Canyon. The include honest cops like Dick Tracy, and fearless investigative reporters, and incorruptible district attorneys, and upstanding young doctors like Doctor Kildare. They include battered but romantic private eyes like Raymond Chandler's Philip Marlowe. They include gentleman knights like Prince Valiant, and Nature's gentlemen like Tarzan and miscellaneous *samurai*, and the martial-arts experts of Bruce Lee. They include Superman and Buck Rogers. They include men about town like Philo Vance, the Saint, and Dashiell Hammett's Nick Charles, and the figures played by Fred Astaire. . . . They include gentlemanly English actors like Ronald Colman and George Sanders, and gentlemanly American ones like Douglas Fairbanks Jr and William Powell, and those immortals Gary Cooper, Spencer Tracy and the rest, who have epitomised native American gallantry and grace.[35]

By contrast with films, individual stars are mentioned much less often in the Bolton questionnaire and only a few get multiple mentions: Jeanette MacDonald (7), Laurel and Hardy (5), Gracie Fields (5) and George Formby (5).

It is important that we should look at film stars in the context of the time and not merely at those who have been retrospectively popular. The fact that some stars have maintained their hold long after their heyday, (Garbo, Bogart, Dietrich, James Dean, Cary Grant, for instance) should not lead us to write cinematic history in a way which gives them undue pre-eminence. Their long-lasting legends tell us more about the present than the past. Why for instance is there no cult for such enduringly popular stars of the thirties as Norma Shearer, Ronald Colman and Wallace Beery? Why – above all – when Astaire and Rogers are timeless symbols of elegance is there no timeless cult of Nelson Eddy and Jeanette MacDonald, who have figured several times in this study and were clearly of major cultural significance? The answer is that in the exaltation of romantic love, melody, sentiment, patriotism, consensus and defined gender images, their films struck a chord with a mass audience that was essentially Victorian in its sensibility. The disappearance of that sensibility undermined the basis of their popularity.

If Raymond Durgnat is right, and you can write the social history of the nation in terms of its preference for star types, and if the stars function as role models, as objects of affection and identification figures, what does Bolton's choice of stars tell us about both Lancashire and Britain in the thirties?

Historians have long seen class-consciousness as crucial in understanding the history of modern industrial society. But recently greater attention has been paid to other ideas transcending class differences. One is the idea of gender roles, the nature and significance of being a man or a woman. Another is the concept of a shared regional identity.

In his important book *Visions of the People*, Patrick Joyce has defined a cultural populism that was essentially consensual rather than conflictual for the nineteenth century, and which emphasised fraternity and social justice rather than egalitarianism and class conflict. Joyce argued that there was no inherent conflict between loyalty to street, to town, to region, to nation or ultimately to Empire, each integrated into the other. Lancashire pride derived partly from the fact that it felt itself to be the industrial heart of Britain and thus of the Empire.

Joyce's argument highlights an important fact. It is that people define themselves in different ways at different times. They define themselves as male or female, as being from a particular family or faith, from an individual town or specific region, from a defined race or class or country. Being proud of being Lancastrian, therefore, did not preclude being proud of being British. Equally some people view the world from a class perspective, others from a moral one, and still more from a gender standpoint. What is interesting to observe is how the Lancashire stars embody, comment on and interpret these multiple identities.

The greatest Lancashire stars were Wigan's George Formby and Rochdale's Gracie Fields. Although not much in evidence in the Bolton questionnaire, they are prominent in Mass-Observation's Blackpool researches, recently published as *Worktowners at Blackpool*. Here Mass-Observation conclude that 'the biggest heroes of the working class are their own Gracie Fields and George Formby' and the manager of the Imperial cinema reported: 'George Formby and Gracie Fields are the two surest draws.'[36] But Fields and Formby were more than simply Lancashire stars. They became national stars: Fields was the top British female star at the cinema box office from 1936 to 1940 and Formby the top male star from 1937 to 1943. Both were rooted in the music hall tradition. Both remained inextinguishably 'Lancashire'. Both became symbols of the people. Both indicate the truth of Patrick Joyce's contention that it was possible for people to be simultaneously loyal to family, street, town, country, nation and empire: Formby and Fields embodied such multiple loyalties.

In his projecting of a spirit of good nature, good humour and goodwill George Formby was able simultaneously to embody Wigan, Lancashire, the working classes, the people and the nation. Gracie's universal appeal derives from her ability simultaneously to represent Rochdale, Lancashire, the working classes, women, England and the British Empire.[37]

It is evident that a careful reading of the popularity of both films and film stars can give us an insight into the minds of the people. Interestingly Formby's films embrace many of the themes Valentine Cunningham identifies as the preoccupations of thirties writers – the proletariat (Formby was a working-class hero), speed (*No Limit* has him riding in the T-T races), the air (*It's in the Air* has him in the RAF), physical fitness (*Keep Fit* has him caught up in the fitness craze) – but the use of contemporary themes did not make him in any sense a modernist figure, as the roots of his appeal, his art and his ethos lie in the nineteenth-century music hall tradition and Lancashire populism.[38] The evidence from Bolton suggests that Lancashire taste and national taste in the thirties were in close alignment, that cinema was in fact nationalising taste and outlook and attitude. It remains true nevertheless that gender and regional identities could be maintained within an overall national identity and the most popular stars achieved their popularity by appealing to all of these multiple identities. In the end what their choice of films shows is that Lancashire folk like the British people in general in the thirties remained to all intents and purposes Victorian in their sensibility and that they conformed more or less exactly to George Orwell's image of them arrived at in *The Lion and the Unicorn* and *The English People*: patriotic, sentimental, decent, private, considerate, anti-intellectual, though whether they were all quite as class-ridden as he suggests remains open to question.

Intellectuals left and right despised Hollywood, denouncing its films for lack of intellectual content, triviality and sentimentality, the glamorisation of false values, luxury and criminality. F.R. Leavis believed that the whole of the mass media, cinema included, stimulated the 'cheapest emotional responses' and 'offer satisfaction at the lowest level'. Aldous Huxley wrote of a million cinemas bringing 'the same stale balderdash', and of audiences who 'soak passively in the tepid bath of nonsense'. T.S. Eliot expressed concern for the minds of 'thousands of people who feast their eyes every night, when in a peculiarly passive state under the hypnotic influence of continuous music upon films the great majority of which have been confected in studios of the Hollywood type'.[39] The poet 'Bryher' spoke for all such commentators when writing of film audiences in the intellectual film journal *Close-up*:

> They hypnotize themselves into an expectation that a given star or theatre or idea will produce a given result. They surrender to this all logical features in abeyance, and achieve complete gratification whatever the material set in front of them provided it is presented in an expected and familiar manner. . . . To watch hypnotically something which has become a habit and which is not recorded as it happens by the brain, differs little from the drugtaker's point of view and it is destructive because it is used as a cover to prevent real consideration of problems, artistic or sociological, and the creation of intelligent English films.[40]

For the likes of 'Bryher', there was an alternative film culture, a network of specialist film societies, intellectual film magazines, and reverence for continental and silent films. But this alternative culture remained an intellectual minority, never commanding the universal support of mainstream commercial cinema. In the end, for some, it was a case of 'if you can't beat them join them'.

As Peter Stead has shown, a succession of British intellectuals took to writing scripts both in Britain and Hollywood – H.G. Wells, J.B. Priestley, Christopher Isherwood, Aldous Huxley, Graham Greene, even the venerable George Bernard Shaw, who was prevailed upon to write new scenes for the 1938 screen version of his *Pygmalion*.[41] For such figures it was, as one wit put it, a case less of 'Art for Art's sake' than of 'Money for God's sake'. In the thirties the mass of the people got their spiritual, intellectual and aesthetic sustenance from the screen, and modernism remained an élite irrelevance.

## NOTES

1. David Vincent, *Literacy and Popular Culture: England 1750–1914* (Cambridge: Cambridge University Press, 1989).

2. Dave Russell, *Popular Music in England, 1860–1914* (Manchester: Manchester University Press, 1987).
3. Patrick Joyce, *Visions of the People* (Cambridge: Cambridge University Press, 1991).
4. Martin Meisel, *Realizations* (Princeton, NJ: Princeton University Press, 1983).
5. Sir Henry Irving, *Theatre, Culture and Society*, ed. Jeffrey Richards (Keele: Keele University Press, 1994), p. 18.
6. Ibid.
7. Suzi Gablik, *Has Modernism Failed?* (London: Thames & Hudson, 1984; 1992 edn), p. 13.
8. John Carey, *The Intellectuals and the Masses, 1880–1939* (London: Faber & Faber, 1992).
9. Commission on Educational and Cultural Films, *The Film in National Life* (London, 1932), p. 78.
10. D. Stone and D.A. Rowe, *The Measurement of Consumers' Expenditure in the UK, 1920–1938* (Cambridge: Cambridge University Press, 1966), p. 81.
11. For a detailed account of cinema and cinema-going in thirties Britain, see Jeffrey Richards, *Age of the Dream Palace* (London: Routledge, 1984).
12. See for instance, E.W. Bakke, *The Unemployed Man* (London: Nisbet, 1933), p. 182.
13. Simon Rowson, 'A Statistical Survey of the Cinema Industry in Great Britain', *Journal of the Royal Statistical Society*, 99 (1936): 67–129.
14. John K. Walton, *Lancashire* (Manchester: Manchester University Press, 1987), pp. 283–324.
15. J.B. Priestley, *English Journey* (London: Heinemann, 1934; 1968 edn), pp. 397–402.
16. Richard Hoggart, *The Uses of Literacy* (Harmondsworth: Penguin, 1958), pp. 102–12.
17. See for instance, Robert Roberts, *The Classic Slum* (Harmondsworth: Pelican, 1973); Don Howarth, *Bright Morning* (London: Methuen, 1990); William Woodruff, *Billy Boy* (Halifax: Ryburn, 1994).
18. Nicholas Pronay and D.W. Spring (eds), *Propaganda, Politics and Film* (London: Macmillan, 1982), p. 235.
19. Leslie Halliwell, *Seats in All Parts* (Manchester: Granada, 1985), p. 12.
20. The questionnaire replies are reprinted in full in Jeffrey Richards and Dorothy Sheridan (eds), *Mass-Observation at the Movies* (London: Routledge, 1987), pp. 41–136.
21. Halliwell, *Seats in All Parts*, p. 54.
22. Henry Kendall, *I Remember Romano's* (London: MacDonald, 1960), p. 115.
23. Halliwell, *Seats in All Parts*, pp. 7, 40, 42, 45, 61.
24. Walton, *Lancashire*, p. 351.
25. Paul Harris, *Social Leadership and Social Attitudes in Bolton, 1919–39* (Lancaster University unpublished PhD thesis, 1973), p. 405.
26. Russell, *Popular Music in England*, p. 240; Ross McKibbin, *Ideologies of Class* (Oxford: Clarendon Press, 1990), pp. 139–66.
27. J. Hutchison, *The Complete Kine Manager* (Kinematograph Publications, 1937), pp. 157–8.
28. Stephen G. Jones, *The British Labour Movement and Film, 1918–39* (London: Routledge, 1987); Bert Hogenkamp, *Deadly Parallels: Film and the Left in Britain, 1929–39* (London: Lawrence & Wishart, 1986); Raphael Samuel, Ewan McColl

and Stuart Cosgrove (eds), *Theatres of the Left: Workers' Theatre Movements in Britain and America 1880–1935* (London: Routledge, 1985).

29. D.L. Le Mahieu, *A Culture for Democracy* (Oxford: Oxford University Press, 1988).

30. Allen Hutt, *The Condition of the Working Class in Britain* (London: Martin Lawrence, 1933), p. 177; Ralph Bond, 'Cinema in the Thirties' in Jon Clark et al. (eds), *Culture and Crisis in Britain in the 1930s* (London: Lawrence & Wishart, 1979), p. 245; Gareth Stedman Jones, *Languages of Class* (Cambridge: Cambridge University Press, 1983), pp. 179–238.

31. Marie Jahoda, 'Some Socio-Psychological Problems of Factory Life', *British Journal of Psychology*, 31 (1940): 191–200; Jack Common, *The Freedom of the Streets* (London: Secker & Warburg, 1938).

32. Board of Trade, Minutes of evidence taken before the Departmental Committee on Cinematic Films, 1936, p. 89.

33. Donald Albrecht, *Designing Dreams* (London: Thames & Hudson, 1986).

34. On the role of the censors in the cinema, see James C. Robertson, *The British Board of Film Censors: film censorship in Britain, 1896–1950* (London: Croom Helm, 1985), and Richards, *Age of the Dream Palace*, pp. 89–152.

35. John Fraser, *America and the Patterns of Chivalry* (Cambridge: Cambridge University Press, 1982), pp. 12, 16.

36. Gary Cross (ed.), *Worktowners in Blackpool* (London: Routledge, 1990), pp. 132–5.

37. On Fields and Formby, see Jeffrey Richards, *Stars in Our Eyes; Lancashire Stars of Stage, Screen and Radio* (Preston: Lancashire County Books, 1994).

38. Valentine Cunningham, *British Writers of the Thirties* (Oxford: Oxford University Press, 1988).

39. Leavis is quoted by Carey, *The Intellectuals and the Masses*, p. 7; Huxley by Peter Miles and Malcolm Smith, *Cinema, Literature and Society* (London: Croom Helm, 1987), p. 109; and Eliot by Cunningham, *British Writers of the Thirties*, p. 282.

40. *Close-up*, 3 (1928): 59–60.

41. Peter Stead, 'Hollywood's Message to the World: the British response in the nineteen thirties', *Historical Journal of Film, Radio and Television*, I (1981): 19–32; 'The People and the Pictures' in Pronay and Spring, *Propaganda, Politics and Film*, pp. 77–97; and *Film and the Working Class* (London: Routledge, 1987), pp. 99–119.

# CHAPTER THIRTEEN

# Blood and Marmalade: Negotiations between the State and the Domestic in George Orwell's Early Novels

LYNETTE HUNTER

Throughout the thirties George Orwell became more and more interested in the kinds of relationship that were built between the individual and the modern nation-state. In the process of addressing those relationships the analytical field of this chapter takes in elements from the rhetoric of the nation-state and its subjects, specifically the way that ideology operates as ethos; the notions of legitimation with which the nation works and the practices demanded by the state of an individual; and the split edges of culture and commodity that the capitalist economics of the modern nation-state constructs.

It is apparent from the collection of pamphlets that Orwell made, now held in the British Library, that he was acutely aware of the theorising around the formation of both entrepreneurial and socialist state capitalism that was going on throughout Europe, North America and the Soviet Union at this time.[1] The thirties is a period during which he becomes increasingly aware of what happens to the individual within the nation-state, while his writing of the forties, possibly focused by the Second World War, indicates a move toward analysis of some of the implications for the state itself. For Orwell the earlier concern with the individual is at least partly the response of someone who knows he belongs to an empowered and privileged group, at the same time as recognising that he is not fully part of that group. He was after all lower-upper-middle-class by self-definition; he had no university education; and he had worked with growing unease in the military section of the colonial service, riding out the end of Empire. For all that he wrote scathingly of intellectuals, he was in exactly that predicament of being in power yet wanting to critique that power that marks the position of an intellectual.[2]

To understand a historical locus for what Orwell was concerned with in terms of the individual within the state, it is helpful to remember that England only achieved male enfranchisement in 1919 and full enfranchisement in 1928. Orwell was born in 1903 and was seventeen years old, on the border of adulthood, when the first enfranchisement occurred. He was not really old enough to have experienced the lack of it, but just old enough to be part of the extraordinary lightness and illusion of freedom and power that marked the energy of the twenties. For whatever reason, possibly because of the appalling losses of the First World War, full enfranchisement did not see those whom it should have benefited asserting themselves. For example, women seem to have been diverted from the continued assertiveness that had gained them the vote, into a compassionate withdrawal. Exacerbated by the slump and the depression years, for the first time working-class English women stopped working within the financial/money economy. So an apparently direct result of women's enfranchisement was the final enclosure of all classes of women within domestic space. The labour movement ran into similar stasis.

It is difficult in the nineties to understand what enfranchisement meant. You get a vote, yes, but what does this imply? After all nowadays in Western Europe and North America, most people grow up simply expecting to vote, treating enfranchisement almost as a 'natural right', certainly taking it for granted. But what if the participation in government had suddenly been achieved after years of struggle and denial? The notion that you could change things, act and therefore have to take responsibility for action, would I suspect be far more immediate in a newly enfranchised population. Technically, every single person could do so. Everyone becomes, suddenly, someone to be listened to. But also immediately apparent must be that the voices are all very different – so how do we listen to each other in this new world? Orwell in the thirties is focusing on guidelines for action, or looking at precisely what the individual could do within the conditions of enfranchised subjectivity in the contemporary nation-state.

To provide a context for what Orwell is doing in his study of individual subjectivities, I would like to ground the discussion in rhetorical approaches to legitimation in politics. Political theory frequently works with the three modes of consensus, corporate and authoritarian decision-making, in its analysis of legitimation.[3] The alliance of nationalism and capitalism in the modern nation-state develops ideology into a particular rhetorical strategy that creates conditions under which the activity of the consensual is repressed, and the corporate continually elides into the authoritarian. This strategy sets up the particular conditions for assent to and participation in the state by the individual.[4]

In the history of Western analysis of the theory of politics, the rhetorically justifiable strategy for ethos – the way the governing group represents itself to those individuals to whom it is responsible – has always been a variety of consensus. In rhetoric, consensus is technically the discussion of and agreement upon grounds for argument, and then the development of decisions leading to action, on those grounds. This will work in governments representing small groups of empowered people such as Greek slave states or early medieval city states, or indeed the small discrete communities described by H.G. Gadamer.[5] However, once one is dealing with larger groups of people consensus decision-making is more difficult and often moves to the corporate. The corporate decision-making set toward action, takes place on the basis of already agreed-upon grounds which the group tacitly accepts. Aristotle discusses the possibility for corporate decision-making in both *Topica* and *Rhetorica* but restricts it to the sciences, saying that it is justified only in small, coherent, mutually constructed groups which make prior agreements about common grounds.[6] Yet even corporate decision-making is difficult to handle if the number of individuals in the represented populace becomes very large: Machiavelli's response to the problem was to describe the authoritarian practices of the 'Prince' – but he was able to do so at precisely the point that they were disintegrating and giving way to representative national governments.

An acute problem, if not *the* problem, of late Renaissance and early modern politics was the growing number of empowered bourgeoisie emerging within a structure of nationalism that produced specific conditions appropriate for capitalist economics. Capitalism needs a broad power base and competitiveness between players who have the possibility of achieving some equity or have at least similar opportunities. Its ethos therefore presents a diverse set of voices, and needs a political system that will diffuse potential conflict between the competing voices, at the least moving conflict out of the overt aggression of force. Early capitalism in England can be seen as an extension of the court system into national politics, with the commonwealth as an attempt to deal with the broader franchise of bourgeois empowerment.[7]

Nationalism, for the first time during this period of the seventeenth century, becomes a political structure that cannot speak directly to the people to whom it is responsible – but it must address them in some way in order to gain legitimacy. Its ethos needs a stable means of mediating its arguments, decisions and actions, and an audience whose reception is constructed as stable. In other words, its needs precisely replicate those of capitalism: both have to have an ethos that stabilises both the perception of the source of power and the receiver of, audience of, subject of power.

From the seventeenth century in Europe, there is an urgent search for stable modes of rhetorical strategy which is usually discussed by current critical discourses in terms of the history and philosophy of science but is also found throughout the humanities, medicine and technology. These recent histories indicate political and institutional structures of nations in Western Europe and North America moving toward state systems because they promise a means of delivering stability. State systems, whether enterprise capitalism or socialist capitalism, construct a corporate ethos currently analysed under the word 'ideology', that uses a set of specific rhetorical strategies to construct a stability of representation that depends upon the public's willingness to forget that it is a representation.[8] This is an appropriate strategy for capitalism with its need to stabilise demand in order to make technology in industry of long-term use and thereby increase profitability. The stabilising of demand becomes a commodification of need through the process of marketing, and is clearly at the heart of Marx's critique of his own time: the moment at which in Europe, technology and industry combine to produce these conditions for profitability. The stabilising of representations of the state also answers the nation's requirement for a fixed and stable ethos, for both the source of power and the subject. This is not only commodification of needs but also a commodification of the individual who is increasingly defined as private, isolated, not responsive to the state, and without community.

Although it has taken centuries to put into effect, for this is no conspiracy theory, ideology solves the problem of the legitimacy of a government of larger spaces and diversified voices simply by denying, evading, hiding and/or ignoring the awareness of a consensual or responsive ethos. This poses its own problems because that consensual ethos can keep the potentially authoritarian dangers of corporate ethos in check; without it the corporate is always on the verge of eliding into the authoritative.[9] Ideology uses the medium of state institutions to imply that there is a norm, a convention, a natural condition for public life. There is no need to question or interact because the norm is the case. The procedure is equivalent to the denial of a need for rhetoric, and the loss of formal rhetoric in Western Europe from the seventeenth century is part of the stabilising effect of ideology and many political theories, including Marxism, are an attempt to remedy that loss.[10]

The rhetoric of the nation-state structures its ethos simultaneously to build a norm as an artificial construction and then to forget that it is artificial. Orwell talked about this extensively in his later work under the term doublethink, and began to understand the incredible stress it puts on the relatively empowered for reasons I shall discuss later. Technically doublethink works from the accepted common grounds of corporate agreement, and uses a representing medium in such a way as to repeat without variation, or with as little as possible. This becomes increasingly realisable as technologies are developed to aid the illusion of invariable and exact repetition.[11] The result is a retarding and eventual repression of responsive change, a commodification of need into desire and a commodification of the individual into the state subject.[12]

If Marx and Engels carefully outlined a description of 'false consciousness', or ideology, created by nation-state capitalism, Freud could be said to have condensed and outlined some of the ramifications for the subject in terms of the repression of the individual, whether that repression be complete, as in narcissism, or ambivalent, as in neurosis, or displaced, as in psychosis. But Freud did not connect this repression with the commodification of the individual by the state, nor did Marxist theorists, often continental, connect state theory with the effects on individual action and responsibility, particularly in a newly enfranchised population. From one perspective it is possible to read the thirties as a decade in which many English writers begin to draw the two together, begin to analyse politics and society in terms of culture and technology with an understanding of commodity reification. This early history is usually constructed at least from the thirties to the early fifties around the figures of Harold Innis, Marshall McLuhan, Roland Barthes and Michel Foucault, none of whom were English although the first two were educated in England. However, many others, and as I shall go on to argue certainly Orwell, can be read as concerned with similar issues.

Most of Orwell's thirties novels describe the problems of the individual within this kind of modern nation-state whose ethos, ideology, requires the public to forget the artificiality of its construction.[13] If we can look at many twentieth-century thinkers as people dealing with the problem of knowing how to handle what it is they are required to forget, you could say that never before have there been such large enfranchised populations. Smaller governing groups are usually from a similar power base, they have similar interests and make decisions on similar grounds. Large populations with many different positions and different needs have to work in other ways. Pluralism doesn't work in large and diverse populations. Representative democratic systems of various kinds control some of the difference, but from the individual's point of view some needs must be foregone, some insisted upon: but how to make the decision? In someone else's system, where you have no vote or political agency, the disempowered revolt around central issues; otherwise there is no need to examine the structure: the system is someone else's, and there is no pressure on the disempowered individual to remember to forget. But since the early part of the twentieth century most people in northern Europe have needed to learn ways of making decisions about what to remember and what to forget.

Orwell is at the heart of this dilemma. He is concerned with the various levels of awareness we can permit ourselves, how far they may be allowed to inform the way we change ourselves, and how difficult it is to manage the continual moral choices that such a system demands, particularly since there is no guarantee of outcome, there is no direct connection between the individual and effective power. Yet the dilemma is especially excruciating for those relatively empowered individuals who are, through some political, social or cultural abutment on to ideology, in contact with policy-making and institutional power.

In the thirties novels Orwell looks at some of the effects of a state system that insists on privacy, and deprives individuals of community the better to isolate and thereby convince them of the 'naturalness' of ideology. But within such a system where does assent and therefore legitimacy lie? Where do loyalty and commitment lie? What does betrayal mean? Can civic, or non-state, communities be constructed as alternative sites of power? If there is no immediate group with similar interests, no necessary concept of non-state community, where can the individual have any consensus-building, any notion of assent to grounds whose construction is held in common with other people? And if the construction of ideology is 'natural' or unseen, then policy change or change in party line, becomes an arbitrary shift in belief in order to maintain loyalty. Loyalty that is blind outweighs other values: it is a loyalty that permits constant change, continual instructions on remembering to forget something once valued. This duplicates the procedures of commodity capitalism in the coming together of technology and the state. Brand loyalties, constructed by advertising, work on notions of the completion of desire – desire that is often cast as need. They build expedient trust and serial loyalty. Just so the commodification of self by capitalism within nation-state ideology, leads directly to a version of pluralism in which the problem of listening to other voices is theorised in terms of them becoming commodities.

All the central characters in Orwell's early novels are isolated individuals, locked into private worlds. They have difficulties with communication, but also difficulties with community. They are all middle-class, and all described as appalled and deprived in different ways by the banality of their class, the compromise it has made between public and private. Take Flory in *Burmese Days*:[14] he doesn't become aware enough of the compromise; therefore he cannot understand the private deprivation of his life which the state requires by making him lead a double life. He is aware of the brutality he mediates as an agent of imperial Britain which simultaneously requires him to think of himself as a civiliser, a mediator of civilisation. In the end, Flory cannot stand the tension and kills himself. A lot of *Burmese Days* is based on the stand-off, central to many discussions of early-twentieth-century politics, between totalitarianism and anarchy. As the franchise extended further and further, in some systems the response of authority was to become more and more total, dividing the public and private even further. Within such a system anarchy appears to be the only response of the individual – a result of enforced privacy: but it is a futile gesture without community; for without community anarchy is equivalent to solipsism or suicide. The character Verrall is the only anarchist who can succeed: but then, he is a member of the ruling class and not only will his anarchic action be delimited by his background, but also aristocratic anarchy is cast by English culture as being a condoned aberration of eccentricity from a defined community.

In similar ways each of the isolated central characters in the other novels is also attempting communication, trying to find a community where the tension or contradiction of the compromise can be discussed. Each turns to different cultures, different races, different gender and different class – this last most clearly and frequently – but they never manage to fit. Through the novels Orwell begins an analysis of the race/class/gender/religion concerns that dominate contemporary cultural studies. He calls into question how we form and/or belong to communities, making us aware that the process is neither self-evident nor often successful: the return to banality is one way of dealing with the alienation proceeding from failure.

Dorothy, in *A Clergyman's Daughter*,[15] is Orwell's only central female character, and she, unlike his male characters but in an interesting pre-seeing of recent feminist searches, turns to religion. Yet she does so not as belief but as a system; indeed the novel is a kind of textbook exercise in consciousness-raising. With Dorothy, Orwell has moved on from observing the frustration of the double-life to depicting the actions/decisions that need to be taken when it is realised that the public institution is a constructed system. Flory views the state not even as monolithic but as natural; but Dorothy is shown in the process of recognising it as artificial. The novel opens by depicting her as a type of a middle-class persona: she has hobbies, arranges flowers. As we gather later from 'The Lion and the Unicorn',[16] these are Orwell's analogues for the English version of the private life: if the state isolates you within a private world you have to fill it with something – things you can do on your own, by yourself. But Orwell's notion of 'choice' is very limited; it is more a matter of selection from already curtailed elements.

Through memory loss Dorothy ceases to be a private person any more, she ceases to have any identity: the text follows her through the reacquisition of a notion of individuality and then to a re-establishment of her private identity that is needed by the public structure. But as it does so, by way of a study of language and psychology, it makes the character and the reader aware every step along the way of the artificiality of ideology. Here the ideological structures are mainly education and the church. In education,

Dorothy tries for a new common ground that will engage both teacher and pupil, but is forced back into rote-learning banality by the head teacher. Finally, she goes back to the church, yet this time aware of its construction and re-entering its clichés *as* clichés.

The negotiations and agreements between personal memory and public history form the primary means by which people engage in public activity in nation-states.[17] There are other narratives that carry public memory, but those of the nation-state are powerful because they are tied to economics. These narratives are mediated by ideology and are therefore bound narratives: what many have come to call master narratives. The individual's need to search for a position within the public history, directs the memory into negotiations between the individual and the social that construct the self: this is the activity of personal memory. But if the self is defined largely by public history, this is an act of forgetting, neglecting the artificial structures of society, taking the nation's conventional narrative as a system of rights and becoming only a private individual, producing a concept of fixed identity: unnerving because it, like the heroic or fame, dissipates when in contact with an immediate community. But also, in maintained privacy, there is one way that an individual can deal with the often overwhelming responsibility of enfranchisement.

Dorothy's self-aware acceptance of doublethink is one way of dealing with the tensions of the public–private separation induced by ideology: but it does little to address the problem. In Gordon Comstock of *Keep the Aspidistra Flying*,[18] Orwell takes the analysis a few steps further. And it is clear that Orwell attributes Gordon's ability to do so to his gender and his class – not only that he is a budding intellectual. If you are aware of the artificiality of the state and its public presence, as well as aware of the doublethink compromise it requires of you, what alternative responses are there? The situation mirrors the postmodern position, which is really only relevant to those people who have a measure of empowerment: the recognition that *even* in an empowered position the individual can do nothing to affect the workings of the state, generates the enervation, melancholia, paranoia and cynicism of postmodern theory. Indeed Orwell's early novels could be read as an anatomy of precisely these responses.

Gordon Comstock is very much the cynic, and he plays the cynic's games with increasing confidence. Gordon constructs his life-before-the-bookstore as alternating between poetry-making and advertising-writing, which are the private and public spheres of his world. He is supremely able to turn himself into whatever the public expects of him; just as he can categorise, type, commodify and reify products for advertising, so he can do it for himself. The early part of the book shows him doing just this: making himself into the person that his different customers expect.

The novel works through the various different ways in which individuals commodify themselves, or negotiate versions of themselves with an institutional public that is the state. Gordon deludes himself by thinking that 'poetry' is his true self, his essential identity. Yet by way of a critique of other analogously 'high' art, such as writing by Dickens and Barrie, illustrations by Rackham, art by Burne-Jones (to which he is introduced by a woman), which is set against the escapist literature of magazines and penny-dreadfuls, he realises that the division between poetry and advertising cannot be made on the grounds of 'true' identity. The world of Dickens and Burne-Jones is just as enclosed and escapist as the magazines – hence the poetry, for Gordon, is just as escapist as the advertising. Both are ways of commodifying the self so it fits: poetry answers the demand for isolated private space, and advertising answers the demand for banal participation in public institutions.

Orwell himself, of course, also offers the obverse of the commodifying process: that if commodification can be a banal response to the imposition of nation-state demands; the identification of needs, the construction of the personal self, may also be responsive. In other words, these generic forms do not only reify; poetry, art, escapist literature and advertisements can also be constructive if undertaken in response to and in engagement with a community, they do not have to be enclosing, cynical and melancholic. In a naïve way, Orwell cartoons this in his bringing together of Gordon and Rosemary in a family. It is the first time that he has permitted his characters *any* lasting relationship, and is an indication of the discussions for supportive structures and strategies for forming communities that he begins to pursue in his essays. The *naïveté* is also an indication of how well Orwell resists bourgeois embarrassment with the strategies of the disempowered: that a community of commitment where you hammer out common grounds restores to you your history, gives you the possibility of personal memory, allows you to re-member yourself, gives you back your body, encourages you to resist the fixities of commodification.

Chronologically, Orwell's novel-writing career was interrupted by the work on *The Road to Wigan Pier* and *Homage to Catalonia*. Although these are significantly different in that they are assessments of contemporary socialism in England and Europe, they are still mediated through fairly isolated characters involved in individual–state negotiations about memory and action. *The Road to Wigan Pier* is damning of the middle class and its intelligentsia, with its inappropriate versions of socialism that simply underwrite the capitalist impetus of the British nation-state. *Homage to Catalonia* is a major step toward the notion of a *personal* identity as opposed to a private essentialism, personal identities being built in response to community needs.[19]

*Coming Up For Air*[20] extends this project of understanding commodification and the ambivalent relationship of the private–personal–public selves.

George Bowling acts out the issues on the stage of a lower-middle-class Britain. He is presented as tensely schizophrenic particularly in response to his family, the wife and children to whom he is alternately verbally cruel and then sentimental, but also with regard to himself as he alternates between the slick sales-talk and heavy irony that undermines the slickness: cliché and parody of cliché. There are occasionally intrusions of a highly unusual domestic male voice, that Orwell develops a little elsewhere, but which from a late-twentieth-century perspective has many similarities to the domestic voices recently created by women writers in order to lay out new common grounds. A topic of particular significance here is that of the self-perception of desirable body shape. But this domestic voice is not given much scope and soon makes way for a grass-roots intellectual voice, also quite different from that anywhere else in Orwell's writing. The introductory section concludes with a series of commentaries on the ersatz, the things that are 'labelled' as one thing for the public yet are actually another: the memorable example being the hot-dog exploding fish ends and offal into the mouth. The ersatz repeats the way Bowling thinks of himself: fat on the outside and thin on the inside.

Bowling attempts to address this schizophrenia by living again his memory of his childhood, and trying to reattach the private and public bits of his life. It is significant that Orwell has him start off on this journey because he has seventeen pounds hidden away: only those who can buy themselves out for a while, buy themselves thinking time, can afford to do this kind of reassessment; and Orwell is quite clear about positioning Bowling's wife Hilda so that this would be impossible for her since she can never get time to herself. Bowling first recounts the historical version of his childhood: the accepted public version of sentiment which is like an ersatz label. Bubbling up into this are isolated fragments of private memory, all associated with violence, with fishing and killing as well as, significantly, with poetry and religion. All the associations are connected to an anarchic violence. He then continues with a recounting of his growing up that presents the private self as contained violence and the public self as ersatz salesman. Finally the character ends up wanting two things: either the destruction of war or escape into the past, either violence or nostalgia; the repressed whether narcissistic, neurotic or psychotic, and the fixed banalities of a stable normative self. The recounting constructs the character's existence as schizophrenic, and more than incidentally paranoid as if he is subliminally aware that outwith the banal there is another set of identities and vice versa, but awareness of one precludes assent to the other. The character has built an early version of the doublethink process narrativised and institutionalised in *Animal Farm* and *Nineteen Eighty Four*.

In George Bowling's present, and as an ending to these memories,

Orwell sends him to a Left Book Club meeting to listen to an anti-fascist speaker. What Bowling hears on one level is about complete manipulation by the state; on another what he hears is a private fear responding with violence. Not only do the fascists hate because of fear, but those against fascism respond to their own fear with violence. There is an argument here that people allow themselves to be motivated toward war because it permits a legitimate expression of the violence engendered by the authoritarianism of the state: an idea that is reiterated explicitly in the opening paragraphs of 'The Lion and the Unicorn' (p. 74). The state manipulates the violence, under the banner of nationalism, as yet another strategy to define its identity, which strategy is also directly analogous to racism.[21] Fear also comes where there are no personally valid grounds for individual decision-making, in other words no community within which to hammer out common bases. This is *how* the state creates fear: as a spin-off from the need for isolation in order to convince of the stable representation of ideology.

Bowling, for this moment, rejects both the violence of war and the nostalgia of the 'decent' people whose 'minds have stopped' – who have forgotten the artificiality of the state entirely. However, the moment is shortlived. Bowling quickly re-enters his schizophrenia. He goes to Lower Binfield, the physical site of his childhood, only to find that his own nostalgia is completely misplaced. Of course it is; he even says to the reader 'you saw this coming, but I didn't'. Only if he had stayed there would his memory have had a chance to change in response to the place; but he left and he commodified it into a fixed thing. With the nostalgia gone Bowling is overwhelmed by feelings of violence: as he comments, the blood gets mixed up with the marmalade, the violence crushes into the banality. The sequence indicates a further parallel, that nostalgia, banality, the possibility of the repetition of nearly exact actions, is one way of controlling the violence engendered by the state. Depriving people of banal repetition unleashes enormous/endless brutality.

With the sides of his self collapsing into one another, Bowling can no longer think of the private and public worlds in terms of true and false, both are part of him. And he has a momentary, frightening glimpse of their simultaneity. But in order to cope he rigidifies his new world; he goes home, where each conversation with his wife, who unlike him has no leisure to reassess and is tied to the economic realities and pressures of this middle-class existence, draws him back into his ability to forget the immediacies of his life. She reminds him to forget until he re-enters the banal. After all, he has run out of money. Yet the writer, through this tale, allows the reader the understanding that the public persona is just as much the actuality as the private self; it is not merely a label but a part of the reality of an individual human being.

As usual Orwell is writing in exemplary style, offering a pastiche and parody of what we need to recognise and be wary of. The writing is postmodern in these generic choices; but also self-consciously so in the statement about the way that those with power don't actually want to change while those with some power are caught in the stress of schizophrenia or doublethink. Any suggestion of change, as he outlines in 'The Lion and the Unicorn' will get people reassessing the social and political basis for the structure of the state in England (p. 88ff). Any suggestion would and will make it all too apparent that those *in* power have been in the business of maintaining state repression to exploit the poorer, the disempowered, the colonial possessions. The powerful especially must remain isolated and private, for if they ever attempted community the stability of the state would be fundamentally challenged.

More pertinently to Orwell's own position, and my own, is what he offers to the analysis of the relatively empowered, for example the intellectual. The relatively empowered hold the position they are in because the state system defines them as such. If they accept the definition then they also accept the grounds upon which it is made and yet the degree of their disempowerment indicates the degree of gap or strain between having to accept those grounds at the same time as recognising that they are beyond assent or question. The relatively empowered have to live with the strain, not of the repressed or forgotten, but of remembering continually to forget. They are on the inside looking out, a position Orwell discusses in depth in *Inside the Whale*[22] as a womb-like position in which one may be simultaneously aware of both violence and sentiment. It is only those who have no effective power who understand the labour involved in the construction of new common grounds – but by definition these often have no money and no time to commit to the labour.

The commodification of self is a way of controlling the schizophrenia of the relatively empowered subject felt by those who have the time, money and leisure to become aware of the contradiction: here and at this time of the enfranchised individual within a representative democratic system still in the hands of the old power. It is clear that Orwell finds the drawbacks in this as well as the needs that are answered. Looking back from the nineties, what he has to say is perhaps most pertinent to the theorising around commodity in terms of the fetish: the notion of the fetish as either banal or reciprocal lies coincident with Orwell's understanding of cliché and community. Orwell goes on to discuss the pros and cons in detail in terms of the artist and writer both in 'The Frontiers of Art and Propaganda' and 'Literature and Totalitarianism'.[23] At one extreme in the totalitarian state, the writer will 'disappear' because totalitarianism will ask all people continually to alter their line on something;[24] and the writer, conventionally, is not there to reproduce the private fixities defined by the state but to open negotiation for communities, to destabilise the representative structures of the state, either their rhetorical strategies or their reified objects: the strategies and images that construct ideology as ethos. But also, the artist or writer is necessary to the state to provide ways of representing, building or constructing acceptable ideology, to provide places where people can agree about evaluation. In doing these things the writer is externalising or articulating the activity of any individual's negotiation between personal memory and public history, which is precisely what concerns many of the novels of the thirties. But also the articulation acts as a focus for making these voices heard; Orwell's novels are exercises in the evaluation and placing of the 'many' voices; they are illustrations of the near impossibility of maintaining a continual assessment of them, or even at all, without a supportive community.

What is interesting is to watch Orwell begin to transfer this theorising out to a global politics; even in 1940 he understood the inevitability of global economics. In 'The Lion and the Unicorn' he looks at the way that 'nations' are becoming important for their cultural identity within global politics (p. 75). It is one step from this recognition to national cultures becoming important because they are being targeted as markets within transnational economy.[25] Again, the commodification is seen as necessary to those markets because it stabilises 'audience' demand. This of course is part of recent economic theory and is not discussed by Orwell, who was still, in 1940, hoping for a non-capitalist socialism. But what he does perceive is that an arbitrarily defined national culture, like the banal commodification of the individual, is not helpful. It leaves a set of pluralist voices within the global, the multinational dream where those who lack power are simply cut to the cloth of those with power: the ethnocentric bazaar that replicates the frustration of enfranchised individuals within a state where all are equal but some are more equal than others.[26]

On the other hand, a responsively constructed national culture, here of course Orwell's socialist revolution of 'The Lion and the Unicorn', could act as the check on the increasingly authoritative tendencies of the corporate power of global agencies. Orwell argues in the essay that 'war' in the context of the Second World War could make this possible in England as nothing else (p. 117). Possibly in an optimistic transfer of his experiences of the Spanish Civil War, and possibly in a propagandic move against the brutalism of the forties' experience of war, he suggests that this 'kind of war' breaks down the notion of private comfort and security, and instead of merely legitimising violence, can be used to get people to commit themselves to work on community. Of course, this 'kind of war' cannot happen, and we have watched time and time again the potential events for political focus fail to draw people together. But the awareness of national culture as civic discourse, not populist, that Orwell's exemplary mode suggests, is vital to the critique of transnational *ethos*. This is particularly so for the nineties because transnational ethos is not yet formulated or understood, and is already being taken for granted in for example post-materialist economics. Without ways of articulating an awareness of its constructed devices, nations run the risk of the intolerable half-awareness of doublethink erupting through cultural commodity into racism and war.

## NOTES

1. Peter Davison, to whom all writers interested in the thirties and in Orwell are indebted, alerted me to the existence of this archive.
2. Edward Said's Reith lectures cover some of this ground from a contemporary point of view, but with the same emphasis.
3. From the political exegesis offered by both Plato and Aristotle on the kinds of agreement that can be made (see especially Aristotle's *Topica*), to among many others D. Beetham's recent account, *The Legitimation of Power* (London: Macmillan, 1991), these three modes recur continually.
4. L. Hunter, 'Ideology as the Ethos of the Nation State', *Rhetorica*, Summer 1996.
5. H.-G. Gadamer, *Reason in the Age of Science*, trans. F.G. Lawrence (London: MIT Press, 1981).
6. See L. Hunter, 'Remember Frankenstein', *Rhetorica*, IX (4), Autumn, 1991.
7. See T. Nairn, *The Break-up of Britain: Crisis and New-Nationalism* (London: New Left Books, 1977).
8. B. Anderson discusses nation-states and forgetting in *Imagined Communities* (London: Verso, 1985); see also T. Eagleton on capitalism and forgetting in 'Nationalism: Irony and Commitment', *Nationalism, Colonialism and Literature*, intro. S. Deane (Minneapolis: University of Minnesota Press, 1990).
9. See W. Rowe and V. Schelling, *Memory and Modernity* (London: Verso, 1991).
10. L. Hunter, *Rhetorical Stance in Modern Literature* (London: Macmillan, 1984), Chapter 3.
11. On the technological control of the media, see among others A. Giddens, *A Contemporary Critique of Historical Materialism* (Aldershot: Gower, 1981).
12. L. Hunter, 'Bodily Functions in Cartesian Space', in S. Chew (ed.), *Borderblur Papers: Essays in Canadian Poetry and Poetics* (Edinburgh: Quadrega, 1996).
13. See E. Gellner, 'Nationalism and the Two Forms of Cohesion in Complex Societies', *Proceedings of the British Academy LXVIII* (London: Oxford University Press, 1983); for a response, see also J. Kellas, *The Politics of Nationalism and Ethnicity* (London: Macmillan, 1991).
14. G. Orwell, *Burmese Days* (London: Penguin 1934; 1969).
15. G. Orwell, *A Clergyman's Daughter* (London: Penguin 1935; 1983).
16. G. Orwell, 'The Lion and the Unicorn' (1941), *Collected Essays, Journalism and Letters of George Orwell*, Vol. 2, ed. S. Orwell and I. Angus (Harmondsworth: Penguin, 1982).

17. See L. Hunter, *Outsider Notes* (forthcoming), part 3, for a fuller account of personal and public memory.
18. G. Orwell, *Keep the Aspidistra Flying* (London: Penguin, 1936; 1975).
19. The notion of 'personal' identity was a central concept in L. Hunter, *George Orwell, the Search for a Voice* (Milton Keynes: Open University Press, 1984).
20. G. Orwell, *Coming Up for Air* (London: Penguin, 1939; 1983).
21. See E. Balibar and I. Wallerstein, *Race, Nation, Class: Ambiguous Identities* (London: Verso, 1991).
22. G. Orwell, 'Inside the Whale' (1940), *Collected Essays, Journalism and Letters of George Orwell*, Vol. 1, ed. S. Orwell and I. Angus (Penguin, 1982).
23. G. Orwell, 'The Frontiers of Art and Propaganda' (1941) and 'Literature and Totalitarianism' (1941), *Collected Essays, Journalism and Letters of George Orwell*, Vol. 2, as above.
24. 'Literature and Totalitarianism', pp. 163–4.
25. See P. Hertner and G. Jones (eds), *Multinationals: Theory and History* (Aldershot: Gower, 1986).
26. R. Rorty advocates this in *Objectivity, Relativism and Truth* (Cambridge: Cambridge University Press, 1991), p. 209.

# Index

*The Adelphi*, 32
Agee, James, 163–77
  *Let Us Now Praise Famous Men*,
    163, 173–7
Albrecht, Daniel, 193
Alexander, Donald, 168
Auden, W.H., 1, 2, 4, 6, 11, 13, 18,
    19, 26, 27, 53–70, 72, 73, 74,
    77, 81, 82, 84, 86, 87, 88, 91–2,
    103, 116, 125–6, 127, 129, 130,
    131, 133, 135, 136, 137, 143, 168
  *Another Time*, 87
  *The Ascent of F6* (with Christopher
    Isherwood), 61–2, 67
  'Honour', 64
  'It's Farewell to the Drawing-
    room's Civilised Cry', 143
  'Letter to Lord Byron', 113, 115
  'In Memory of W.B. Yeats', 73
  *The Orators: An English Study*,
    53–5, 58–67, 126, 131
  'September 1, 1939', 73, 74
  'Sir, no man's enemy', 111
  'Spain', 17, 111
Aragon, Louis, 28

Bakhtin, M.M., 4, 16, 116
Baldwin, Stanley, 64, 65
Barke, James, 3, 4, 11, 18, 20
  *Major Operation: A Novel*, 7–16,
    18–19
Barker, George, 125, 136
  *Thirty Preliminary Poems*, 124
Bell, Julian, 77, 78–9, 81
Bergonzi, Bernard, 86
Bernal, J.D., 26
Bérubé, Michael, 6
Betjeman, John, 2, 112–13, 114
  'The Outer Suburbs', 112
  'Slough', 111, 114, 115, 120

Bond, Ralph, 168, 206
Bradbrook, Muriel, 38, 39
Brandt, Bill, 173
Bridges, Robert, 126, 127, 129
  *Testament of Beauty*, 126
Brittain, Vera, 38, 39–43, 48, 49, 50
  *Honourable Estate*, 48–9
  *Testament of Friendship*, 42, 48
  *Testament of Youth*, 41–2, 48
Britten, Benjamin, 142, 168
  *Ballad of Heroes*, 142–3
Brooke, Rupert, 129, 144
Brown, Alex, 30, 31, 34
Bryden, Samuel, 62–3
Bukharin, Nikolai, 14, 17, 18
Bunting, Basil, 2, 92, 97, 103
  *Briggflatts*, 102, 106
  'Chomei at Toyama', 106
  'Villon', 98, 99–102, 104, 107
  'The Well at Lycopolis', 102
Bush, Alan, 19, 21, 142

Calder-Marshall, Arthur, 18
*Cambridge Left*, 24, 26–7, 28
Cameron, Norman, 28
Carey, John, 183
Carpenter, Humphrey, 65
Carritt, Gabriel, 66
Caudwell, Christopher, 13, 32, 77, 83
  *Illusion and Reality*, 76
Chase, Richard, 6
Common, Jack, 192
Communism, 3, 5, 10, 11, 12, 13,
    18, 26, 32, 74, 76, 78, 80, 83–4,
    125, 126, 130, 132, 133, 139,
    141, 148, 152
Communist Party of Great Britain,
    65–6, 70, 125, 127, 130
Constable, John, 79
*Contemporary Poetry and Prose*, 126

Cornford, John, 27, 34, 79
Cournos, John, 32
*Criterion*, 32, 53, 77–8, 80, 126
Cronin, A.J., 194, 195
Cunard, Nancy, 127, 142
Cunningham, Valentine, 112, 113, 198

*Daily Worker*, 14, 127, 130
Day Lewis, Cecil, 6, 12, 26, 27,
    29–31, 81, 103, 129, 130, 135,
    136, 137
  'Letter to a Young Revolutionary',
    114
  *The Magnetic Mountain*, 11, 114–15,
    133
  'Newsreel', 115
  'The Poet and Revolution', 26
  'Revolution and Poetry', 31
Derrida, Jacques, 19
Dimitrov, Georgy, 28–9
Dos Passos, John, 13, 14, 126
Driberg, Tom, 53

Eagleton, Terry, 89
Edwards, Ness; *The Workers' Theatre*,
    148–9
Ehrenburg, Ilya, 15, 16
Eliot, T.S., 2, 4, 6, 7, 11, 12, 13, 15,
    18, 19, 22, 25, 27, 32, 53–70,
    74, 75–6, 77–9, 80–5, 87–8, 92,
    103, 126, 127, 136, 144, 145,
    199
  *Ash-Wednesday*, 63, 91
  *A Choice of Kipling's Verse*, 20–1
  'Dante', 61
  *Four Quartets*, 54, 78, 91
  'The Function of Criticism', 58
  *The Idea of a Christian Society*,
    73–4
  'Little Gidding', 66–7
  *Murder in the Cathedral*, 21
  'Religion and Literature', 75
  *The Rock*, 21
  *Selected Essays*, 56–7, 58
  'Shakespeare and the Stoicism of
    Seneca', 61
  'Tradition and the Individual
    Talent', 56–7
  *The Use of Poetry and the Use of
    Criticism*, 56–7, 82

*The Waste Land*, 18, 21, 31, 53,
    54–6, 57, 58, 59, 81–2, 98
Ermolaev, Herman, 25
Ervine, St John, 148, 149, 152, 153,
    156
Evans, Walker, 163, 172, 174, 176

Facism, 3, 11, 29, 33–4, 47, 54, 113,
    125, 150, 166, 170, 212
Flanagan, Hallie, 172
Foucault, Michel, 16, 206
Fox, Ralph, 13, 14, 18, 33, 34
Fraser, John, 196
Freeman, Joseph, 6
Freud, Sigmund, 2, 206

Gablik, Suzi, 183
Gadamer, H.G., 204
Galsworthy, John, 149
Garman, Douglas; *The Jaded Hero*, 127
Gide, André, 84
Glasgow Unity Theatre, 14
Gold, Michael, 6
Golding, Louis, 194, 195
Gorky, Maxim, 25, 124
Grassic Gibbon, Lewis, 14, 15, 30
  *Grey Granite*, 16
Graves, Robert, 18, 28
Gray, Terence, 150, 151–2, 156, 158,
    160
  *The Degradation of Drama*, 152
Greene, Graham, 199
Greenwood, Walter, 195
Grierson, John, 165
  *Drifters*, 165–6
Griffith, Hubert; *Red Sunday*, 156
Grigson, Geoffrey, 27, 126, 136

Hall, Radclyffe; *The Well of Loneliness*,
    50
Halliwell, Leslie, 190
  *Seats in All Parts*, 185–6
Hardy, Thomas, 126
Harlem Renaissance, 6
Harrison, Jane, 51
Harrisson, Tom, 185, 186
Hawkins, Desmond, 128
Hay, Ian, 1
Hayward, John, 53
Henderson, Philip, 18, 32–3, 81, 89

Heslop, Harold, 15
Hoggart, Richard, 185
Holtby, Winifred, 2, 3, 38–43,
    49–50, 195
  *South Riding*, 42–3, 49
  *Virginia Woolf*, 38–40, 43, 50
Hope, Francis, 114
Hosking, Geoffrey, 25–6
Houseman, A.E., 126, 129
Huxley, Aldous, 127, 199
  *Brave New World*, 110
Hutt, Allen, 192
Hynes, Samuel; *The Auden Generation*,
    71, 130

Innis, Harold, 206
Irigaray, Luce, 44, 47
Isherwood, Christopher, 17, 74, 77,
    91–2, 170, 199

Jahoda, Marie, 192
Jakobson, Roman, 180
Jameson, Storm, 33, 166–7, 168, 174,
    177
Jeffares, A. Norman, 95, 96
Jennings, Humphrey, 168
Jolas, Eugene, 57
Jones, Gareth Stedman, 192
Joyce, James, 1, 2, 3, 4, 10, 13, 14,
    15, 19, 25, 27, 126
  *Finnegan's Wake*, 1, 91
  *Ulysses*, 12, 13, 17, 18, 21, 31, 59,
    102
Joyce, Patrick, 182, 197, 198

Kermode, Frank, 179
Kendall, Henry, 184
Kipling, Rudyard, 7, 20–1
Kisch, Egon Erwin, 166, 168
Knights, L.C., 32

Lane, Homer, 2
Lawrence, D.H., 2, 6, 15, 83, 95, 127
Leavis, F.R., 2, 127, 136, 199
Leavis, Q.D., 2, 32, 39
*Left Review*, 3, 11, 15, 23, 24, 28–34,
    130, 142
*The Left Song Book*, 19, 142
Lehmann, Rosamund, 6
Levin, Harry, 56

Lewis, Wyndham, 11, 28
Lindsay, Jack, 14, 126, 127
Lukács, Georg, 38, 50

MacAlastair, Somhairle, 21
MacColl, Ewan, 148
MacDiarmid, Hugh, 28, 30, 66
MacDonald, Ramsay, 63–4, 65
McLuhan, Marshall, 206
MacNeice, Louis, 2, 28, 74, 77, 82,
    86–7, 120, 122
  *Autumn Journal*, 71–4, 87, 118–19
  'Birmingham', 117–18, 119
McPherson, Aimée Semple, 20
Madge, Charles, 31
Le Mahieu, D.L., 191–2
Marx, Karl, 2, 77, 205, 206
Mason, H.A., 32
Mirsky, Prince, 13
Mitchison, Naomi, 17, 26
Morton, A.L., 127
Moscow Writer's Congress, 11, 12,
    13, 14, 15, 17, 24–5, 27, 28,
    31–2
Muir, Edwin, 28
Murry, John Middleton, 26

*New English Weekly*, 31–2
*New Masses*, 6, 172
*New Verse*, 27–8, 32, 126
Nixon, Barbara, 150

Odets, Clifford; *Waiting for Lefty*, 152,
    157, 158, 162
Orwell, George, 2, 3, 163–77,
    202–15
  *Animal Farm*, 211
  *Burmese Days*, 207–8
  *A Clergyman's Daughter*, 208–9
  *Coming Up For Air*, 210–2
  'The English People', 198
  'The Frontiers of Art and
    Propaganda', 213
  *Homage to Catalonia*, 163, 171, 210
  *Inside the Whale*, 213
  *Keep the Aspidistra Flying*, 209–10
  'The Lion and the Unicorn', 170,
    198, 208, 212, 213, 214
  'Literature and Totalitarianism',
    213

*The Road to Wigan Pier*, 33, 111, 163, 164, 166, 167, 168–71, 172, 174, 210

Peck, David, 163–4
Porché, Francois *Tsar Lénine*, 148, 154–7, 161
Pound, Ezra, 1, 2, 6, 15, 56, 57–8, 81, 88, 92–3, 95, 97, 101, 102–3, 104
 'Canto XXIII', 103–4
 *The Cantos*, 91, 105
 *Le Testament de Villon*, 98
 *The Spirit of Romance*, 98
Priestley, J.B., 2, 110, 111, 112, 113, 115, 118, 194, 195, 199
 *English Journey*, 108–9, 122, 178–9, 184–5
 *The Good Companions*, 39
*Problems of Soviet Literature*, 5, 15, 24, 31, 32
Promethean Society, 132
Pudney, John, 125
 *Spring Encounter*, 124

Radek, Karl, 13, 14, 15, 16, 17, 25
*The Red Flag*, 20
Reed, John; *Ten Days That Shook the World*, 165
Rhys, Jean, 91
Richards, I.A., 2, 56, 57, 58, 68, 81–4, 85–6
 *The Principles of Literary Criticism*, 82–3
 *Science and Poetry*, 81, 87
Rickword, Edgell, 127
Riding, Laura, 27, 125
 *Poet: A Lying Word*, 124
Roberts, Michael, 26, 82
 *New Country*, 129, 133
 *New Signatures*, 116–17, 129

*Scrutiny*, 32
Shaw, George Bernard, 28, 149, 199
Shaw, Irwin; *Bury the Dead*, 148, 157–9, 162
Shlovski, Viktor, 17
Sitwell, Edith, 127
 *Aspects of Modern Poetry*, 55

Slater, Montagu, 149–50, 152, 159, 168
 *Easter 1916*, 153–4
 *Stay Down Miner*, 152–3
Smith, Stan, 89, 90
Smith, Stevie, 91
 'Suburb', 119–20
 'The Suburban Classes', 121
Socialist Realism, 1, 2, 3, 13, 14, 16, 23–34, 193
Sommerfield, John; *May Day*, 14, 16
Spender, Stephen, 2, 6, 17, 27, 30, 57, 74, 77, 79–80, 81, 87, 109, 111, 121, 129, 130, 135, 136
 *The Destructive Element*, 75
 'The Express', 122
 *Forward from Liberalism*, 75–6, 110, 113
 'Landscape Near An Aerodrome', 122–3
 *The New Realism. A Discussion*, 76
 *Poems*, 133
 *The Still Centre*, 79
 *The Thirties and After*, 15
Squire, Jack, 126
Stead, Christina, 29, 32
Stead, Peter, 199
Stott, William, 173
Swingler, Randall, 3, 19, 21, 33–4, 124–144
 'Crisis', 142
 *Crucifixus*, 131–2, 133
 *Difficult Morning*, 124, 134–5, 136, 142
 'Funeral March', 143
 'Imperial June', 134–5
 *No Escape*, 139–41, 142
 'Ode to a Plane Above the City', 129
 'Peace and Prosperity', 142
 *Poems*, 128–9, 131, 133
 *Reconstruction*, 129–30, 131, 133
 'Revolutionary Poem', 131
 'Sandbag Follies', 142
 'Spain', 142
 'Sunset Over Camden Town', 133–4
 'The Swans', 136
 *To Town*, 142
Symons, Julian, 50
Synge, J.M., 96, 97, 100